LINCOLN CHRISTIAN COLLEGE

P9-DIG-878

Participating
in *Worship*

Participating
in *Worship*

History, Theory, and Practice

Craig Douglas Erickson

Westminster/John Knox Press
LOUISVILLE

Unless otherwise indicated Scripture quotations are from the Revised Standard Version of the Holy Bible, copyright, 1946, 1952, and © 1971, 1973 by the Division of Christian Education, National Council of the Churches of Christ in the U.S.A. and used by permission.

Acknowledgment is made for permission to reprint the following material:

To Augsburg Publishing House for Psalm 100 and psalm tone 10 from LUTHERAN BOOK OF WORSHIP and measures 6–9 from Psalm 32 by Paul Weber. Psalm 100 is from BOOK OF COMMON PRAYER (1979). Psalm tone 10 is reprinted from LUTHERAN BOOK OF WORSHIP, copyright © 1978, by permission of Augsburg Publishing House. Reprinted by permission from PSALM 32 by Paul Weber, copyright © 1979 Augsburg Publishing House.

To Collins Publishers for the setting of Psalm 27, music by John Lemon. From THE PSALMS: A NEW TRANSLATION FOR WORSHIP © English text 1976, 1977 David L. Frost, John A. Emerton, Andrew A. Macintosh, all rights reserved. © printing 1976, 1977 Wm. Collins Sons & Co. Ltd.

To G.I.A. Publications, Inc. for the music of "The sacrifice you accept, O God, is a humble spirit" by David Clark Isele. Copyright © 1979 G.I.A. Publications, Inc., Chicago, Illinois. All rights reserved. For Psalm 83 from *30 Psalms and Two Canticles.* Copyright © 1959 Ladies of the Grail (England). Used by permission of G.I.A. Publications, Inc., Chicago, Illinois, exclusive agent. All rights reserved. For "Jubilate, Servite" by Jacques Berthier. Copyright © 1978, 1980, 1981 Les Presses de Taizé (France). Used by permission of G.I.A. Publications, Inc., Chicago, Illinois, exclusive agent. All rights reserved.

To The Westminster Press for HERE IT IS! from Singing Psalms of Joy and Praise. Words © 1986 Fred R. Anderson; from SINGING PSALMS OF JOY AND PRAISE. Used by permission of The Westminster Press.

Library of Congress Cataloging-in-Publication Data

Erickson, Craig Douglas, 1948–
     Participating in worship : history, theory, and practice / Craig Douglas Erickson.
          p. cm.
     Bibliography: p.
     List of works by Craig Douglas Erickson: p.
     Includes index.
     ISBN 0-8042-1900-1 :
     1. Public worship. 2. Liturgics.   I. Title.
BV15.E75 1989
264—dc19   88-31153
     CIP

© copyright Craig Douglas Erickson 1989
10 9 8 7 6 5 4 3 2 1
Printed in the United States of America
Westminster/John Knox Press
Louisville, Kentucky 40202

Dedication

To my teachers, especially Mary Ann Lampa, Billy Graham, Ralph T. Dirksen, Zenos Hawkinson, Michael Houlahan, Calvin Katter, Karl Olsson, Douglas Cedarleaf, Karlfried Froehlich, Arlo Duba, John Gallen, Leonel Mitchell, James F. White, John Chandler, Robert Taft, and Edward J. Kilmartin.

To Robert and Carolyn Berghoff, who believed in and supported my education.

And to the members of my family who lavishly provided hospitality and encouragement while this book was written: Beverle J. Huey; and Jeanne Marie, Michelena Louisa, and Nathaniel Lukas Huey Erickson.

In memoriam
R. Curtis Huey
1931–88

Abbreviations

ApTrad	*La Tradition Apostolique de Hippolyte. Essai de reconstitution.* Bernard Botte, ed. Paris: Éditions du Cerf, 1984; *The Apostolic Tradition of Hippolytus.* Gregory Dix, ed. London, UK: S.P.C.K., 1968; Burton Scott Easton, ed. Cambridge, UK: Archon, 1962.
ASB	*The Alternative Service Book 1980* (Church of England). Cambridge, UK: Cambridge University, 1980.
BCP	*Book of Common Prayer* (American Episcopal). New York, NY: Church Hymnal Corporation and Seabury, 1977.
BEM	*Baptism, Eucharist, Ministry.* Faith and Order Paper, 111. Geneva: World Council of Churches, 1982.
CC	*Corpus Christianorum.* Series latina, vols. 1–62. Turnholti: Typographi Brepols, 1971.
FC	*Fathers of the Church: A New Translation,* vols. 1–78. New York: Fathers of the Church, Inc. and Washington, DC: The Catholic University of America Press, Inc., 1947–88.
H82	*The Hymnal 1982,* vols. 1 & 2. New York, NY: Church Hymnal Corporation, 1982.
ICET	International Consultation on English Texts
LBW	*Lutheran Book of Worship.* Minneapolis, MN: Augsburg, 1978.
LCC	*Library of Christian Classics,* vols. 1–26. Philadelphia, PA: Westminster Press, 1953–68.
NCE	*New Catholic Encyclopedia.* New York, NY: McGraw-Hill, 1967.

NPNF	*Nicene and Post-Nicene Fathers.* First Series, vols. 1–14. Buffalo and New York, NY: Christian Literature Co., 1886–90. Second Series, vols. 1–14. New York, NY: Scribner's, 1890–1900.
PG	J. P. Migne, ed. *Patrologiae cursus completus: Series graeca,* 161 vols. Paris: 1857–66.
PGIS	*Praise God in Song,* ed. William G. Storey and John Allyn Melloh. Chicago, IL: G.I.A., 1979.
PL	J. P. Migne, ed. *Patrologiae cursus completus: Series latina,* 221 vols. Paris: 1844–55.
RIL	*Rejoice in the Lord,* ed. Erik Routley. Grand Rapids, MI: Wm. B. Eerdmans, 1985.
Sac	*The Sacramentary.* Collegeville, MN: Liturgical, 1974.
SC	*Sources Chrétiennes,* vols. 1–281. Paris: Éditions du Cerf, 1955–81.
SLR	Supplementary Liturgical Resources (Presbyterian). Philadelphia, PA: Westminster, 1984–.
SWR	Supplemental Worship Resources, vols. 1–12 (United Methodist). Nashville, TN: Abingdon or United Methodist Publishing, 1972–82.
WB	*Worshipbook.* Philadelphia, PA: Westminster, 1972.
Worship3	*Worship: A Hymnal and Service Book for Roman Catholics,* 3rd ed. Chicago, IL: G.I.A., 1986.

Preface

The widespread concern for and interest in liturgical participation raises important questions:

— Why must Christian worship be participatory?
— What shape should participation take?
— How can new forms be implemented?
— Are some types of participation superior to others?
— What is the relationship of participation in worship to the spiritual renewal of the church?
— What is the underlying significance of all liturgical participation?

In approaching these questions, this book advances a theory of participation that is biblically rooted. It provides a theological framework for comprehending diverse types of liturgical participation and for holding them in a harmonic balance.

This book is also written from an ecumenical perspective. Encouraging active participation in worship involves similar problems across denominational and communal lines. The church catholic exhibits a rich diversity of styles of liturgical participation. This book approaches them objectively, evaluating them as options for the experience of prayer and transcendence within any tradition.

Lastly, this book has a pastoral perspective. Written with the interests of the person in the pew in mind, it is about how

Christians participate in worship and what the significance of that participation is. It touches on liturgical leadership only inasmuch as it enhances (or inhibits) congregational participation. Shaped by the author's pastoral ministry, it contains practical suggestions for deepening liturgical participation in the local parish. The illustrations and guidelines for implementation arise out of churches large and small, black and white, rural and urban.

This study is not exhaustive. There are doubtless many forms of participation, some of which are deeply cherished, in traditions other than those with which the author is familiar. The reader is encouraged to situate these within the broad framework that is provided.

This book is written for worship leaders who desire to involve their flocks more deeply in the corporate prayer of the church, the corporate prayer that is collectively embraced and owned. It does not contain quick fixes or gimmicks. Rather, it offers long-range directions for those willing to undertake a sustained effort toward an ever-elusive goal. It is for parish worship committees, whose main task of promoting a fuller level of participation in worship is all too often eclipsed by the secondary tasks of lining up ushers and acolytes, etc. It is for liturgical commissions, entrusted by denominations and communions with the weighty task of developing worship resources that invite the fervent participation of all. It is for seminarians who are beginning to reflect upon ways of actively involving themselves and future parishioners in worship. Finally, it is a book for all Christians, regardless of denomination or communion, who care deeply about the renewal and unity of the church.

The worship of Almighty God lies at the heart of that renewal. It is the activity through which the church is most visible, through which it most fully reveals its character and essence as the body of Christ. It is hoped that this study will enrich the prayer of the church, which, by the power of the Holy Spirit, is joined to the prayer of Christ who intercedes continuously in our behalf before the Father.

The author gratefully acknowledges the assistance of many in writing this book. The Central Presbyterian Church and Valley Covenant Church, both of Eugene, Oregon, generously provided office space. Newton Thurber and J. Wilbur Patterson of the Program Agency of the Presbyterian Church (U.S.A.) encouraged the use of a missionary furlough-sabbatical for this purpose. Their ecumenical vision and personal support were a great inspiration. Special recognition is due James Gaderlund and John Grabner, who graciously provided editorial assistance in the preparation of the manuscript, furnishing many invaluable suggestions along the way. They have sharpened and amplified this book at many points, and I am deeply grateful to them. Corlyss McCullough's help on chapter 3 was yet another manifestation of a ministry that has made a deep and lasting impression. Raleigh McVicker made important contributions to chapter 5. Editors Peter Bower and Fr. Michael Marx, O.S.B., permitted the use of materials from previously published articles.[1] My students at the University of Dubuque Theological Seminary in Iowa gave a thoughtful reaction to this book when it was presented as a series of lectures in the fall of 1986.

Lastly, I wish to thank the members of the congregations that I have been privileged to serve as a minister of Christ. In one way or another they have encouraged me to attempt this work. The extent to which it is helpful and clearly focused is due in large part to their ministry to me.

— Craig Douglas Erickson
Tokyo Union Church, Tokyo, Japan

Contents

1

Participatory Worship and the Priesthood of the Church

A Priestly Community

In a baptismal sermon written to early Christians undergoing fierce persecution, the author of First Peter gives this timeless description of the church:

> Come to him, to that living stone, rejected by men but in God's sight chosen and precious; and like living stones be yourselves built into a spiritual house, to be a holy priesthood, to offer spiritual sacrifices acceptable to God through Jesus Christ.
>
> . . . you are a chosen race, a royal priesthood, a holy nation, God's own people, that you may declare the wonderful deeds of him who called you out of darkness into his marvelous light. Once you were no people but now you are God's people; once you had not received mercy but now you have received mercy. (1 Peter 2:4–5, 9–10)

The church is a royal priesthood. In worship, its identity is most fully revealed. Because the church is a priestly body and a royal dwelling place of the Holy Spirit, its worship ought to be participatory. It is only natural that the church should demonstrate collectively its character in worship. A clergy-dominated performance of the liturgy before a passive congregation obscures the priestly character of the entire church.[1]

Participatory worship was a lively issue for New Testament Christians. While still a Jewish sect, the church was forced to reinterpret such concepts as priesthood, sacrifice, and temple in a way that was consonant with the new covenant. To accomplish this, the Christian community drew upon the more progressive trends in Jewish thought.[2]

The concept of priesthood was radically transformed. In the new Israel, when the church gathers for worship, it does so as a collective priesthood. Christians celebrate the mysteries together. As a body of priests, they offer sacrifices pleasing to God. What is the nature of these sacrifices? They are sacrifices of praise and thanksgiving. Most vitally, they symbolize the fact that the holiness of the church is for the sake of the world. The lifestyle of Christians is to be sacrificial. As St. Paul writes:

> I appeal to you therefore, brethren, by the mercies of God, to present your bodies as a living sacrifice, holy and acceptable to God, which is your spiritual worship. (Rom. 12:1)

"Spiritual worship" refers to the presence of the Holy Spirit, who is understood to reside in each Christian through the grace of baptism. The New Testament awards the concept of temple to the bodies of individual Christians, who are temples of God's Holy Spirit. The writer of First Peter also likens the baptized to living stones built into a spiritual house or temple (1 Peter 2:5).

The church is a priesthood. All Christians, as temples of the Holy Spirit, are to offer their lives as sacrifices. Reflecting this identity, Christian worship ought to be participatory worship. Such is the right and duty of the faithful, who through baptism join a "chosen race, a royal priesthood, a holy nation, God's own people." Because all of the members of the church constitute a priestly community, its worship deserves to be participatory.

Objections from the Pew

Despite firm biblical evidence in favor of participatory worship, it is not a concept that is warmly embraced by all. Many are resistant to more active levels of participation for a variety of reasons.

The level of participation in worship may be affected by

personal problems, e.g., marital difficulties, ill-health, guilt, low self-esteem, a crisis of or a lack of faith. This book cannot deal directly with the many personal barriers to full liturgical participation. Suffice it to note that it is unfortunate when Christians who most need the healing power of the liturgy are least able to participate in it. Although worship joins forces with other forms of ministry to bring about healing and strengthen faith, its beginning and ending purpose is the praise and glorification of God.

Another major barrier to participatory worship is fueled in part by a consumeristic orientation. Christians generally understand that they are both to give and to receive in worship. Yet, there exists a natural tendency to focus inwardly more upon the receiving than the giving. In this context Jesus' words are most apt: "It is more blessed to give than to receive" (Acts 20:35).

The personal motive for worship is crucial to the level of participation experienced therein. The starting point for authentic participation is the individual Christian's own heartfelt and genuine response of praise and thanksgiving before the presence of God:

My vows to thee I must perform, O God;
     I will render thank offerings to thee.
For thou hast delivered my soul from death,
     yea, my feet from falling,
that I may walk before God in the light of life. (Ps. 55[56]:12–13)

Participatory worship is founded upon *pietas* or piety—that personal trust in and reverence for God that inclines the heart to true worship and devotion. Piety is that quality of openness to God that is itself a gift of the Spirit of God. Without piety participatory forms of worship are of little avail. This is not to deny the evangelistic potential of the liturgy, which is considerable. Nor is it to suggest that liturgy is powerless to prompt and awaken the disposition that is proper to worship. Rather it is to emphasize the fact that major responsibility for participation in worship lies with the individual Christian. This responsibility involves much more than a momentary or nostalgic desire or the fulfillment of one's Lord's Day obligation. Authentic participation in worship arises out of the heart that is actively engaged in the Christian life with all of its moral and spiritual demands, including preparation for worship through prayer, Bible study, meditation, and fasting.

This duty on the part of each Christian in no way reduces the responsibility borne by those entrusted with the design of corporate worship. They are called to provide for the faith community structures of worship that can accommodate multiple levels of participation so that the liturgy is collectively an authentic expression of faith.

Participation in worship may also be affected by church problems. Differences in preference for forms of active participation are to be found in every local congregation. These can be a source of either creative or hurtful conflict. Differences also exist between congregations, denominations, and communions. Similarly, these can be a source of either helpful or destructive conflict. Over the centuries Christians have often grouped themselves according to patterns of participation in worship. Denominations and, in some cases, religious orders within communions have institutionalized and hardened such differences. Granted, these actions may have been necessary to preserve the peace of the church. However, such divisions are costly. While they may be positive ways of declaring religious identity, they can also result in isolation, inhibiting a hardier strain of Christian faith by preventing cross-fertilization. An example of this isolation is the polarization between some Protestants and Roman Catholics, which has made a desirable balance between biblical proclamation and eucharistic celebration difficult to achieve on either side.

Because participation in worship is a church problem, an ecumenical study needs to take into account the reasons why people react in the way that they do. It must consider: Reformed Christians, who may display uneasiness over certain liturgical gestures, fearing them as religious encroachments from Rome; evangelicals, who may resist what they perceive as cold formalism in written liturgies; Anglo-Catholics, who may be threatened by the extemporaneous acclamations of a black or charismatic congregation; Eastern Rite Christians, who may be scandalized at the thought of a woman being the celebrant at the Eucharist.

Participatory worship is a concept that is guaranteed to raise the blood pressure of some members of congregations. Therefore, before any liturgical reform is attempted, it is important that, among the people who will be affected, a consensus exist on the desirability and appropriateness of participatory worship.

Participation in worship is so integral to Christian faith and life that a fresh look is in order. On December 4, 1963, the Second Vatican Council promulgated the "Constitution on the Sacred Liturgy." Contained within this reform-minded document is a terse but pregnant statement about liturgical participation. The faithful, it says, should take part "knowingly, actively, and fruitfully." Perhaps here is a beginning point at which Christians of diverse affiliation may discover some common concerns.[3]

To Participate Knowingly

Knowledgeable participation in worship requires personal illumination. The illumination of the heart originates with conversion, the gift of personal faith in God, which is either anticipated in or ratified by baptism. St. John writes that Christ came into the world for judgment, "that those who do not see may see, and that those who see may become blind" (John 9:39). Faith creates a new vision (Acts 26:18; Rom. 8:5; Rev./Apoc. 21:5). The experience of Christian worship is most fully accessible only to those who have been illumined, to those whose eyes have been opened to the mystery (John 1:14, 14:9). In fulfillment of the promise of baptism, their lives continue to be sanctified by the Holy Spirit. It is the Spirit who makes possible a more profound participation in the worship of the church. To participate knowingly requires this inward illumination, which is given through the grace of baptism.

The vision of faith is analogous to human love. Persons who enjoy a deep marital commitment of love see things in each other that no one else does. They comprehend things about each other that others cannot, and they grow more deeply in their love in a way that is unique to them.

The personal appropriation of faith and the illumination of the Holy Spirit bring one into that kind of marriage with God and the church. For the nonbeliever, Christian worship may seem like utter nonsense. But, for the believer, Christian worship is never nonsense. It may not make perfect sense, but since when did logic rule over love? Conversion, then, is necessary to participate in worship knowingly.

Illumination of the heart must be complemented by illumination of the mind. To worship knowingly requires an intensive study of the Bible and the liturgy. Ongoing Bible study, based upon an ardent and living love for God's word, is a vital ingredient of growth in the Christian faith. It prepares the heart and the mind for the worship of God.

The link between the Bible and worship is especially productive when the liturgy in question is a biblical one. The classic liturgies that have evolved over the centuries are imbued with Scripture. Within them are an abundance of citations, paraphrases, and scriptural allusions, all artistically woven together. Indeed, the great liturgies are celebrations of God's Holy Word. The well-conceived liturgy imparts a wealth of Scripture, proclaiming the gospel through a medium that is unique.

Furthermore, the interpretation of Scripture is at times informed by the liturgy. For example, a rich liturgical tradition sheds light upon: Ephesians 5:2 ("Walk in love, as Christ loved us and gave himself up for us, a fragrant offering and sacrifice to God") as a reference to the use of incense in worship; or Ephesians 4:22–24 ("Put off your old nature which belongs to your former manner . . . and put on the new nature.") as a reference to the custom of disrobing and of dressing in baptismal garments; or the several references to white garments in Revelation/Apocalypse as allusions to liturgical vesture. Knowledge of Scripture helps to make sense out of the liturgy and vice versa. For those who are concerned about a decline in biblical literacy, the possibilities opened up by the interplay between liturgy and Scripture are worth pondering.[4]

Illumination, both of the heart and of the mind, is necessary to participate knowingly. Without understanding, all ritual, regardless of its level of simplicity, is prone to misunderstanding. Intelligibility is necessary to apprehending the Christian faith through one's knowledgeable participation in worship.

To Participate Actively

Active participation is what the documents of Vatican II refer to as *actuoso participatio*. *Actuoso* refers to that which is full of activity, with the added idea of zeal. Thus *actuoso participatio* is stirring, pulsating, energetic, effective participation.

The church's worship requires worshipers who are open to active participation. To this end, it is necessary to increase familiarity with various types of participation and to cultivate an appreciation for them, an appreciation that can only arise out of a love for God's people, the church. Such a process is likely to be only a beginning.

As previously noted, much resistance to participatory worship is centered here at the starting point. Many a worship leader can empathize with a cheerleader who attempts in vain to rouse fans whose team lags hopelessly behind. The level of active participation in worship mirrors deep-seated factors that cannot be ignored.

More than cultural inhibitions stand in the way of active participation. An invitation to more active participation in worship directly challenges current levels of personal faith and commitment to Christ and the church. Feelings of discomfort over what is going on in worship and possibly over those who are leading and sharing in it will need to be dealt with creatively. For many, a more active level of participation will occur only as the result of a faith awakening nurtured by exceptional pastoral skills.

Of course, the activity levels of liturgical participation do not always reflect the efforts and intentions of the congregation. I once gently scolded a rural congregation because their singing, in my opinion, lacked exuberance. I issued a challenge to their lung power: "See that chip of loose paint dangling up there on the ceiling? I want you to stand and sing this hymn so that it will come down." The members of the congregation rose to the occasion and sang as lustily as they could. To no avail. Not only did the paint flake not even quiver, but the sound level did not go up one decibel. Reflecting on this, I realized that *they* were not the problem at all. The sanctuary had thick, wall-to-wall carpeting. There was a large velvet curtain around the reredos behind the altar-table. There were lush curtains on the side windows. There was padding on every pew. And, because it was winter, virtually everyone was wearing wool, a sound-absorbent fabric. Their best attempts at active participation were being thwarted by the acoustics of their worship space. Incidentally, while I couldn't do much for their singing, I did manage to get the sanctuary repainted.

Active participation requires the rooting out of patterns of passivity, patterns that may not be obvious. The same forms of worship that called for the active energy of one generation may require little from the next, which thereby lapses into passivity. The call for more active participation needs to be a continual one. Typically, it will sound like an alarm that rings an hour early.

Søren Kierkegaard, a nineteenth-century Danish theologian, sensed this problem about worship. In an oft-quoted analogy, he likened Christian worship to the theatre. Many Christians, he wrote, tend to view the minister/priest as the actor, God as the prompter, and the congregation as the audience. But actually, according to Kierkegaard, the congregation is the actor, the minister/priest merely the prompter, and God the audience.[5]

Active participation means that the congregation takes its place upon the stage in the light that emanates from heaven. For a priestly people, this is meet and right.

To Participate Fruitfully

The term *fruitful* has biblical overtones. There is the negative association with trees that bear evil fruit and are to be cut down and cast into the fire (Matt. 7:19). The worshiper who is not open to the ministry of the Spirit engages in an act of hypocrisy against which God's judgment is inevitable.

There is a positive image as well. Those who pray for openness to God's presence will experience the transformative power of the Holy Spirit in their lives, as promised in baptism. Fruitful participation in worship manifests itself in the fruit of the Spirit —"love, joy, peace, patience, kindness, goodness, faithfulness, gentleness, self-control; against such there is no law" (Gal. 5:22–23). Fruitful participation issues forth in mission as acts of charity and as efforts in behalf of social justice and world peace. In this sense the liturgy of the sanctuary and the liturgy of life are integral to each other. The purpose of liturgical participation is not simply to do the liturgy better. Its twofold purpose is the glorification of God and the equipping of Christians with power to carry out the witness and mission of the church in the world. These two dimensions of liturgy are inseparable.

There are innumerable testimonies to fruitful participation in the liturgy. Few would be more eloquent than that of the African martyrs of Abilinitina during the fierce persecution under Diocletian (c.e. 303–305). These early saints were willing to risk their lives to attend the eucharistic assembly. Its transformative power was so real to them that life without it was inconceivable. Meeting for worship in defiance of the authorities, they were arrested, tried, and executed. At their trial, they defended their actions. "We cannot survive without the Eucharist," they said. "The eucharistic celebration cannot be superseded."[6]

The church of Christ is a royal priesthood. Individual Christians are temples of God's Holy Spirit. Consequently, worship that fully expresses this identity will be participatory. Faithful Christians may be vigorously encouraged to take part knowingly, actively, and fruitfully.

Study Guide

1. The author contends that participatory worship is necessary given the nature of the church as a priesthood. Do you agree?

Why, or why not?

2. What inhibitions to active participation in worship exist within your congregation? Within you?

3. Illumination of the heart and of the mind is necessary to full participation in worship. How might education about worship occur in your context? How is the heart illumined?

4. How is worship linked to the ways in which you perceive the world and live out your faith in it?

2

Perspectives on Participation

The larger goal is clear. Christian worship is to be participatory worship. But this claim does not explain how creatively to enhance liturgical participation. Instead, it raises important and difficult questions:

—How does participation occur?
—In promoting liturgical participation, which investments will pay richer dividends?
—What levels of participation are desirable and possible?
—What are the options for types of participation?
—How may different types of participation be balanced together?

Answering these questions entails constructing a comprehensive theory of ritual engagement.

Beyond Bipolarity

When Christians describe their personal preferences in worship or make distinctions among the various liturgical traditions, they may often rely upon bipolar terminology. Terms like *formal* and *informal, high church* and *low church, free* and *structured, liturgical* and *nonliturgical* are common parlance for clergy and laity alike, and they serve as shorthand descriptions of styles of worship.

In some contexts these classifications may be very helpful. A bishop interviewing an applicant whose profile includes the description, "flat-footed low church," will be able to make a judicious placement. A newcomer to a community may pick up reliable clues in selecting a new church home where the worship is called "informal." A session or church council may function more harmoniously knowing that the 11:00 A.M. worshipers prefer a more "structured" service. Within limited contexts such bipolar systems of classification have obvious value.

In broader contexts, however, they may not only lose their value but also become imprecise, divisive, and restrictive. Bipolar terms quickly become unreliable indicators because, based upon subjective experience and perception, they are relative, and therefore biased, judgments. What is "structured" to one person may be "free" to the next. What is "high church" for one may be quite "low" for another. Much like the political labels of "conservative" and "liberal," these terms are meaningful only within a narrowly defined context. Beyond that context they become less precise.

The term *informal* is illustrative in this regard. "Informal worship" often connotes an intimate atmosphere created through an emotive worship leader, a warm, personal interaction between worshipers, and a de-emphasis on form and structure. This connotation can be traced to cultural patterns of informality. However, for someone from a different culture, such patterns may be perceived as being highly formal. Those things that Americans consider to be informal are actually complex formalities of their culture. An inability to convince Americans that their informal manners are but cultural formalities does not alter the facts. Viewed from a cross-cultural perspective, parishioners' demands for "informal worship" are judged to arise out of a preference for one type of formality over another, and for one in which vital aspects, such as a transcendental dimension, may be diminished.[1]

Bipolar terminology generally works to divide, not unify, the church. When, as is actually the case, a whole range of liturgical styles exists, a use of bipolar terms functions restrictively. Such words polarize the church by creating the false impression that there are only two mutually exclusive options.

A bipolar mindset further restricts possibilities for the spiritual growth of churches. A proposed innovation, and perhaps the very innovation that a given worshiping community may really need, may be discarded merely because it is perceived as being "too high church" or "too informal." Positive directions for spiritual growth are thereby precluded, because they originate "in the other camp" and consequently are held in suspicion.

The evolution of American Presbyterian worship over the last 150–200 years provides classic examples of this restrictiveness. Parishes were divided and in some cases pastorates ended prematurely as such things as Christmas and Holy Week were revitalized, choirs and vestments appeared, and sermon and prayer texts were introduced. Congregations came to view these changes as capitulations to the enemy—the formalism of Roman Catholic and Episcopal communions.[2] In retrospect it is obvious that formalism was not the enemy at all! Rather, the enemy was an inhibited experience of corporate prayer—worship in which the levels of participation were perceived to be less than maximal. Today, the spiritual benefits of these and other innovations are plain to most, if not all, American Presbyterians. Meanwhile, the battle lines between what is perceived to be formal and what is deemed informal (or "Catholic" and "Protestant") are being drawn elsewhere, and the trench warfare continues.

Such is an unfortunate and self-defeating cycle. The lenses through which we view reality are crucial to our spiritual well-being as Christians in worshiping communities. If that perception is restricted, we can look at reality with only limited vision at best. At worst, our vision is distorted, resulting in senseless and unduly prolonged conflict, paralysis, inertia, and the like.

Ritual

The keynote of Christian worship is authenticity. Outer forms of liturgical participation are inescapably wed to the inner motivation to worship. To grasp this, it will be necessary to explore how ritual works and what its ends are.

The term *ritual* refers to "the prescribed form of words which constitute an act of worship." Its etymology is a straightforward one. It comes from the Latin adjective *ritualis,* which is derived from the noun *ritus* meaning "the form and manner of religious observances; a religious custom, usage, ceremony."[3] So defined, ritual is applicable to any pattern of Christian worship, because it refers simply to the form and manner of religious observances be they well developed symbolically or otherwise.

For some, the term *ritual* has negative connotations. These may arise from religious perspectives and temperaments that are averse to anything that is perceived to be an excessive devotion to ritual or to what is judged to be an extravagant and empty use of symbols. The basis for this aversion is a desire to avoid the vain and empty use of ritual, against which Jesus rightly protested (Matt. 23:23–26). However, what is being eschewed by Jesus is not ritual but an excessive devotion to ritual, which is better labeled as ritual*ism.*

An excessive devotion to ritual is undesirable for the practice of the Christian faith. But, if ritualism is not what is wanted, then what term describes the experience that *is* desired? No such term exists. Ritual is not the opposite of ritualism. It is neutral, denoting merely a prescribed form of words that constitutes an act of worship. It indicates nothing about the level of interaction between worshipers and the prescribed forms. A new term is needed. Here we suggest that the term *synergistic ritual* can fill that need.

Synergistic Ritual

Ritualism is the result of a breakdown of the various elements working together in ritual. For instance, a certain ritual may be ill-suited to drawing a congregation into an act of prayer. Or, the worship leader may be inept at celebrating it. Perhaps a problem exists within the life of the congregation with the result that discord remains unresolved. Or, there may be barriers in the hearts of individuals who are not open to the movement of the

Holy Spirit through the medium of the liturgy. For ritual to succeed, the respective agents involved must work together cooperatively.

In the New Testament the Greek word *synergos* describes a special relationship among fellow workers united in purpose. St. Paul calls the Corinthian Christians "fellow workers [*synergoi*] for God" (1 Cor. 3:9, author's translation). The term *synergos* reflects a cooperative working relationship among the respective agents such that the total effect is greater than the sum of each agent acting alone. For ritual to succeed it must be synergistic, that is, involving persons, church, and liturgy in a cooperative relationship of mutual enrichment. The harmonious interaction of these agents is orchestrated by the Holy Spirit.

When worshipers, by the power of the Spirit, participate knowingly, actively, and fruitfully in the liturgy, the individual person, the church, and the liturgy are joined together in synergistic ritual. In synergistic ritual, each agent is mutually enriched: personal faith responses are confirmed in substance, upheld in solidarity, deepened in perception, and poised for action in the world. The church is strengthened as its individual members bear witness to their essential unity in the Spirit, grow in the prayer of the church, function more harmoniously as the body of Christ, and prefigure the kingdom of God. The liturgy itself is benefited also inasmuch as it is further appropriated as the prayer of the church, the corporate prayer that is collectively embraced and owned.

Worship strives for synergistic ritual. Obviously, this can occur through the use of a wide variety of rituals. It is less important which precise forms of ritual are used to achieve synergistic ritual *than it is that synergistic ritual actually occurs.* Synergistic ritual ought to be the goal of all liturgical reform, of all liturgical innovation, of all liturgical indigenization.

Ritualism

A more precise definition of ritualism now becomes possible. When persons, church, and liturgy do not function as coworkers, worship becomes ritualistic. In ritualistic worship church members have difficulty recognizing and appropriating the liturgy as an authentic expression of their own faith. Consequently, they are no longer able to participate knowingly, actively, and fruitfully. While active participation may continue to be evident at the exterior level, there is no corresponding level of participation on the interior level. The synergistic relationship among persons, church, and liturgy has become dysfunctional. Devotion to God is eclipsed by a sole recourse to ritual which thereby becomes excessive because the reality behind the ritual has "fallen away."

Some may assume that ritualism is more of a problem within those liturgical traditions that are relatively well developed and lavishly employ symbols, gestures, and other sensory stimuli. But, if ritualism is defined in contradistinction to synergistic ritual, such an assumption is unfounded. Because ritualism is the result of a dysfunctional relationship among persons, church, and liturgy, it is possible within all liturgical and ecclesial traditions. None is more immune or more resistant to ritualistic worship than the others.

The reasons for dysfunction may be moral, such as when an individual participates in worship with an ingenuine spirit. Or, the breakdown may be due to unintentional reasons, such as was reported by a missionary who, after teaching nineteenth-century American gospel hymns to Thai nationals, discovered that Western musical idioms conflicted with the tonal nature of the Thai language. In this particular case an ascending line of music, which, contextually, connoted to Western musical sensitivities the triumph of Easter, connoted to Thai linguistic sensitivities the despair of the tomb.

Ritualism reflects a breakdown, a disintegration of synergistic ritual. Not only can churches with well-developed liturgical traditions profit from perpetual vigilance against ritualism, but traditions that are more free church in nature can also benefit by taking similar precautions. Ritualism is a church-wide problem because it has to do with individual worshipers whose hearts and minds may or may not be able, for one reason or another, to pray through the liturgy regardless of its degree of development.

Levels of Signification

Pure synergistic ritual and pure ritualism are polarities that may be viewed as the two endpoints of a continuum. Between the two ends every degree of liturgical participation involves a mixture of ritualism and synergistic ritual.

SCALE OF LITURGICAL PARTICIPATION

Pure   Pure
Ritualism   ├──┼──┼──┼──┼──┼──┼──┼──┼──┤   Synergistic
       1 2 3 4 5 6 7 8 9 10   Ritual

As desirable as the goal of synergistic ritual is, it remains precisely that, a goal. The perfect synergistic ritual cannot be achieved on this side of the Parousia. It must await the fullness of the kingdom that is coming. Full liturgical participation is only what the saints in glory experience in the ritual of the New Jerusalem. Earthly saints or mystics may occasionally register at "10," but for the rest of us the experience of liturgical participation routinely falls lower on the scale.

Likewise, occasions of pure ritualism are equally rare. Where the presence of ritualism is suspected, there is usually some vestigial meaning present, however slight, some redeeming level of authenticity, no matter how confused the theological justification may be.

Participation in worship occurs at multiple levels of signification. Participants engage in worship through words, gestures, and symbols at levels that are unique to each person. For example, the sign of the cross may register at level "8" for one person and at level "2" for another. In such liturgical matters there are no black-and-white distinctions, but only subtle gradations of meaningfulness. Moreover, these levels of meaning are fluid. They change during the course of a person's life due to changes in the experiences that one brings to worship. Liturgy is like art in this respect. Persons who encounter a work of art over a period of time apprehend it at differing levels of meaningfulness with each encounter.

Among the modern art exhibits at the Art Institute of Chicago is a ten-foot, pincher-type clothespin standing upright, the flared edges (where one pinches) forming the "legs" of the sculpture. On many occasions I passed this sculpture, reacting as many do to modern art, scratching my head at how easily fame and fortune come to some. Then, one day, my reaction of "that's art!?!" was utterly transformed. I happened to walk by the work one March day just as the late afternoon sunlight was moving across its top. I was transfixed. Suddenly, it was no longer a giant clothespin, but two human beings—standing, embracing, breasts touching, kissing, their midsections bound tightly together by the spring, and their faces illuminated by joy at the discovery of their new-found love. At that instant, the work had ceased to be a clothespin and had become a statement about human emotions, sexuality, and the *imago Dei*.[4]

The meaningfulness of words, gestures, and symbols in worship registers at different points on the scale of liturgical participation for different persons at different times in their lives. In light of this fact, *good worship will provide an artistic transparency that patiently awaits subjective human encounter.* Meaning is often enhanced through familiarity. Each church must learn to tolerate the dilemma that what for one is ritualistic, for another is more fully synergistic, and for hosts of others lies somewhere between the two extremes. The level of participation in worship inevitably varies from person to person, a situation that cannot be altered!

This is an admonition to iconoclasts, to those who are quick to judge, to those who would discount certain acts of worship as pure ritualism. It is peremptory to impose one's personal scale of liturgical meaningfulness and timetable upon the experience and needs of the whole. Such individuals would more profitably seek after the Spirit's gift of patience (Gal. 5:22).

The Law of Retroactive Engagement

The recognition of multiple levels of signification highlights the hidden value of another troublesome term, *repetition.* How far some are from seeing positive value in liturgical repetition is illustrated by the story of a young minister with strong liturgical training who interviewed for a job as pastor of a congregation. Aware that the candidate possessed these specialized skills, the committee inquired as to the liturgical program he envisioned for the church. He began to enumerate several goals: more frequent eucharistic celebration; an enriched Holy Week; focus on the lectionary; revitalization of participation, etc. Before he had proceeded very far, he was interrupted by a thirty-five-year-old member of the committee, his voice filled with ennui, "But we've already tried all that."

Worship is not something that is done only once. Ritual thrives on repetition. Our cultural tendency to identify TV reruns with the off-season is deadly to worship. The experience of worship is deepened through repetition. It is repetition that provides the context within which artistic transparency may patiently await subjective human perception. Like the clothespin that was encountered on many occasions before it was apprehended as a work of art, so must worship be granted the time and exposure that are needed for spiritual engagement to occur. Moreover, liturgical participation is not confined to the liturgy. It extends and occurs out beyond the liturgy. Worship frequently serves to rehearse the person for a religious encounter at a later point in life—perhaps in connection with a personal crisis or tragedy. At such moments some liturgical element, e.g., a Scripture song, a hymn, a *Kyrie,* a psalm response, or a sermon, is appropriated to great effect by the power of the Holy Spirit working through the richness of the human imagination. The liturgy is a seed planted in the soul that grows in secret and reaches fruition as a miracle of God's grace (Mark 4:26–29).

Sometimes this shift in meaningfulness can be a dramatic one. One woman cited her experience of "rattling through the Lord's Prayer every Sunday in church." Then came a time when she was critically ill. The Catholic hospital, where she lay near death, daily broadcasts a celebration of Evening Prayer into each room. As the Lord's Prayer was read over the intercom, this woman, as she herself expressed it, "suddenly prayed it for the first time."

The consumeristic demand for immediate rewards from worship is a misleading criterion for judging the actual level of participation. Liturgy rehearses one for life as well as for life eternal. Repetition makes possible the moment when synergistic ritual may engage retroactively.

By extending this logic, it is evident that all earthly worship is ritualistic to a certain extent, for it merely foreshadows heavenly worship in which spirits will be *fully* attentive upon God. In the heavenly sanctuary the veil will be removed and we shall behold God "face to face" (1 Cor. 13:12). Only then will the saints, the liturgy, and the Spirit be united in perfect synergistic ritual (Rev./Apoc. 19:6–8). While the maximum level of participation is not realizable in this life, repetition can help to approximate the future liturgy in heaven. C. S. Lewis intimated as much in his suggestive analogy:

> As long as you notice, and have to count, the steps, you are not yet dancing but only learning to dance. A good shoe is a shoe you don't notice. Good reading becomes possible when you need not consciously think about eyes, or light, or print, or spelling. The perfect church service would be one we were almost unaware of; our attention would have been on God.[5]

Patterns of Liturgical Participation

What is needed for liturgical renewal is a new framework, new filters through which to perceive reality. What is needed is a system of descriptions that is precise rather than imprecise and that opens up new possibilities by working for, not against, spiritual growth and by promoting, not inhibiting, the peace, purity, and unity of the church, the body of Christ.

How might such a framework be constructed? A place to begin is by asking: what are Christians attempting to describe when they use terms such as high church/low church, formal/ informal, liturgical/nonliturgical, free/structured, and the like? Is it not *the style of participation* in Christian worship? If it is, we have discovered a positive basis upon which to construct an alternative way of looking at the diversity of participatory styles.

Christians affirm the *theoretical* importance of striving for a high level, if not the highest level, of participation in worship. Granted, disagreements arise over the methods used to achieve fuller participation. But, if consensus exists on the desirability of a maximum level of participation in worship, have we not found a new entryway through which to approach the varieties of liturgical practices? Freed from the rancor of sectarianism that formerly brought us in through a different gate, we will now examine more rationally six types of liturgical participation. We will scrutinize each from the same perspective with the same question in mind: what potential is there for enhancing liturgical participation?

As a result of our examination, we will no longer conceptualize worshiping Christians as painfully and artificially divided between high and low, structured and free, formal and informal, liturgical and nonliturgical. Instead we will view these patterns through new lenses and see Christians from a wide variety of liturgical traditions, all striving toward a common objective: maximal liturgical participation.

The goal of liturgical participation is synergistic ritual, which always exists in a creative tension with ritualism. Many paths may lead to this goal, each of which is determined by a variety of cultural, theological, historical, pastoral, and personal considerations.

An examination of different forms of Christian worship reveals the existence of distinct modes or types of liturgical participation. Despite popular tendencies to classify these types strictly according to bipolar categories, there are, in actual fact, many patterns. In any given worshiping community one or more types will usually predominate, while the remaining types will be less evident. The weaves among them are rich and varied and should remain so.

Each of the following six chapters examines a type of participation: Spontaneous Involvement, Silent Engagement, Interiorized Verbal Participation, Prophetic Verbal Participation, Lay Leadership, Multisensate Participation. This system of classification, which may be used by a worshiping community within any ecclesial tradition, is beneficial for many reasons: it illumines the nature of liturgical participation from a theoretical standpoint; it measures the diversity of worship styles and emphases within a congregation or grouping of congregations; it is an advance over the simplistic and mutually exclusive bipolarities, which divide the church and hamper much liturgical innovation; it clarifies preferences and suggests options for liturgical enrichment; it provides a framework for guiding liturgical change coherently and in the direction of synergistic ritual; and it helps those developing new resources to derive balanced patterns of participation.

The six types of participation are complementary. Each is thoroughly biblical. Each holds a venerable place in the history of worship and is essential to a balanced liturgical life. Furthermore, each type of participation projects an image of the nature of God, the Christian faith, and the church.

Study Guide

1. Discuss your feelings about ritual.

2. Can you point to examples of ritualism in your congregation's life? Are these completely ritualistic? Or, are there some dimensions of authenticity and meaning present or potentially present?

3. What are some of your most meaningful experiences in life? How has repetition been instrumental in creating and sustaining them? How does repetition deepen liturgical participation?

4. The author compares good worship to art in that worship provides "an artistic transparency that patiently awaits subjective human encounter." How do you feel about having a liturgy that is somewhat opaque, i.e., that allows you space to "grow into"? The author cites as an example the story of a woman who, when gravely ill, suddenly prayed the Lord's Prayer "for the first time." Has such a shift in the level of meaning ever occurred for you?

5. How would you classify your congregation's worship:

high church or low church
formal or informal
structured or free
liturgical or nonliturgical

Do you agree with the author that such categories are imprecise, divisive, and restrictive? Why, or why not?

6. An implication of the Law of Retroactive Engagement is that lower levels of liturgical participation are to a certain degree tolerable. Do you agree?

3

As the Spirit Gives Utterance

Freedom and Structure

No pastor would be surprised to hear that people use different instruments to measure the vital signs of a congregation. Some have their antennae up for displays of spontaneity. Others monitor the pulse of a regular, set format.

There are biblical and theological bases for the validity of both systems of measurement. Freedom and structure enjoy a reciprocal relationship: one cannot exist without the other. St. Paul encouraged the spiritual gifts, both for the edification of the church and the manifestation of the presence of the risen Lord in the worshiping assembly (1 Cor. 14:25–26). But Paul also counseled that worship should be conducted decently and in order (1 Cor. 14:40). The Spirit moves through spontaneity. The Spirit also moves through form and structure. Obviously, for Paul both dimensions are vital to the dynamics of worship.

As many worship leaders will attest, a balance between structure and freedom is easier to attain in theory than in practice. The tension between the two can become a source of discord within a congregation. The pastoral challenge is to maintain a creative balance amidst these two constantly shifting elements.

Tension between freedom and structure is an inevitable one. It is not fomented by querulous parishioners. It is unavoidable because of the nature of the Christian faith itself. God is a covenanting God who enters into binding relationships with God's people. Yet God is also a sovereign, free Spirit who is elusive, not to be taken for granted, hidden, wholly other. This paradox is expressed in Calvinist sacramental theology, which affirms that the sacraments are means of grace but also that God is bound neither to them nor by them. Typically, such contradictory, dialectical language is intended to convey an accentuated appreciation for the sacraments as the gracious and free gifts of God.[1]

The tension between liturgical structure and freedom as an experience of God's presence has always existed. From the simplest of *berākôth*[2] (short blessings) to the most elaborate of Temple liturgies, God has been and is present in ritual. But God's presence is also experienced through another mode—the prophetic. The modes of ritual and prophecy reflect the difference between:

predictability	and	surprise
comfort	and	discomfort
familiarity	and	unfamiliarity
composition	and	improvisation
the habitual	and	the fresh
corporate	and	individual creativity

Inasmuch as liturgy is a mirror of Christian faith and practice, both structure and freedom are necessary to its balance. The presence of both structure and freedom is an expression of the fullness of the Godhead.

The focus of this chapter is on freedom. More precisely, whereas there is also freedom within structure, its focus is on unstructured liturgical participation. There are numerous possibilities for Spontaneous Involvement in the liturgy. In examining some of them, we will be mindful of the reciprocal relationship that freedom enjoys with structure, a relationship that keeps disorder from quenching the Spirit.

The Gifts of God for the People of God

"Over My Head"

I first experienced spontaneous singing as a young person while visiting another congregation. During the distribution of the communion, the silence was broken by a solo voice intoning a spiritual that was familiar to those in the congregation. Immediately, all joined in, at first on the melody line, then breaking into four-part then eight-plus-part harmonies, all a cappella. Every voice blended together in a marvelous symmetry. The congregation breathed together, modulated together, moved together, prayed together, as though they were a choir that had rehearsed many times before. Yet the song was simple enough that it invited the participation of those who were unfamiliar with it. The sense that this congregation was one with its Lord and one with each other was profound.

The spontaneous singing of spirituals, Scripture songs, hymns, and psalms is an expression of God's abiding presence by the power of the Holy Spirit, as well as a powerful way of experiencing that presence. Like all effective worship, spontaneous singing must be cultivated. The act of an individual choosing a song is done with the consensus of the community; familiarity and appropriateness are crucial factors that determine the choice. Spiritual discipline is also necessary. When the congregation joins in with the person who initiates the singing, it is indicating its willingness to be led by the one whom the Spirit is prompting.

Spontaneous and improvisational singing developed into an art form among American blacks who, in the preliterate, antebellum era, combined African singing patterns with biblical texts and images to produce a rich expression of spiritual solidarity and longing. Today this tradition lives on in many congregations. An old Negro spiritual often sung in this fashion summarizes in poignant simplicity the feelings that this kind of liturgical participation can evoke:

Over my head I hear music in the air.
  Over my head I hear music in the air.

Over my head I hear music in the air,
    There must be a God somewhere.[3]

Spontaneous Prayer

The virtues of "free prayer" and "set prayer" were exhaus-
tively debated in the Calvinist Puritan traditions of the seven-
teenth–nineteenth centuries. Little could be added to that debate
except a more reasoned verdict: biblical and theological reflec-
tion establishes a place for both.[4]

Within the structure of modern liturgies, where may spontaneous prayer of the faithful occur? The goal is a constructive
balance between structure and freedom in prayer. There are
various points at which this type of prayer is especially appropriate and should be encouraged.

For example, free space for Spontaneous Involvement should
routinely be allowed during the intercessory Prayers of the
People. These prayers are patterned on the bidding prayers of the
early church.[5] Regarding the scope of such prayer, the writer of
First Timothy urges:

> that supplications, prayers, intercessions, and thanksgivings be
> made for all men, for kings and all who are in high positions, that we
> may lead a quiet and peaceable life, godly and respectful in every
> way. (2:1–2)[6]

The bidding prayer format utilizes short petitions that cover a
traditional range of topics, similar to those alluded to in 1
Timothy 2:1–2. As each petition is concluded, it is embraced by
the whole worshiping body through a common response, such as
"Lord, have mercy" or "Lord, hear our prayer."

The Prayers of the People were restored into Roman Catholic
usage by the reforms of Vatican II. This restoration has influenced much Protestant practice, where the prayers are properly
viewed as the successor to the Pastoral Prayer. The Pastoral
Prayer, in which a minister composes and offers the intercessions
of a church, is a priestly usurpation of the people's prayer if ever
there was one.[7] The order of worship that contains both prayer
forms is comparable to a new color TV that sits atop an old black-
and-white console.

The Prayers of the People, being of the people, are preferably offered by laypersons or deacons in order to reveal more fully the identity of the prayers as belonging to the church. On special occasions representatives of church organizations may share in leading them, e.g., prayer circles, confirmation classes, or young peoples' groups. As a sign that the Prayers of the People are a priestly act of the congregation, standing is appropriate for these prayers. Commendable models may be found in the *BCP* (pp. 383–95), which may easily be adapted to non-Episcopal usage.[8]

Spontaneous Involvement should be allowed at some point during these prayers. The litany should pause and the faithful be bidden to articulate their personal petitions. An effective method is for the leader to say, "Now let us offer up those names and concerns that have been entrusted to our prayers." The silence that follows should be of sufficient length to invite the articulation of petitions. This free space for spontaneous prayers may be concluded with an invitation by the leader for all to embrace these prayers, e.g., "For these prayers and the silent petitions of our hearts, Lord in your mercy, *Hear our prayer.*" A concluding collect would then follow.

This method is recommended over the practice of the minister collecting prayer requests and then repeating each petition, often stumbling through index cards and balking at unfamiliar pronunciations. While this may be a good method for securing data for pastoral duties, it retards and interrupts the flow of worship. People who are able to vocalize a name or prayer request to a worship leader are probably as capable of uttering the same words within the context of the prayer itself. A consistent pattern to the Prayers of the People is important in eliciting spontaneity.

Other places for Spontaneous Involvement in prayer are within some well-established eucharistic prayers, which provide free space for the articulation of names (e.g., Roman Canon, "Eucharistic Prayer," # 1; *BCP,* "Prayer D," p. 375). Because this practice solicits the names of departed loved ones, it is especially appropriate on All Saints' Day. Any Eucharistic Prayer may pause for spontaneous expressions of thanksgiving and praise. The Prayer of Confession may also pause for spontaneous expression of personal confessions.

Less frequent and sometimes unpredictable occurrences call for flexibility and spontaneity. The liturgist who relies solely upon prayerbooks will come up short when there is a heart attack in the pew or someone responds to a liturgical invitation to make a faith commitment to Christ. Exceptional circumstances often call forth the gift of extemporaneous prayer. How is such a gift cultivated? Classic prayers can serve as models for free prayer. Familiarity with their rhythm, progression, phraseology, and spirit will suggest an appropriate prayer for the occasion to the leader who is sensitive to the guidance of the Spirit.

Spontaneous, unstructured prayer carries with it a demand for discipline. Congregations should be instructed so that this type of prayer complements the liturgy. It must reflect the norms that the local community establishes concerning length, content, and style. Like all liturgical prayer, this unstructured prayer expresses the mystery of one God in three persons. It should be understood as originating from the Father, and, through the name of Christ and in the presence and power of the Holy Spirit, it is to be offered to the Father in return.[9]

Spontaneous prayer should neither intrude upon other prayers nor be repetitious. *But it should occur,* and free space can be provided for it, especially where the worshiping body is not large. Its primary and regular place is within the Prayers of the People.

Kiss of Peace

The Kiss of Peace belongs to the "first stratum" of the liturgy.[10] Its origin probably lies in Jewish table customs. Luke 7:45 notes Christ's reproach to Simon the Pharisee who neglected the customary kiss. A liturgical kiss is mentioned frequently in the New Testament (Rom. 16:16; 1 Cor. 16:20; 2 Cor. 13:12; 1 Thess. 5:26; 1 Peter 5:14) and is mentioned in most ancient liturgical sources.

In the early liturgies, the Peace comes before the Offertory (the movement of bread and wine to the altar-table). So placed, it is a symbol for the peace and unity of the church, which is a prerequisite for eucharistic celebration. Significant efforts were made to insure that the Peace did not "degenerate into a formality."[11]

Matthew 5:23–24 instructs worshipers first to be reconciled with other Christians before offering gifts at the altar. Similarly, Didache 14 counsels:

> On every Lord's Day—his special day—come together and break bread and give thanks, first confessing your sins so that your sacrifice may be pure. Anyone at variance with his neighbor must not join you, until they are reconciled, lest your sacrifice be defiled. For it was of this sacrifice that the Lord said, "Always and everywhere offer me a pure sacrifice; for I am a great King, says the Lord, and my name is marveled at by the nations."[12]

In modern practice the position of the Peace in the order of worship varies. It may occur after the penitential rite (SLR); after the Prayers of the People (*LBW, BCP,* SWR, Coptic and Abyssinian rites); or after the Lord's Prayer, prior to communion *(Sac).* Wherever it occurs, it is vital that it be exchanged with sincerity and reverence. The imposition of casual, street language is inappropriate. Liturgy is poetry. The way in which we greet one another in a liturgical context is stylized out of deference to the uniqueness of the occasion: Christians in the house of the Lord greeting one another in the Spirit.

The Peace is an act of spontaneity set within the confines of structure. Obviously, there is much room here for indigenization. Local cultures will determine which gestures are appropriate. However, spontaneity does not give license to what one pastor labeled the "abominable greeting." The Peace should be peaceful and reverent, not tumultuous.

The Peace is a spiritual encounter. Each Christian is a vehicle of God's grace, and thus a primordial sacrament. When the Peace is exchanged, persons become means of grace to each other. Warmth, genuineness, and spontaneity best convey that peace which passes all understanding.

Adapting the Peace

The exchange of the Peace may be tailored to particular occasions in which the liturgy marks personal transitions. When Paul and Barnabas prepared to embark upon one of their missionary journeys, the church gathered around them and extended to them "the right hand of fellowship" (Gal. 2:9). The image seems to suggest a handshake, but it does not necessarily imply a handshake given the variety of greeting gestures among the world's cultures.[13] For Paul and Barnabas, the gesture was a sign of solidarity of purpose, a recognition of equality and partnership, a pledge of cooperation and support as they undertook their mission to the Gentiles.

At the occasion of a baptism the Peace may be spontaneously transformed into an act of welcome. Such a display of affection is often found among the Brethren and Mennonites. At a wedding, it may flow out of the nuptial kiss and thereby express congregational solidarity with the bride and groom in their new covenant relationship. At an ordination or commissioning, the Peace may communicate a recognition of equality and partnership in ministry. Upon the occasion of a leave-taking, the Peace may be transformed into a spontaneous gesture of Godspeed.

The congregation may be trusted as to how best to exchange the Peace on such special occasions. The important thing is to provide sensitively a free space for its gift of discretion. This free space will help insure that the Peace does not degenerate into a formality.

The Power of God

Spontaneous Involvement can also occur during preaching. A curious transformation occurs in many folks on every Sunday morning. The very people, who on the day before whistle, stomp, and boo at an athletic event, give a standing ovation to a concert violinist, let a political orator know he's "right on," or clap their hands to the rhythm of a folk artist, are miraculously transformed by sermon time the next day. When the gospel, the power of God unto salvation, is preached, these same persons become like Zechariah in the Temple, struck dumb, strangely subdued, hushed as though dazzled by the elocutions from the pulpit.

The word of God, theologians tell us, is *an event,* a bold proclamation of the person who stands at the center of all of history, Jesus Christ. In preaching, the human word is transformed by the power of the Holy Spirit into the divine word. In the New Testament we read of persons being seized by the Holy Spirit as God's word is preached to them (Acts 10:44–45). Hebrews 4:12–13 tells us how this happens:

> For the word of God is living and active, sharper than any two-edged sword, piercing to the division of soul and spirit, of joints and marrow, and discerning the thoughts and intentions of the heart. And before him no creature is hidden, but all are open and laid bare to the eyes of him with whom we have to do.

I once attended a Good Friday service that was sponsored by the black congregations in town. A three-hour preaching marathon, it afforded the opportunity of sampling every black preacher in town in one sitting. Of course, in such a context competition among preachers is inevitable. One preacher had to follow a particularly tough act. He was so unnerved by this task that he stammered through the first ten minutes of his sermon, despite the earnest encouragement of his faithful followers scattered among the other worshipers.

Suddenly, the preacher stopped in midsentence and pled with the entire congregation: "Gimme some hep! Ah need yo hep! Ah can't do dis without your hep, *please* hep me now." A shot of adrenaline bolted the congregation out of its lethargy. They responded as though they had been asked to pull a drowning child from a lake. With loud "Amens," hand-clapping, and shouts of encouragement from all quarters, the preacher ventured on, but now far, far above his previous, meager level of ability. It wasn't the best sermon that afternoon, but it was surely the most exciting. The preacher didn't preach that sermon; the congregation did. It became *their* sermon! Would that the rest of us poor preachers felt free to plead for that kind of "hep."

Mysteries in the Spirit

An emphasis on giftedness pervades the New Testament. In St. Paul's writings spiritual gifts are referred to as *charismata.*

The New Testament clearly understands these spiritual gifts as manifestations of God's grace. Lists of gifts or *charismata* are usually drawn from three passages:

Romans 12:4–8	*1 Corinthians 12:4–11, 28–31*	*Ephesians 4:11*
teaching	utterances of wisdom	apostles
exhortation	utterances of knowledge	prophets
contributions	faith	evangelists
giving of aid	healing	pastors
	miracles	teachers
acts of mercy	prophecy	
	discernment of spirits	
	tongues	
	interpretation of tongues	
	helpers	
	administrators	

Such lists are hardly exhaustive. In fact, the New Testament mentions other gifts, such as singing (1 Cor. 14:15; Eph. 5:19; Col. 3:16) and prayer (Rom. 8:15–16, 26–27; 1 Cor. 14:14–17; Eph. 6:18). The gifts listed in these passages reflect merely those with which the writers are familiar and those of pastoral relevance to their purposes.

The expansiveness of such lists confirms what baptismal theology also teaches: that every Christian is a charismatic. Each has a unique combination of gifts that the Holy Spirit gives to fulfill the Lord's purpose (1 Cor. 7:7). Each is a recipient of God's gift of salvation and eternal life and is empowered by God's Spirit to the new life in Christ (Acts 2:38; Rom. 3:24; 6:23; Col. 3:12–17). Each receives charisms as the call of God that empowers the recipient to a particular ministry within the community of faith.[14]

Certain Christians refer to themselves as Charismatics, a practice that highlights the fact that all Christians are such. The modern Charismatic Movement, in both its Pentecostal and neo-

Pentecostal (i.e., Roman Catholic and mainline Protestant) forms, brings to the church an intensified awareness of God's personal gifts, as is found in the New Testament. The movement is characterized by an awareness of the personal indwelling and empowering of the Holy Spirit (1 John 3:24) who moves the person to glorify the risen Christ, to witness and worship at a level of abundance as described in Acts and the epistles, to love God's word, and to live in the power of the Holy Spirit. In this way of life charismatic manifestations are frequently evident.

The twentieth-century resurgence of charismatic emphases received great impetus from revivals in the early 1900s, which led to the formation of the classical Pentecostal churches. In the 1960s the Charismatic Movement made inroads into the mainline churches, Catholic, Protestant, and Orthodox. This neo-Pentecostal movement is now widespread and of very great influence among Christians throughout the world.

As in any movement, not all who are associated with it articulate its goals and tenets accurately or in the most constructive way possible. The Charismatic Movement is at once a gift and a challenge to mainline churches, as is any reformation. It is a gift inasmuch as it is an obvious manifestation of the renewing power of the Holy Spirit. It is a challenge in that churches must be flexible in creating free space for these gifts in ministry.

The local congregation that is blessed with the ministry of Charismatics should explore ways of enhancing liturgical participation utilizing these gifts. This is a delicate process, requiring patience, openness, sensitivity, respect, education, encouragement, and discernment. The Spirit moves in a myriad of ways. A tolerance for diversity is a prerequisite to enhancing liturgical participation. The church that would display its note of catholicity will need to feel comfortable with a variety of forms of liturgical participation.[15]

Certain *charismata* lend themselves readily to spontaneous involvement in worship. When used in public worship, speaking in tongues (glossolalia), to be in order, must be accompanied by an interpretation of tongues in faithfulness to Scripture (1 Cor. 14:5). The interpretation is the vernacular of God's message that was uttered in tongues, which is usually in an unidentifiable language. This form of communication may be likened to abstract painting or surrealist poetry, forms that also transcend earthly realism and human rationality.[16]

St. Paul, himself very capable of speaking in tongues (1 Cor. 14:18), understood the motive behind the practice. It is not surprising that Paul would interrupt a careful theological treatise with an ecstatic hymn of praise:

> O the depth of the riches and wisdom and knowledge of God! How unsearchable are his judgments and how inscrutable his ways!
> "For who has known the mind of the Lord,
> or who has been his counselor?"
> "Or who has given a gift to him
> that he might be repaid?"
> For from him and through him and to him are all things. To him be glory for ever. Amen. (Rom. 11:33–36)

Speaking in tongues may be joined to unknown and unrehearsed music in a spiritual phenomenon known as "singing in the Spirit" (1 Cor. 14:15). The effect of this combination is an unusual, ethereal sound, one that is very beautiful and wonderfully harmonious. It begins softly, builds into a crescendo, then gradually subsides into silence, a silence that participants often describe as being pregnant with the presence of God.

For St. Paul more desirable than speaking in tongues is the gift of prophecy (1 Cor. 14:1–5). Prophecy is a message from God for a congregation, communicated in a comprehensible language. The Holy Spirit expresses itself directly through a prophet. This communication may consist of words of encouragement, consolation, edification, insight, instruction, exhortation, or admonishment. It may be couched in insider's language, such as that contained in St. John's Revelation/Apocalypse. Prophecy differs from speaking in tongues in that it is of greater benefit to the whole worshiping body. It is also more persuasive to unbelievers who are more likely to be convicted by it than they are by the gift of tongues (1 Cor. 14:24).[17]

Just as St. Paul placed strictures on speaking in tongues by insisting upon an interpretation, so prophecy is paired with another gift, the discernment of spirits. "The spirits of prophets are subject to prophets. For God is not a God of confusion but of peace" (1 Cor. 14:32; cf. 1 Thess. 5:19–22).

The *charismata* are gifts primarily for a church, not the individual. The overriding criterion for evaluating their worth is that they be used for the edification of the church (1 Cor. 14:26, 31). Indeed, this is an appropriate guideline for all forms of Spontaneous Involvement in worship.[18]

Patterns of Spontaneous Involvement

Christian theology affirms the dialectical truth that the God who is transcendent, totally above and beyond creation, is also immanent. God is everywhere present (Ps. 138[139]). God's handiwork and invisible nature are clearly perceived throughout creation (Ps. 18[19]:1; Rom. 1:20). For Christians the personal experience of God's immanence is through the indwelling Spirit, a fact that illumines the nature of liturgical spontaneity. The word *spontaneous* comes from the Latin *sponte* which means "of one's own accord, willingly, unaided." However, Spontaneous Involvement in worship does not originate in the spontaneity of individuals. When Christians act willingly, it is actually the will of the Holy Spirit that prompts them. Spontaneous Involvement is an act of one's own accord only inasmuch as it conforms to that of the Holy Spirit. While it appears to be unaided by structures of worship, it is dependent upon the Spirit both in its articulation and in its reception. True spontaneity originates with God's free Spirit. It is a sign of the new life in Christ within the communion of the Holy Spirit.

The purpose of spontaneous participation is widely underestimated, if not misunderstood. Its true purpose is not to make worship less formal, more friendly, or more "folksy"; nor is it to make worshipers feel more comfortable with each other (reasons often advanced in defense of informal worship). Least of all is it to reduce the encounter with the Holy One to more manageable proportions. The purpose of spontaneity is a very specific one:

the edification of the church, the building up of Christ's body (1 Cor. 14:26). A true charism is given for the service of the community. It is bestowed in the interests of others. Spontaneity in worship that does not advance this sole criterion under the direction of the Spirit does not add to worship and, in some cases, may even detract from it (e.g., 1 Cor. 12:3). All Spontaneous Involvement must flow from the Spirit's ministry to edify the church. For this reason, it is desirable only to the extent that it is subject to the discipline of worshiping communities. This subjection will insure that it is faithful to its calling: the upbuilding of the church by the power of the Holy Spirit.

Spontaneous Involvement will flourish only as truly free space is generously provided for it. Social pressure and judgment, as well as narrow views of liturgical decency and order, can inhibit the development of this free space. Spontaneous Involvement indeed adds a dimension of unpredictability to worship. However, sometimes God surprises. Those with the gift of liturgical leadership must here (as always!) defer to the liturgical leadership of the Holy Spirit. After all, the dynamics of worship can hardly be circumscribed by prayerbooks or rubrics, which are merely starting points. Structure and freedom are complementary modes of God's presence. Although the church may be filled with the Spirit, it does not own the Spirit. Let all things be done decently and in order (1 Cor. 14:40), but do not quench the Spirit (1 Thess. 5:19)!

Spontaneous Involvement typifies in a more vivid way certain ideals for all forms of liturgical participation: it springs from the heart; it cannot be coerced and must be voluntary; it is unconscious of forms; it enjoys an immediacy with the Holy Spirit. A pupil of Pablo Casals once performed flawlessly a difficult work. After the recital, he proudly sought out the affirmation of his revered teacher. The maestro agreed, "Yes," he exclaimed, "the notes, they were perfect—*but there was no music!*" Spontaneous Involvement demonstrates for all liturgical participation a level of communion in the Spirit that transforms notes into music.

Study Guide

1. The author lists as examples of Spontaneous Involvement:

spontaneous song
spontaneous prayer
the passing of the Peace
verbal responses to preaching
the charismata

Are any of these present in your congregation's worship? Should they be? Why, or why not? What are some assets of this type of participation? What are some liabilities?

2. In your opinion, to what degree might Spontaneous Involvement impinge upon needed liturgical order?

3. What is the true purpose of Spontaneous Involvement? How is the criterion of edification to be applied to the expression of this type of participation?

For Further Reading

Bradford, Brick. "Releasing the Power of the Holy Spirit." Oklahoma City, OK: Presbyterian Charismatic Communion, 1983.

Dobson, Theodore E. *How to Pray for Spiritual Growth.* Ramsey, NJ: Paulist, 1982.

Koenig, John. *Charismata: God's Gifts for God's People.* Philadelphia, PA: Westminster, 1978.

McDonnell, Kilian. *Presence, Power, Praise: Documents on Charismatic Renewal.* 3 Vols. Collegeville, MN: Liturgical, 1980.

MacNutt, Francis. *Healing.* Notre Dame, IN: Ave Maria, 1974.

Martin, Ralph P. *The Spirit and the Congregation: Studies in 1 Corinthians 12—15.* Grand Rapids, MI: Eerdmans, 1984.

O'Connor, Edward D. *The Pentecostal Movement in the Catholic Church.* Notre Dame, IN: University of Notre Dame, 1974.

_____. *Perspectives on Charismatic Renewal.* Notre Dame, IN: University of Notre Dame, 1975.

_____. "Charismatic Renewal, Catholic." *NCE,* 17.104–6.

Sherrill, John L. *They Speak with Other Tongues.* Old Tappan, NJ: Fleming H. Revell, 1964.

Songs of Zion. SWR, 12. Nashville, TN: Abingdon, 1981.

4

The Still, Small Voice of Calm

Creative Silence

The silence of worship is more than the absence of sound. Liturgical silence provides a context, a frame for the hearing of God's word. It is waiting "patiently for the Lord" (Ps. 39[40]:1), being open to the "still, small voice of calm."[1]

Silence is a favorite metaphor of an early father of the church, St. Ignatius of Antioch. For those who wonder whether silence is less possible in these faster-paced times, consider the fact that Ignatius knew little of it, at least outwardly. He was a busy pastor of a major church in a bustling city. The religious movement with which he was affiliated had a serious public-relations problem in Antioch. One day, during a local persecution of Christians, Ignatius himself was arrested. Tried and convicted, he was sentenced to die. A squadron of soldiers marched him overland toward the Coliseum in Rome. Surrounded by gawkers, despisers, and the coarse military language of his guards (his "ten leopards"), the bishop dictated letters to churches en route to Rome.[2]

In these epistles there are references to the silence of God, which for Ignatius is a symbol for the primordial mystery. This silence is not a void. It is a creative, pregnant silence out of which God moves. Mary's virginity, he writes, was hidden from the prince of this world, as was the birth of Christ and his death upon the cross. These "mysteries of a cry . . . were done in the stillness of God." The silence of Christ before Pilate, he continues, also reflects the primordial silence of God. These "unheralded events of salvation cry out their meaning to those who are able to grasp their significance." Similarly, Christians may appropriately keep silent in certain circumstances. Their silence can be an eloquent testimony to their faith:

> It is better to be silent and to be than while speaking not to be. . . . Those who have truly mastered the utterances of Jesus will also be able to apprehend his silence, and thus reach full spiritual maturity, so that their own words will have the force of actions and their silences the significance of speech.[3]

Ignatius reminds us that liturgical silence is more than the absence of sound. It is not the silence of gaps in liturgical execution as, for example, when an organist fumbles for the music, or when a deacon is dispatched to the sacristy during a baptism because the ewer contains no water, or when the logistics of communion distribution are needlessly prolonged. Such silence serves no positive function. It is simply a void that is distracting and confusing. It interrupts the flow of the service and detracts from the creative and pregnant silence out of which issues forth God's wisdom.

How does silence play a positive role in worship? Because it is an amorphous symbol, the context determines its meaning. When silence occurs in worship, it is defined by how it is framed.

The Silence of Preparation

> The present state of the world and the whole of life is diseased. If I were a doctor and were asked for my advice, I should reply: "Create silence! Bring everyone to silence." The Word of God cannot be heard in the noisy world of today. And even if it were blazoned forth with all the panoply of noise, so that it could be heard in the midst of all the other noise, then it would no longer be the Word of God. Therefore, create silence.
>
> (Søren Kierkegaard)

Creating silence is easier said than done. Our senses are bombarded by the cacophony of modern existence. In order to worship God we must first silence the welter of anxious concerns for the morrow. We must extinguish the commercialism that is drummed into our psyches. We must filter out human words as we listen intently for the transcendent word. To prepare to enter into the mode of worship requires considerable effort. Just as an athlete must train before entering into competition, so must the worshiper prepare for worship through prayer, meditation, Bible study, and physical rest, so that bodies and minds will "be alert to the privileges and responsibilities of the Lord's Day."[4]

The need for worship preparation argues favorably for a preacher's use of a lectionary. How much more fruitful will be the silence of preparation when it is focused upon those lessons that will be read and proclaimed during the liturgy. More than one pastor has heard a parishioner remark: "Since I've started studying the lectionary, it's amazing how much your preaching has improved." Whether preachers utilize the church's lectionary or their own, it is important that they give advance notice of the lessons for the liturgy. This is only fair to the worshipers who need every available assistance toward entering into the act of worship.

Meditation upon God's word prior to worship creates additional free space for the ministry of the Holy Spirit whose field of operation includes the richness of human imagination. The Spirit moves as minds are actively engaged with God's word. During periods of incubation, the Spirit secretly prepares each soul for an encounter with God's word as read and proclaimed in the eucharistic assembly.

The silence of preparation is also important for worship leaders. In particular, the preacher must faithfully set aside time alone to listen for the still, small voice through meditating upon the preaching texts. How much time is needed? That is difficult to say. Some sermons come relatively quickly. Others require extensive research and time-consuming wrestling with the texts. Over the long term, a good rule of thumb is one hour of preparation for every minute in the pulpit. Celebrants should prepare for their role by meditating upon the prayers of the liturgy. Familiarity enhances the execution of prayers. It is vital for the celebrant's spirit to be resonant with the Holy Spirit who prays through the liturgy.

The Silence of Centering

Let all mortal flesh keep silence,
    And with fear and trembling stand;
Ponder nothing earthly-minded,
    For with blessing in his hand,
Christ our God to earth descendeth,
    Our full homage to demand.
                    From the Liturgy of St. James for Good Friday, fifth century

One summer while home from college, I attended a church at which a former music teacher was the organist. I revered her as my teacher and was proud that she was employed at such a large and prestigious congregation. Looking forward to hearing her play, I arrived early and took a seat behind the organ console. She put up works by Alain and Messiaien and executed them flawlessly. By then, folks were beginning to arrive. There were friendly exchanges of greetings going on in the sanctuary and, as more persons gathered, the noise level grew. Some minutes before the service was scheduled to begin, the ministers entered the sanctuary, walking through the congregation, boisterously greeting worshipers. By this time, the organist was forced to switch to musical pabulum, because she was unable to compete with the din. It was a distressing scene. A congregation had hired an accomplished artist; however, instead of using her talents fully, it in effect reduced her to the level of Muzak (innocuous or nondescript background music) in order to cover its social chatter before worship. The service began without any provisions for centering on the activity at hand, the worship of Almighty God.

It is said that the rabbis in Jesus' time encouraged an hour of silence before the beginning of synagogue worship. The moments that immediately precede the beginning of the liturgy are crucial to participation. Just as a runner spends the final moments before a race stretching tendons and warming muscles in preparation, so worshipers need this time for centering. Centering prayer cleanses the inner spirit of worldly worries and concerns. It integrates the entire person into a deep and fruitful disposition for worship. It involves an intentional focusing *of* the inner person, but the focus is not *on* the inner person. Centering is contemplation of the triune God. It means taking one's place with the angels and archangels, with cherubim and seraphim and all the heavenly host, before the throne of God in anticipation of the liturgy of heaven.

Effective aids for centering include hymn texts, Scripture readings, and composed prayers of preparation. Worship spaces furnished with kneelers afford the additional benefit of letting bodies help engage spirits for worship. The use of short repetitive prayers that clear the mind of distractions and orient one's spirit toward God can also be effective.[5]

Announcements made at the beginning of worship may negate the centering that has taken place earlier. If that negation occurs, additional concentrated silence is then needed to reorient persons toward the act of worship. Although announcements are legitimate expressions of the life of the faith community, they should ordinarily be conveyed through the medium of print. When this is not possible, oral announcements ought to be brief and in suitable taste.

Congregations in which an initial centering does not occur may profit by exploring this issue. The entire congregation should be invited into dialogue on the question. Changes in practice may need to be approached cautiously. The usual justification given for the "social-greeting pattern of worship preliminaries" is that the congregation is an open, caring, and friendly one and naturally displays this quality as it gathers for worship. In encouraging a shift to silence, care should be taken so that this is not perceived as "an intrusion of cold formalism." Dialogue within the congregation will reveal alternative ways through which it might demonstrate its level of friendliness. Surely a "friendly congregation" would also desire to be known as a "house of prayer." Such images of a church need not be mutually exclusive.

Points of centering prayer also occur throughout the service and should be carefully observed by the celebrant. Liturgy is like a dance. If you move ahead of the beat, you will step on your partner's toes. The invitation to prayer should be routinely punctuated with silence. The ancient rhythm of the collect, in which rubrics stipulate a pause for silence, is a commendable example of this pattern:

> Let us pray:
> *(Pause for silent prayer)*
> Father in heaven, author of all truth,
> a people once in darkness has listened to your Word
> and followed your Son as he rose from the tomb.
> Hear the prayer of this newborn people
> and strengthen your Church to answer your call.
> May we rise and come forth into the light of day
> to stand in your presence until eternity dawns.
> We ask this through Christ our Lord.
> *(All respond):* AMEN.[6]

The same, ancient pattern of silent punctuation also occurs in the Prayers of the People (see *BCP*, pp. 383–93) and the Prayers after the Communion (see *Sac*).

A regular pattern of silent punctuation allows time for the community to center for prayer. Breathing is synchronized. The worshipers become integrated. Thoughts are focused. Attuned to the words articulated by the leader, the congregation enters more fully into the expression of the prayer. The silence of centering is a collective gathering of focus.

Navy veterans describe the wartime experience of a ship's crew being instantly awakened in the middle of the night by the engines being cut off. No matter how soundly each had been sleeping, all were immediately drawn together in silent awareness that something of great import was imminent. The silence of centering serves a similar function in worship. It is a frame that announces the graceful advent of God. It is a moment of anticipation, a hush when "shadows hold their breath."[7]

The Silence of Confession

And the foundations of the thresholds shook at the voice of him who called, and the house was filled with smoke. And I said: "Woe is me! For I am lost; for I am a man of unclean lips, and I dwell in the midst of a people of unclean lips; for my eyes have seen the King, the LORD of hosts!" (Isa. 6:4–5)

The biblical response to the fullness of the presence of the Lord is one of contrition. The holiness of God reveals the unworthiness of humanity. In worship the presence of the Holy One is acknowledged with an opening penitential rite. The Prayer of Confession appropriately includes a generous free space for silent, personal confessions of sin. This silence is an inviting moment in which to surrender sin to God "to whom all hearts are open, all desires known, and from whom no secrets are hid."[8]

The silence of confession reaches its high point in the liturgy for Good Friday. In solemn procession the ministers enter in silence, and all kneel in prayer. In some traditions the celebrants prostrate themselves before the cross. Such gestures are powerful expressions of the doctrine of utter depravity. In this prolonged silence of confession, we suffer "the loss of all things, and count them as refuse" in order that we may gain Christ (Phil. 3:8).

The church is accused by some of perpetuating guilt, of promoting too low a view of the human state. In some instances there is truth to that, unfortunately. Yet the silence of confession is a form of reality therapy. It is a frank admission of responsibility, the full acceptance of which dignifies, rather than degrades, our humanity. Problems arise only when those who enter into that silence are unable to embrace God's promise in faith.

Confession would not be possible were it not for the fact that God's mercy surpasses our sin. The silence of confession sets the stage for the graceful advent of the Savior, as so beautifully expressed in the words of a popular Christmas carol:

How silently, how silently
     The wondrous Gift is given!
So God imparts to human hearts
     The blessings of His heaven.
No ear may hear His coming,
     But in this world of sin,
Where meek souls will receive Him still,
     The dear Christ enters in.

Phillips Brooks,
"O Little Town of Bethlehem"

The Silence of Listening

The Resonance of God's Word

Because this book is written from the perspective of the pew, the discussion of Silent Engagement appropriately includes mention of preaching. The preacher's task is made easier only by the knowledge of that of which St. Paul writes: "The word is near you, on your lips and in your heart (that is, the word of faith which we preach)" (Rom. 10:8). The Apostle's words contain the secret to active participation in worship through Silent Engagement when God's word is read and proclaimed. An analogy from modern art will assist our understanding.

Sculptor Harry Bertoia, of the "Structure Sonores" movement, has created a number of untitled sounding sculptures. The grandest of these is a "wind barn." Standing within it are several clusters of upright metal rods, ranging in height from a few inches to several feet. The rods are made of various metals—copper, brass, stainless steel, and bronze sheeting. The upper end of each is enlarged, which makes the clusters resemble a stand of cattails. When the wind blows through the building, the rods resonate, causing them to strike adjacent ones. Some undulate with a mere breeze, others require winds of greater velocity. Standing within the barn, one hears soft whistling chimes, watery sighs, and resonant gongs. It is a wind chime and a magic music box of enormous proportions. What is significant about this work is that it is only when the sculpture resonates in the wind that it becomes what it really is. Only when it is making music does it affirm its true identity by fulfilling the purpose for which it was created.

God's word, read and proclaimed, is much like the wind animating those rods. When God's Spirit breathes, it causes a sympathetic resonance, because it corresponds with the same word that is already there "on your lips and in your hearts." It is a word that reaffirms our identity. The musical resonance that God's word creates is a declaration of who we really are—the Lord's redeemed.

There are further considerations to be drawn from this analogy. First, it is tempting and, alas, even fashionable to fault the efforts of preachers. The wind sculpture analogy suggests that such criticisms may be misplaced. No matter how hard the wind blows, nothing resonates that is immovable. The first requirement of a good sermon is a receptive audience. The sermon that is criticized may actually reflect a case of a listener who is inflexible to the breath of the Spirit.

That may be a painful perspective from which to critique a sermon but is, I would suggest, a proper place to begin. This is not to deny that bad preaching exists, for it does. Nor is it to excuse inadequate preparation, the main reason for poor sermons. It is to suggest, however, that there is usually something of value even in a mediocre sermon. If the word is truly near you, "on your lips and in your heart," you will resonate with it when it is read and proclaimed. "The wind blows where it wills, and you hear the sound of it, but you do not know whence it comes or whither it goes; so it is with every one who is born of the Spirit" (John 3:8).

Secondly, the wind sculpture analogy illustrates that a preacher's task is to resonate with the faith of the church. The preacher is not called to reveal new truth. Christians, by their baptism, already possess all knowledge and all wisdom in Christ (1 John 2:27; Eph. 1:9). Rather, a preacher's task is to illumine the Scriptures, to articulate the faith of the church in such a way that the church recognizes and appropriates what already belongs to it. Preaching becomes highly participatory when it expresses a congregation's own faith, including its fears, hopes, anger, joy, doubt, and gratitude.[9]

Preachers, then, do not stand over and against their churches. Preachers stand with their churches, speaking for them, prompting a process of mutual discernment of the Spirit. Therefore, it is incumbent upon listeners to pray both for preachers in their difficult task and for openness to the Spirit, "that the word of the Lord may speed on and triumph" (2 Thess. 3:1).

Discerning God's wisdom is hard work; it requires a radical openness of spirit. Preoccupation with worldly concerns, distractions, even negative feelings about the preacher—these must all be set aside for the sake of a much larger concern: hearing God's word spoken through human words. The best preaching in the world cannot cut through the elaborate network of interference that many erect. Only the listener can bring an intensity of openness for the secret wisdom of God that is otherwise so easily drowned out by the din of the world.

The silence of listening occurs when God's word is read and proclaimed and during the reflective silence that follows. It is hardly a passive form of liturgical participation. Indeed, it is a very active one. It is active engagement with God's word by the power of the Holy Spirit. The silence of listening is an act of prayer, prayer that human words will be transformed into God's word and resonate with God's glory.

The Silence of Adoration

Be still, and know that I am God. (Ps. 45[46]:10)

There are certain precious moments in life that naturally evoke a response of silence. They are moments of awe, of being overwhelmed by transcendence. When a mother gives birth to a child, there are often shouts of relief and gratitude. But shortly thereafter, in that miracle of miracles, the participants will be silent, at a loss for words to express their wonder at the gift of new life. The response of silence may be prompted by a telescopic glimpse of the marvelous garden of the heavens. It may be the contemplation of a rose or, as with the seventeenth-century Carmelite Brother Lawrence, an oak tree. It may be the death of a loved one, when interspersed among displays of grief there is a deepened reverence for the sanctity of life. For those of religious faith and for those without, life has its transcendent moments.

The cycle of Christian worship contains its own interludes of awe. Over the centuries, the liturgy has learned to recognize when it is standing on holy ground, there to pause in adoration.

–When hands are laid on the heads of ordinands, there is a hushed silence; it is obvious that the Holy Spirit is moving to call, to empower, to seal.

–When bride and groom turn to each other for the first time as husband and wife, their kiss is beheld in silence, an instinctive recognition of the transcendent dimensions of this union.

–When the faithful gather on Good Friday, they meditate on the cross in silence, awestruck at the magnitude and costliness of God's reconciliation.

–At the Paschal Vigil, as worshipers in darkness await the entrance proclamation, "The light of Christ," there is an anticipatory silence that precedes an announcement of great import.

–When an invitation is given to receive Christ as Savior and Lord, there is a respectful silence as the Holy Spirit secretly works in the heart that is restless.

–When the candles of Christmas Eve are lighted, there is an unspoken awareness of solidarity among Christians throughout the world on that holiest of nights.

–When bread and wine are elevated for all to see, there is silence, an appropriate recognition of the real presence of Christ, the living Lord.

Moments of awe are naturally shrouded in silence. Their sanctity demands it. In silence worshipers may contemplate the "dearest freshness deep down things."[10]

The Silence of Communion

The LORD is in his holy temple;
   let all the earth keep silence before him. (Hab. 2:20)

The indwelling of God in the church, the temple of God, is most evident in the celebration of the Eucharist. Before this great mystery, words fail and symbols fall short. As great a theologian as John Calvin faltered before it:

Although my mind can think beyond what my tongue can utter, yet even my mind is conquered and overwhelmed by the greatness of the thing [Lord's Supper]. Therefore, nothing remains but to break forth in wonder at this mystery, which plainly neither the mind is able to conceive nor the tongue to express.[11]

The high mystery of the Eucharist is owed to the real presence of Christ by the power of the Holy Spirit. The awareness of this mystery yields to that which alone can adequately begin to express it: silence. The silence of communion is one of the richest moments in the liturgy. In it the church surrenders itself fully to the Holy Spirit who gives this silence its content, its orientation, its profundity. The Spirit ministers personally to each person according to the need that is unique to each. The Spirit binds all together in a mystical union. Calvin describes this as being lifted up into heaven. Orthodox Christians refer to it as a foretaste of paradise.

To maximize participation in this silence, it is vital that the moment be framed well. Framing should highlight the joyful presence of the risen Lord with the church. Black robes, dour faces, and a sterile worship environment tend not to be the most suitable framing. The celebrant should not intrude upon the silence of communion with commentary, or compete with it by giving directions, or violate it by conveying a sense of uneasiness about it. Restraint is among the greatest of liturgical virtues. Here the celebrant must allow the actions to speak for themselves, trusting in the ministry of the Holy Spirit to fill the silence and to transform subjective freedom into the experience of communion.

Patterns of Silent Engagement

Wisdom manifests itself, and is yet hidden. The more it hides, the more it is manifest, and the more it is manifest the more it is hidden. For God is known when He is apprehended as unknown, and He is heard when we realize that we do not know the sound of His voice. The words He utters are words full of silence, and they are bait to draw us into silence. The truths He manifests are full of hiddenness, and their function is to hide us, with themselves, in God from whom they proceed.

(Thomas Merton)[12]

To reach spiritual maturity, one must apprehend the silence of God. In worship it is the silence that is the stepping-stone to maturity. Silent Engagement mirrors a transcendent, sovereign God, glorious in majesty, upon whom all exist in utter depen-

dence. What transpires within this silence is of utmost importance to liturgical participation. Liturgical silence is not a void or
a gap. It is a creative and pregnant silence, from which issues
forth the wisdom of God. Therefore, Silent Engagement, despite
its appearance of passivity, is a very *active* form of liturgical
participation, in that through it one is engaged by the ministry of
the Holy Spirit. The church that is absorbed in fruitful silence
images itself as a faithful flock of Christ's own, whose prayer is
that of Mary: "Behold, I am the handmaid of the Lord; let it be to
me according to your word" (Luke 1:38).

Silent Engagement thrives on a stable rhythm, in which the
liturgy regularly pauses for the silence of preparation, of centering, confession, listening, adoration, and communion. These
pauses must be consistent in length, so that they are not awkward. They must be ample. They must be framed with restraint, a
most desirable gift in liturgical leadership. The temptation to
flood this silence with a torrent of words, to make worship more
"active" or more "interesting," ought absolutely to be resisted.
The environment of worship is here to be surrendered to the
Spirit.

The gift of liturgical leadership includes the gracious sense of
how to step aside, of when to defer to the Spirit so that the people
may pray, of when one good symbol is worth more than a
thousand words. After all, worship leaders, there is one greater
than you. He must increase, you must decrease (John 3:30).
There is power in the still, small voice of calm!

Study Guide

1. In what ways does silence in worship make you feel comfortable or uncomfortable?

2. How might silence have a more fruitful place in the worship life of your congregation? Is its current framing adequate?

3. Do you prepare for worship? In what ways? Are there
additional disciplines that you could undertake?

4. How can you get more out of the sermon/homily? How can
your preacher/homilist put more into it?

5. Have any of your most meaningful religious encounters occurred in the context of silence?

For Further Reading

Craddock, Fred B. *Preaching.* Nashville, TN: Abingdon, 1985.

Erickson, Craig Douglas. *Under the Shadow of Your Wings: Ten Lenten Sermons on Covenant Themes.* Lima, OH: C.S.S., 1986.

Ignatius of Loyola. *The Spiritual Exercises of St. Ignatius.* Tr. Anthony Mottola. Garden City, NY: Doubleday, 1964.

Kelsey, Morton T. *The Other Side of Silence.* Paramus, NJ: Paulist, 1976.

Merton, Thomas. *Seasons of Celebration.* New York, NY: Farrar, Straus, and Giroux, 1965.

Micks, Marianne H. "The Sounds of Silence." Pp. 70–85 in *The Future Present.* New York, NY: Seabury, 1970.

Pennington, M. Basil. *Centering Prayer.* Garden City, NY: Doubleday, 1980.

Thielicke, Helmut. *The Silence of God.* Grand Rapids, MI: Eerdmans, 1962.

5

A Memorial Before God

Memory and Saving Presence

And God heard their groaning, and God remembered his covenant
with Abraham, with Isaac, and with Jacob. (Exod. 2:23–24)

Abraham Joshua Heschel has aptly commented, "Much of what
the Bible demands can be comprised in one word: *Remember.*"[1]
The obligation to remember is applied to both the divine and the
human. When God remembers, his saving presence draws near.
In remembering the covenant, God acts in conformity with it.
The Lord intervenes for Israel, acting in Israel's behalf (Gen.
9:15; 30:22; Exod. 2:24; 6:5; Lev. 26:42; 1 Sam. 1:19; Pss.
104[105]:8, 42; 97[98]:3; Luke 1:54, 72). For this reason, Hebrew
prayers (e.g., Pss. 82[83]:4; 87[88]:5; 105[106]:4; Lam. 5:1) often
petition God to remember, it being understood that when this
occurs, the Lord moves to make his saving presence known.

Israel, created in the image of the God who remembers, is
itself obliged to remember. The covenant is not unconditional. In
response to divine promises and blessings Israel must also as-
sume responsibilities. "You shall remember the LORD your God"
(Deut. 8:18). "Remember this day, in which you came out from
Egypt" (Exod. 13:3). "Remember the sabbath day" (Exod. 20:8).
The memory of God's wondrous saving deeds is the way in which
Israel is instructed to approach a gracious God:

Seek the LORD and his strength,
  seek his presence continually!
Remember the wonderful works that he has done,
  his miracles, and the judgments he uttered. (Ps. 104[105]:4–5)

The covenant is God's promise to remember Israel. The covenant also obligates Israel to remember God.

The biblical sense of memory implies much more than mental recollection. Here memory has a spiritual, not a psychological, structure. Memory is essential to being present not only to oneself and to others but also to God. Consequently, memory in the biblical sense may be applied not only to the past but to the present or the future as well. When Israel remembers, it moves toward God. When Israel remembers, it acts in faithfulness to God's law. Biblical memory brings to mind something by which to live and hope, as Passover Haggadah explains:

Even if all of us were wise,
all of us people of understanding,
all of us learned in Torah,
it would still be our obligation to
tell the story of the Exodus from Egypt. . . .
For Redemption is not yet complete.[2]

Christian worship functions as a living memorial before God. It helps the community call into conscious memory what it has received (1 Cor. 11:23–26) and already knows or should know.[3]

Differing theories attempt to explain the relationship of human memory to God's saving presence in worship. According to one school of thought, memory renders saving events objectively present to the believer.[4] This viewpoint is problematical in that to speak as though historical events are temporally movable is to adopt a nonbiblical and mythical conceptualization of time.[5]

Another possible explanation of the relationship of memory to saving presence is that memory renders the worshiper present to past events central to salvation history, a perspective seemingly expressed in the beloved spiritual: "Were you there, when they crucified my Lord?" However, this explanation neglects the role of the Holy Spirit and the uniqueness of biblical memory as prayer.

A preferable explanation is that through the remembrance of God's wondrous saving deeds the worshiper participates in the mystery of the God who is eternally present. For example, in the Jewish Haggadah the events of the Passover are remembered before God. In so doing, these become events that reverberate throughout a remembered history. Specifically recalling them enables the Jew to enter into the same redemptive reality. In this sense the father instructs the child: "It is because of what the Lord did *for me* when *I* went free from Egypt."[6] Although the participants are separated in time and space from the arena of God's acts, the historical gulf is spanned through remembrance. Israel remembers and thereby approaches the God who is, who was, and who shall be present to all of history.[7]

For Christians, to celebrate the liturgy is to reminisce in the Spirit and so to be in communion with the saints of God. To remember is to know and therefore to participate in the saving acts of God (Mic. 6:5). This is why all liturgical prayer properly begins with memory. In worship human memory is the avenue to encounter with God. As St. Augustine commented, memory permits the soul to live, to be present to itself. In worship human memory invokes communion with God.

The Rule of Prayer

Interiorized Verbal Participation is an expression of faithfulness to God's command to remember. It is verbal language that resonates in the sanctuary of the heart, the interior of the soul. It employs prayers, Scripture, responses, and poetry (psalms, canticles, and hymns) in a wide variety of idioms. What all of these have in common is their relationship to memory. To the degree that they are interiorized, they enjoy a quality of language that lies close at hand to the seat of spiritual encounter, language that is either learned or otherwise so familiar as to be easily recognizable and appropriated as prayer. Through repetition these expressions are woven into the fabric of the spirit, thereby becoming the matrix of the spiritual life.

The elements of Interiorized Verbal Participation are comfortable, beloved, and timeless—of proven value to God's people over the centuries, who by using them have come into ownership of them. This type of participation understands worship as a discipline of prayer and the liturgy as an objective standard that invites worshipers to conform themselves to it.[8] This conception stands in sharp contrast to the perspective that concludes that, because the liturgy seems irrelevant, there is something wrong with *it* rather than with the spiritual state of the person who professes an inability to relate to it.

Interiorized Verbal Participation knows well the value of repetition. It understands that when overly inundated with the new, regardless of quality, a congregation finds it difficult to participate fully in the worship. Beethoven's "Fifth Symphony" is not famous simply because a large number of people have heard it only once and liked it. It is a great, even monumental work because it grows better and better with each successive hearing. Its well-crafted phrases provide enormous satisfaction by being both majestic and familiar. One is always uplifted by the work, which is why it is enduring. Similarly, an effective liturgy grows better each time it is celebrated. Participation in it rises in direct proportion to the degree of recognition present within the participants.

Some may protest that invariability is a formula for uninteresting worship. Ironically, the most tedious worship is that in which new words and happenings are piled on, overwhelming the participant. Liturgy of this style is like a wine tasting. You don't get enough of any one wine really to enjoy it. After awhile it is difficult to distinguish among those wines already tasted. Repetition makes possible a deeper level of meaning in many of life's experiences, whether it be eating, bathing, lovemaking, or worshiping. Familiar, repetitious patterns provide stability and order within which true creativity and enjoyment are possible.

Is this an argument against the creativity of worship leaders?

Not at all. It argues instead for the primary investment of those gifts in making the liturgical tradition come alive. Excess creative energies might better be applied to those energies already invested in preaching. There, let the prophetic voice and individual creativity have full rein, but elsewhere let familiarity through repetition deepen the level of participation. Let the prayers flow from measured cadences and well-worn phrases. Let the tongue that articulates them delight in knowing it has passed that way before and will pass that way again.

Interiorized Verbal Participation, operating in the ritual mode, thrives on repetition, the key to a deeper level of participation over a lifetime. Repetition enhances participation because of the marvelous capacity of the Holy Spirit to work through the human imagination. The prayer that is said again and again prepares the heart for the graceful advent of the Lord whose Spirit will, in God's own time, work to engage retroactively the level of participation in utterly unpredictable ways.

The Mind as Living Memorial

Familiarity is of greatest value at the level of memorization. Through repetition certain elements of the liturgy are freed from the medium of print, thereby becoming more immediately available to the soul upon the occasion of its divine encounter. "To know by heart" is to bring something into closer proximity to the center of one's being. Committing God's word to memory dignifies the mind as a living memorial before the Lord. The memorization of music and portions of the liturgy, either intentionally or through repetitive usage, is an act of stewardship, an act that offers the mind as a living memorial before God.

The human mind, that most marvelous of all of God's creations, holds a truly awesome capacity for knowledge, reasoning, and psychological and spiritual sensitivities. Not surprisingly, such greatness of potential is matched by greatness of liability. An unfortunate by-product of this ability is that the human mind also has the capacity to accumulate much extraneous and unwanted data. Sophisticated advertising techniques, well aware of the mind's retentive capabilities, exploit these fully in order to embed commercial messages deep within the psyche. For those people who are vulnerable to the bombardment of these techniques, the mind can rapidly become a memorial to consumerism, making memory an avenue to material acquisition. With messages stored where they are immediately available, consumers are moved closer to a product they have learned to trust.

The modern attempt to instill a few hymns, responses, Scripture passages and psalms into the overloaded circuitry of parishioners' minds is an uphill battle. Yet, if Christians are to be transformed by the renewal of their minds, that they may "prove what is the will of God, what is good and acceptable and perfect" (Rom. 12:2), this effort must surely be made. The memorization of liturgical elements, such as hymns, Scripture verses, prayers, and responses, places the gospel where it may be immediately and directly appropriated by the Holy Spirit, whenever an association or a need arises. This discipline strives toward the scriptural mandate:

> If then you have been raised with Christ, seek the things that are above, where Christ is, seated at the right hand of God. Set your minds on things that are above, not on things that are on earth. (Col. 3:1–2)

A Treasury of Spirituality: The Prayerbook

Within certain communions the concept of the prayer of the church (the corporate prayer that is collectively owned and embraced) is integral to specific orders of worship, forms of prayer, and formulae of prayer that have recognized standing. Prayerbook worship is worship that arises out of these established formularies. The use of a prayerbook accurately estimates the formative impact of worship upon faith. Because it is conceived collectively, it is less prone to theological and linguistic inadequacies. Consequently, such worship more readily rises above the personality of the celebrant. Use of a prayerbook rescues worship from subjectivism by lifting it above the level of individual preoccupation and vision. The breadth of the prayerbook invites the worshiper to unfold layer upon layer of meaning and to apply the rule of prayer to the rule of faith.

The prayerbook tradition is almost synonymous with the *Book of Common Prayer* in its various Episcopal and Anglican editions. These are carefully crafted works, undergirded by impressive scholarship and a deep respect for tradition. They are profoundly biblical. The scope of prayers is hardly parochial. There are no distractions of grammar, ineloquence, or syntax. Symmetry abounds. They uphold a tradition of linguistic excellence, despite the fact that when revised editions appear Anglicans may grouse about some phrases. Nowhere more evident than in this prayerbook tradition is the power of eloquent prose to exalt the soul unto God.

It would be difficult to overestimate this tradition's influence throughout some four hundred years, upon both other liturgical traditions and the English language itself. Even within the Calvinist tradition, which reacted strongly against an ill-advised imposition of the prayerbook in Scotland in 1637, its influence is evident. Modern Reformed prayerbooks have borrowed extensively from various editions.[9]

The secret of any prayerbook's creative influence on participation is the element of familiarity. Its potential for enrichment increases with usage. The tongue relishes exquisite language, rejoicing that it has passed this way before and will pass this way again. Through regular usage a prayerbook becomes a mirror for the soul that reveals God's "inestimable love in the redemption of the world," that expresses an inmost devotion "with gladness and singleness of heart," and that affirms the "inquiring and discerning heart, the courage to will and to persevere, a spirit to know and to love (God), and the gift of joy and wonder in all (God's) works." Here one may "delight in the law of God." Here may the soul magnify the greatness of God, who has "brought us out of error into truth, out of sin into righteousness, out of death into life."[10]

For those who feel overwhelmed by the majesty of God, for those whose steps in the courts of the Most High are tentative and uncertain, a prayerbook establishes patterns of discourse.

For those whose spiritual discipline suffers from a lack of organization and focus, a prayerbook is able to transpose chaos into firmament. The language of prayerbook worship does this by providing a matrix that reverberates with the memory of God's people, the memory that invokes communion with God.

A Gracious Dialogue: Liturgical Responses

Within civilization ritualized patterns of interaction define the character of space as belonging to a culture or subculture. These patterns help to situate persons within recognizable entities. Each culture determines its own linguistic structures for greeting, attentiveness, cordiality, cooperation, gratitude, leave-taking, etc. Conformity to them expresses and creates a sense of identity and belonging. This behavior is *learned.* It may not feel natural at first. Rather than imposing an inhibition, teaching a child socially acceptable responses is actually a liberation for the child, who is thereby made free to function within a society.

The dialogue of worship accomplishes this liberation for Christians. It identifies them as a people set apart, a holy nation, a royal priesthood. The nature of their calling demands distinctive forms of interaction. For this reason intrusions of secular patterns, e.g., the greeting "Good morning," are simply inadequate for the liturgical action by which the church of Jesus Christ is actualized. Such an occasion calls for language that reveals and communicates much more. The liturgy should reverberate with a stylized dialogue that identifies the people of God and the sacred act that they undertake. The use of traditional and ecumenically accepted liturgical responses situates that identity within the largest boundaries possible.

Amen

The fundamental liturgical response is *Amen.* The word is a transliteration of the Hebrew verb *'mn* which means "to be faithful, reliable, steadfast." The meaning of *Amen* has been variously rendered as "firm" or "established" or "so be it."[11] From Jewish synagogue and Temple usage *Amen* has passed untranslated into the worship, both Christian and Muslim, of many languages.

In biblical usage *Amen* is a formula that is spoken by the congregation at the end of the liturgy (e.g., 1 Chron. 16:36) or at the end of a doxology (e.g., Rom. 1:25). In the New Testament *Amen* also appears as an asseverative particle, an indicator that a solemn truth is about to be uttered. For example, many of Jesus' sayings are prefaced with "Amen, amen" (translated into English as "Verily, verily" or "Truly, truly"). This distinctive usage is a self-ratification, indicating that what follows is trustworthy and reliable, indeed God's certain word. This occurrence at the beginning of Jesus' proclamations echoes the New Testament's claim of Christ as "God's Amen" (Rev./Apoc. 3:14; 2 Cor. 1:20). The asseverative usage of *Amen* survives in the Orthodox Liturgy of St. Chrysostom.

Other traditional liturgical occurrences of *Amen* reveal many shades of meaning. It is frequently an assent. Those who utter it indicate that they agree with what is being affirmed. As Augustine wrote, "To say *Amen* is to subscribe."[12] This is often the intended sense of a spontaneous *Amen* during the proclamation of God's word. In many congregations it is this simple acclamation that makes preaching the overtly participatory event that it is.

As an expression of corporate assent *Amen* occurs at the conclusion of any prayer. This usage constitutes a communal embrace, a congregational appropriation of the prayer that has been articulated by one member as properly belonging to the whole body. The *Amen* at the conclusion of the Eucharistic Prayer is illustrative. Because the church is a community of priests, an entire congregation may be properly understood as celebrant in the sacrament, despite the fact that, for reasons of church order, its prayer is articulated by one person. The *Amen* that concludes the Great Thanksgiving both demonstrates this priestly identity and ratifies the prayer. "This is *our* faith. This is *our* offering, this is *our* memorial." Here is the church's assent to being the body of Christ, which, through him, with him, and in him, in the unity and power of the Holy Spirit gives all honor and glory to the Father. No wonder that St. Jerome boasted that his congregation's *Amen* could be heard "like thunder shaking the empty temples of the idols"![13]

Amen can express unanimity of belief. This is the predominant sense at the conclusion of the creeds. *Amen* can also be a congregational seal that ratifies a covenant, as, for instance, the covenant of baptism:

> N., I baptize you in the Name of the Father, and of the Son, and of the Holy Spirit. AMEN.

or marriage:

> Those whom God has joined together let no one put asunder.
> People: AMEN (*BCP*, p. 428).

Lastly, it may be an indication of personal commitment, as in the reception of communion:

> The Body of Christ, the bread of heaven. AMEN.
> The Blood of Christ, the cup of salvation. AMEN.

In this context the response is essentially the communicants' prayer for the indwelling of Christ, that they may be the real presence of Christ in and for the world.

Despite a mild scarcity of *Amens*, in some contexts the acclamation is inappropriate. The *Amen* at the conclusion of congregational hymns is passé, it being based upon an erroneous assumption. The practice was unknown prior to the nineteenth century when Anglican hymnal editors began to append this word to hymns, incorrectly citing as models the monastic hymns and antiphonal psalmody of the Middle Ages. However, modern hymns are sung by the entire congregation, which makes an *Amen* redundant. Modern hymnal editors, aware of this error, now omit the *Amens* that are not original to the poems.[14] The practice of worship leaders soloing the *Amen* at the conclusion of their own prayers should be resisted. Because *Amen* is the people's acclamation, such acts represent a priestly usurpation. Moreover, they are nonsensical, the equivalent of people talking to themselves, of saying *both* "Thank you" *and* "You're welcome." An *Amen* signifies a church's agreement with and ownership of a prayer. Congregations that are too lazy to reply and expect their ministers to say their response for them should at least pay them extra for their double duty.

The use of *Amen* is a bench mark for liturgical participation, a fact so basic that it is often overlooked by those promoting liturgical renewal. If a congregation's *Amens* are routine, uncoordinated, noncommittal, or nonexistent, there is no better place to begin work on participation in worship than right here. It is helpful, particularly in congregations that are unaccustomed to saying *Amen,* that instruction be given regarding the nature and structure of liturgical prayers. Timing should also be discussed. The lengthy doxological conclusions to prayers can disperse or subdue the entrance of the congregation's *Amen.* This problem has a simple remedy. Those who regularly offer prayers can elicit a unified *Amen* through the inflection of the voice. For example, the leaders of prayer may regularly signal the congregation by dropping their voices by an interval that approximates a musical third:

... through Jesus Christ our Lord, who lives and reigns with you and the Holy Spirit, one God for ever and e‑
                                                      ver. AMEN.

Once a pattern of tonality is adopted, care should be taken to insure that it remains consistent.

The Christian Greeting

The Lord be with you
And also with you.[15]

This ancient greeting identifies the people of God. It acknowledges their mutual prayer that each Christian will be filled with God's grace. "The LORD be with you" (Ruth 2:4)—these are words of assurance: "here you are welcome"; "here you will find sustenance"; "here, under the shadow of God's wings, you are protected" (Ps. 35[36]:7). It is a greeting that expresses the Lord's favor (Luke 1:28). Contained therein is a declaration of the true nature of the encounter that occurs when Christians greet one another. Thomas Howard writes:

It builds into the very structure of the act of worship itself the glorious antiphons of charity that ring back and forth in heaven and all across the cosmos, among all the creatures of God. It is charity, greeting the other and wishing that other one well. In its antiphonal ("responsive") character it echoes the very rhythms of heaven. Deep calls to deep. Day answers to night. Mountain calls to valley. One angel calls to another. Love greets love. The place of God's dwelling rings with these joyful antiphons of charity. Hell hates this. It can only hiss, *Out of my way, fool.* But heaven says, *The Lord be with you.* This is what was said to us in the Incarnation. This is what the Divine Love always says.[16]

The Christian greeting dispels fear. It scatters the darkness of our hearts. It reassures us that all things are indeed ours. It introduces heaven into earth by announcing the graceful advent of God.

The Gathering of Focus

The Call to Worship or Opening Dialogue ought to be one that naturally engages the soul. Although the favored versicles and responses vary from tradition to tradition, the principle of a ritualized pattern of interaction remains the same. If worship is begun with the proclamation, "Our help is in the name of the Lord," the response should be automatic, like thunder following lightning, *"Who made heaven and earth."* American Episcopal usage employs an opening blessing similar to that in the Byzantine liturgy:

Leader: Blessed be God: Father, Son, and Holy Spirit.
People: And blessed be his kingdom, now and forever.

During Lent and on other penitential occasions the versicle and response are more subdued:

Leader: Bless the Lord who forgives all our sins.
People: His mercy endures forever.

During Eastertide the resurrection theme is woven into the Opening Dialogue:

Leader: Alleluia. Christ is risen.
People: The Lord is risen indeed. ALLELUIA. (*BCP*, 355)

The Welcoming of God's Word

In Western practice, when God's word is read, the lesson is often concluded with this dialogue:

Lector: (This is) the Word of the Lord.
People: Thanks be to God!

The dialogue surrounding the reading of the gospel may be more elaborate:

Lector: A reading from the holy Gospel according to St. _____.
People: Glory to you, Lord.
    (The reading of the Gospel)
Lector: This is the Gospel of the Lord.
People: Praise to you, Lord Jesus Christ.

When God's word is read, it is like a revered guest entering into our house. How are we to show hospitality? What etiquette is appropriate to such an occasion? Answer: one that is gracious. Liturgical responses put words of thanksgiving and praise on our lips, so that we who are so honored by this divine presence may respond appropriately.

A Consensus of Prayer Intentions

In the early church bidding prayers were offered by individual worshipers and then embraced by the whole. In modern practice this custom is being restored in the Prayers of the People, short intercessions offered for the church and the world. The common assent of the body of Christ is given through designated responses that vary with local custom, e.g., *"Lord, have mercy"* or *"Lord, hear our prayer."* Seasonal variants may be used (e.g., during Eastertide, *"King of glory, hear our prayer"*), although it is best to resist a wide diversity of responses so that concentration may be centered on the prayers themselves.

A Sacrifice Acceptable to God

Celebrant: The Lord be with you.
People: And also with you.
Celebrant: Lift up your hearts.
People: We lift them to the Lord.

Celebrant: Let us give thanks to the Lord our God.
People: It is right to give thanks and praise.

This dialogue, the ancient *Sursum corda*, is both an invitation
to prayer and an indication of the readiness of the congregation
to celebrate the Eucharist. The Eucharistic Prayer is trinitarian
in its structure, focusing in turn on the three persons of the
trinity. Each section may be concluded with an acclamation of
the people. The first section, focusing on the Father, traditionally
concludes with the ancient acclamation that symbolizes the unity
of the Church Triumphant with the Church Militant, intoning
the heavenly hymn of praise to the Father:

> *Holy, holy, holy Lord, God of power and might,*
> *Heaven and earth are full of your glory.*
> > *Hosanna in the highest.*
> *Blessed is he who comes in the name of the Lord.*
> > *Hosanna in the highest.*

The christological section of the prayer recalls in particular
Christ's death, resurrection, and ascension. In modern prayers
the christological focus often concludes with a memorial acclamation, the most common of which is:

> *Christ has died,*
> *Christ is risen,*
> *Christ will come again.*[17]

The Eucharistic Prayer's concluding focus on the Holy Spirit be-
seeches the Spirit's blessing upon the sacrament, the church, and
its mission in the world. It is followed by a third acclamation, the
basic element of which is *Amen* but which may be expanded to
include the entire doxology, such as:

> *Through him, with him, in him, in the unity of the Holy Spirit, all*
> *glory and honor is yours, Almighty Father, for ever and ever. AMEN.*
> *(RS)*

The dialogue of grace prior to the communion takes many
forms. The Roman Mass provides a prayer of preparation (based
upon biblical references: John 1:29; Rev./Apoc. 19:9; and Matt.
8:8):

Celebrant: This is the Lamb of God, who takes away the sin of the
              world. Happy are those who are called to his feast.
People: *Lord, I am not worthy to receive you, but only say the*
              word and I shall be healed.

Many traditions place the Our Father prior to the act of communion, the modern and preferred version of which is:

Our Father in heaven,
*   hallowed be your Name,*
*   your kingdom come,*
*   your will be done,*
*   on earth as in heaven.*
Give us today our daily bread.
Forgive us our sins
*   as we forgive those who sin against us.*
Save us from the time of trial
*   and deliver us from evil.*
For the kingdom, the power, and the glory are yours
*   now and forever. AMEN.*[18]

Internalization of communion responses reveals the true nature of the Eucharist as a corporate act by a priestly body. They express the sacrifice of praise and thanksgiving as the offering of the church that is acceptable to God.

A Gracious Departing

The liturgy concludes with a blessing, to which the people respond, *"Amen."* The Roman and Episcopal traditions, during seasons and on festival days, often use clusters of blessings that are punctuated by the response, *"Amen."* It is a form of blessing that deserves the consideration of the whole church. The way in which the multiple themes of a festival day or a season are recapitulated and applied to the lives of the worshipers is illustrated by this Solemn/Seasonal Blessing for the Day of Pentecost:

May Almighty God, who enlightened the minds of the disciples by pouring out upon them the Holy Spirit, make you rich with his blessing, that you may abound more and more in that Spirit for ever. *Amen.*

May God, who sent the Holy Spirit as a flame of fire that rested upon the heads of the disciples, burn out all evil from your hearts, and make them shine with the pure light of his presence. *Amen.*

May God, who by the Holy Spirit caused those of many tongues to proclaim Jesus as Lord, strengthen your faith and send you out to bear witness to him in word and deed. *Amen.*

And the blessing of God Almighty, the Father, the Son (+) and the Holy Spirit, be among you, and remain with you always. *Amen.*[19]

The dismissal, the final note in the gracious dialogue of the liturgy, resounds with thanksgiving. The incipit may vary—"Let us go forth in the name of Christ," "Go in peace to love and serve the Lord," "Let us bless the Lord," etc.—but the response is typically, *"Thanks be to God."* (*BCP,* p. 368).

A gracious dialogue is a declaration of who we are: a chosen race, a royal priesthood, a holy nation, God's own people. It is formal, court language—the language of the courts of heaven—which mirrors the etiquette with which angels beckon to each other and heaven calls to earth. As language appropriate to worship, it is more than politeness. This gladsome dialogue communicates charity, peace, joy, and hope. Above all it is infused with reverence, reverence before God, reverence within the fellowship of God's people. Those who enter into its spirit declare the wonderful deeds of the one who has called us out of darkness into light, and they consent to the gentle rule of the kingdom of God.

The Music of Worship

Be filled with the Spirit, addressing one another in psalms and hymns and spiritual songs, singing and making melody to the Lord with all your heart. (Eph. 5:18–19)

Christians participate in worship through four major types of music: psalms, canticles, liturgical music, and hymns.

Psalmody: The Praises of Zion

The Psalter is the Bible's hymnbook. More precisely, it is the hymnbook of the Second Temple, the postexilic Jewish community that collected, arranged, and edited these poems for the official worship of the Temple in Jerusalem. Although many psalms reflect a preexilic setting (i.e., before 586 B.C.E.), the collection as we know it was completed in the fourth–second centuries B.C.E.

Modern biblical scholarship has focused on the literary genre of the psalms and how they were employed in the setting of worship. Various schemes have been devised by which to classify them. Frequently, there are three major categories: (1) *hymns* extol God's greatness and goodness; (2) *laments* are occasioned by difficult times, and they usually represent complaints offered within a context of praise; (3) *thanksgivings* contain personal testimony to what God has done and express gratitude to the Lord as the rescuer.

Some scholars make further distinctions, e.g., Royal or Enthronement Psalms, Wisdom Psalms, Liturgical Psalms, Historical Psalms. While agreement may not exist on the exact classification of each psalm, it is evident that they were composed according to poetic convention and that many were conceived with specific liturgical uses in mind, namely, the feasts and festivals of the Temple.

Psalms are corporate expressions of prayer. Although many of them may have been composed by individuals and purport to recount individual life situations, they came to be embraced as the common expression of all, much as are modern hymns when disseminated through hymnbooks. Even when psalms are voiced in the first person singular, it is usually understood that the entire community joins together in this act of prayer, for in ancient Israel the individual relates to God only as a member of the community. Praise to God is therefore rendered in solidarity with others in the covenant: "O magnify the Lord with me, and let us exalt his name together!" (Ps. 33[34]:3).[20]

Originally the psalms were sung. Evidence for this lies in the mysterious musical and liturgical notations (e.g., *selāh*) that have survived in the Hebrew texts down to the present, despite the fact that the ancient methods of intonation have long since perished.

As the heartbeat of Jewish piety, psalms were central to the piety of Jesus who even cited one from the cross. They are, from beginning to end, ceaseless praise. They exude a joyful dependence upon the God who is the source and center of our being. "Whether the mood was elation or sorrow, bewilderment or confidence, these songs were intended as anthems to the glory of

God."[21] It is little wonder that they were revered by Christians and given a major place in the worship of the early church. The church that would keep this treasury of spirituality alive as a means of prayer will use them regularly and in a variety of styles. The following methods may be recited or sung, either simply or elaborately.

Direct Recitation

Direct recitation consists of the intonation or reading of a whole psalm, or portion of a psalm, in unison. Two methods are well known. The choral psalm anthem may be an independent work or an excerpt from a larger work. Such anthems should comprise a significant portion of the choir's repertoire.

Direct recitation is also the method employed in Metrical Psalmody. Originating with the rise of modern harmony and the spread of literacy, it is the distinctive contribution of the Calvinist churches and a hallmark of their worship. Metrical Psalmody is a successor to plainsong, of which the most popular form is Gregorian chant. Although this ancient and venerable style had produced psalm settings of extraordinary beauty and integrity, its musical form and linguistic idiom (Latin) made it ill suited for general use by lay congregations. By contrast, Metrical Psalmody provided a vernacular means by which entire lay congregations could sing the Psalter. John Calvin commissioned the French court poet Clément Marot to set the psalms into meter (verse) and Louis Bourgeois provided the tunes in four to six voices. The resulting Geneva Psalter of 1562 was an enormous success, the effects of which may be seen down to the present day. Some of the more familiar metrical psalms remain as standard entries in modern hymnbooks of many churches in many lands, e.g., Psalms 99(100) ("All People That on Earth Do Dwell," sung to "Old Hundreth" [*RIL,* 120]) and 120(121) ("I to the Hills Will Lift My Eyes," sung to "Dundee" [*RIL,* 131]). With the modern resurgence of psalmody, new metrical psalms are appearing. Here is a Fred R. Anderson setting of Psalm 144(145):1–4, 11–13, to the tune of "Ellers" ("Savior, Again to Thy Dear Name We Raise"):

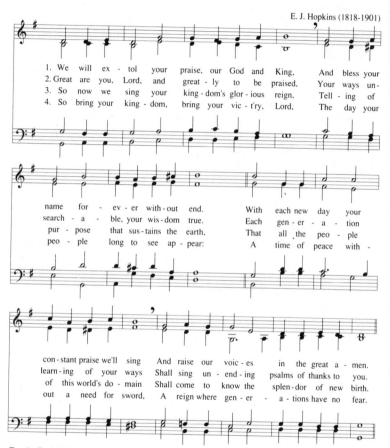

E. J. Hopkins (1818-1901)

1. We will ex - tol your praise, our God and King, And bless your
2. Great are you, Lord, and great - ly to be praised, Your ways un-
3. So now we sing your king - dom's glor - ious reign, Tell - ing of
4. So bring your king - dom, bring your vic - t'ry, Lord, The day your

name for - ev - er with - out end. With each new day your
search - a - ble, your wis - dom true. Each gen - er - a - tion
pur - pose that sus - tains the earth, That all the peo - ple
peo - ple long to see ap - pear: A time of peace with -

con - stant praise we'll sing And raise our voic - es in the great a - men.
learn - ing of your ways Shall sing un - end - ing psalms of thanks to you.
of this world's do - main Shall come to know the splen - dor of new birth.
out a need for sword, A reign where gen - er - a - tions have no fear.

Text by Fred Anderson, from *Singing Psalms of Joy and Praise*, copyright © 1986 Wesminster Press.

Metrical psalms may be sung to more than one tune. Alternate tunes may be selected by noting the metrical notation and consulting the metrical index of tunes in a hymnbook. Care must be taken that the alternate tune will match the spirit of the text and that the musical meter complements the versical meter. In the example above the psalm may be sung to "Toulon," "National Hymn," or "Woodlands" but not to "O Quanta Qualia," which, although the same meter (10.10.10.10.), breaks the text awkwardly.[22]

The continuing success of Metrical Psalmody is owed to its setting of psalm texts into a common poetic idiom. When texts are joined to simple, robust tunes, one's memory is more deeply engaged. The interiorization that results provides a rich opportunity for praying the psalms "without ceasing."[23]

Antiphonal Recitation

Antiphonal recitation consists of a verse-by-verse alternation between groups of singers or readers. This alternation may occur between a choir and congregation, or between one side of the congregation and the other. Oftentimes, the alternate recitation of the psalm concludes with the *Gloria Patri* or with a refrain (sometimes and misleadingly termed the *Antiphon*) recited in unison.

Antiphonal recitation is used frequently in the celebration of the Daily Office and is understandably popular in religious communities or wherever a tradition of plainsong continues. In parishes, two psalm-tone methods lend themselves well to antiphonal recitation. The familiar Anglican Chant, a harmonized and stylized development from plainsong, has endured over the centuries and continues to inspire new expressions. Here is the *Alternative Service Book* setting of Psalm 26(27):1–6:

1 The Lord is my light and my salvation * whom then I shall I I fear?:
the Lord is the stronghold of my life * of whom I shall I I be
aIfraid?

2 When the wicked even my enemies and my foes * come upon me I
to deIvour me:
they shall I stumble I and I fall.

3 If an army encamp against me * my heart shall I not · be alfraid:
and if war should rise algainst me I yet · will I I trust.

4 One thing I have asked from the Lord which I I will relquire:
that I may dwell in the house of the Lord I all the I days · of my I
life,

† 5 To see the fair I beauty · of the I Lord:
and to I seek his I will · in his I temple.

6 For he will hide me under his shelter in the I day of I trouble:
and conceal me in the shadow of his tent * and set me I high
uplon a I rock.

7 And now he will lift I up my I head:
above my I ene·mies I round albout me.

† 8 And I will offer sacrifices in his sanctuary with I exulltation:
I will sing I will sing I praises I to the I Lord.[24]

Like any method, Anglican Chant requires a certain degree of
inculcation. When it is led by a well-trained, four-part choir, the
effect can be glorious. However, the subtleties of the pointing do
require instruction. In the previous example, a break in the text
(I) indicates movement to the next measure of music; singers take

a breath at the asterisks (*); the second half of the double chant is used for the stanzas marked with daggers (†).

A simpler method has recently been introduced by American Lutherans. An abridged, pointed psalter and ten simple psalm tones provide a method of intonation that is closer to the musical abilities of the average, especially non-Anglican, congregation. In this method, a whole note (o) is the reciting tone, on which most of the syllables are sung; an accent (ʹ) indicates the syllable or word upon which the singer moves from the reciting tone to the "black notes"; an asterisk (*) indicates how the verse division fits the tone division. Here is Psalm 99(100) set to *LBW* psalm tone # 10.

¹ Be joyful in the LORD, áll you lands;*
   serve the LORD with gladness
   and come before his presence
   ẃith a song.
² Know this: The LORD himśelf is God;*
   he himself has made us,
   and we are his;
   we are his people
   and the sheep óf his pasture.
³ Enter his gates with thanksgiving;
   go into his ćourts with praise;*
   give thanks to him
   and call upón his name.
⁴ For the LORD is good;
   his mercy is éverlasting;*
   and his faithfulness endures
   from áge to age.²⁵

The methods of Anglican Chant and *LBW* psalm tones are well suited to antiphonal recitation, which enables all participants to pray the psalm both actively and in silence. One group listens while the other ministers to it, and then "sounds in answer," inspired to minister in return.

Responsorial Recitation

In responsorial recitation the verses of a psalm are read or intoned usually by a solo voice. The choir and congregation listen and then reply with a response after each verse or group of verses. The response is often called an antiphon, although this designation should not be allowed to confuse the responsorial method with the antiphonal method of psalm recitation, which is group against group.

The responsorial recitation of psalms is the method of preference for an expanding repertoire of psalmody.[26] Modern hymnals, such as *Worship3*, are now including responsorial psalms. In performing them, the response, which may be printed in the service bulletin, should first be played by the accompanying instrument, then sung a cappella by the soloist, then echoed by the congregation, whereupon the psalm stanzas begin immediately. Having thereby learned the response, the congregation is on its own to repeat it after each stanza. On the facing page is the response (antiphon) to Psalm 50(51) by David Clark Isele for use in Morning Prayer and on penitential occasions.[27]

Not only is the responsorial method breathing new life into the Psalms, the prayer of the ages, it is an effective antidote to the problem of minds that, having succumbed to the appeals of modern advertising, are memorials to consumerism. Through the act of singing the response four–five times, the worshiper interiorizes it. The commitment of this response to memory furthers the inner transformation of the mind. The recalling of the response, as prompted by the Spirit, engages anew the heart with the psalmist's prayer.

The responsorial method can also be applied to psalm anthems. Such application transforms the normally passive role of the congregation during a choral work into active participation. Paul D. Weber's choral setting of Psalm 31(32) draws the congregation into the performance of the psalm through the lovely antiphon on page 78.[28]

In a psalm anthem the music must be composed so that the point at which the congregation enters is obvious. The choir director, if visible, may assist the congregation with its entry.

Gelineau Psalms are frequently sung according to the responsorial method. The French composer Joseph Gelineau began his important work with a fresh translation of the Psalter that both

rendered faithfully its meaning and reproduced Hebrew poetic rhythm and verse structure. The texts are set to psalm tones that are inspired by Gregorian, Ambrosian, and other ancient diatonic psalm tones. Gelineau Psalmody requires only a trained soloist or cantor, an accompanist who can count one beat per measure, and a willing congregation. It is well suited to worship settings both large and small.

The principle of intonation is a simple one. It is what Gerard Manley Hopkins called "sprung rhythm." Each line of a Gelineau Psalm has a specified number of accented or stressed syllables, although the number of intervening (unstressed) syllables varies. Each measure has only one beat, which coincides with the stressed syllable. The beat must occur with absolute metronomic regularity and must not vary in the transitions from psalm text to response to psalm text. Moreover, the pulse must not be exaggerated in any way. The unstressed syllables that fall in between are to be sung "with the natural rhythm of careful speech," and every effort to give them a mechanical regularity, as though they had note values, is to be resisted.[29]

Gelineau Psalmody is deceptively simple. Perhaps for this reason, even talented musicians sometimes execute these psalms poorly. The performance of a Gelineau Psalm will not be done well until the method has been mastered. Because Gelineau Psalms are now making their appearance in hymnbooks, wherein methodological considerations cannot always be detailed, the reader is referred to the clear explanation of the method that is found on the first pages of the original English collections.[30]

The genius of Gelineau Psalmody is that it renders the text faithfully and intelligibly in natural speech rhythms. Through repetition the responses are interiorized in the memory of the worshiper. As summaries of psalms, they become brief prayers that the Spirit may recall within the heart long after the liturgy has concluded.

Responsive Recitation

In responsive recitation the minister/lector alternates with the congregation verse by verse. From the standpoint of active participation, this method is preferable to the entire psalm simply being read by the lector. Regrettably, the method is not well suited to song. The *BCP* Psalter divides each verse into two parts with an asterisk. Some hymnals contain an appendix of respon-

Ps. 83 (84) HOW LOVELY IS YOUR DWELLING PLACE

Antiphon I *(Obligatory before verse 1)*

(Mode: Ray. Tonic: D)

♩ = 𝅝 of psalm

How love-ly is your dwell-ing place, O Lord of hosts.

UNISON ONLY

PSALM

(A.G.M.)

1. My soul is longing and yearning, is yearning for the courts of the Lord.
2. The sparrow herself finds a home and the swallow a nest for her brood;
3. They are happy who dwell in your house, for ever singing your praise.
4. As they go through the Bitter Valley, they make it a place of springs,
5. O Lord God of hosts, hear my prayer, give ear, O God of Jacob.
6. One day within your courts is better than a thousand elsewhere.
7. For the Lord God is a rampart, a shield; he will give us his favour and glory.
8. Give praise to the Father Almighty, to his Son, Jesus Christ, the Lord,

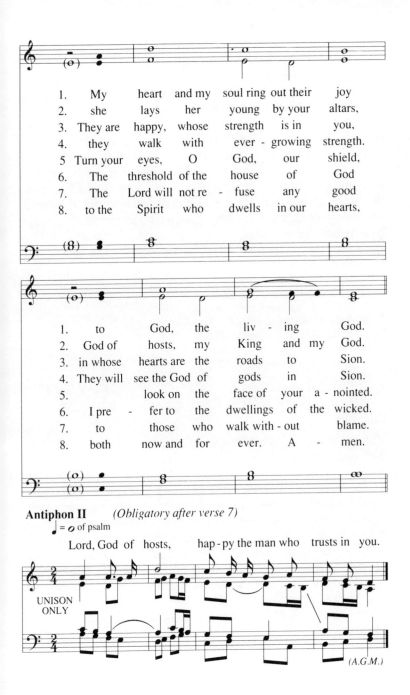

1. My heart and my soul ring out their joy
2. she lays her young by your altars,
3. They are happy, whose strength is in you,
4. they walk with ever - growing strength.
5 Turn your eyes, O God, our shield,
6. The threshold of the house of God
7. The Lord will not re - fuse any good
8. to the Spirit who dwells in our hearts,

1. to God, the liv - ing God.
2. God of hosts, my King and my God.
3. in whose hearts are the roads to Sion.
4. They will see the God of gods in Sion.
5. look on the face of your a - nointed.
6. I pre - fer to the dwellings of the wicked.
7. to those who walk with - out blame.
8. both now and for ever. A - men.

Antiphon II *(Obligatory after verse 7)*

♩ = 𝅝 of psalm

Lord, God of hosts, hap - py the man who trusts in you.

UNISON
ONLY

(A.G.M.)

sive readings. A similar effect can be achieved through reading alternate verses from pew Bibles.

Psalm means praise. The church exists to give praise to God. Any effort to enhance liturgical participation must give generous place to the Psalms. Happily, there is a growing abundance of psalm settings in a variety of methods that invite this use. The well-guided congregation will settle upon those few approaches that serve it well, so that it will not have to "count the steps" while praying them. The congregation that knows and loves the Psalms will be enriched beyond measure and will acquire a spiritual vitality that reverberates throughout the length and breadth of creation:

> The Church with Psalms must shout,
>   No door can keep them out:
> But above all, the heart
>   Must bear the longest part.
> Let all the world in every corner sing,
>   My God and King.

George Herbert (1593–1632)

Canticles

Canticles are biblical songs or prayers outside the Psalter. Although appropriate within any liturgical context, they are particularly related to the celebrations of the Divine Office, such as Morning and Evening Prayer. The most commonly used canticles are the *Benedictus* (or "The Song of Zechariah"; Luke 1:68–79), the *Benedicite* (or "The Song of Creation"; from the Apocryphal "Song of the Three Young Men," 35–65), the *Nunc Dimittis* (or "The Song of Simeon"; Luke 2:29–32), and the *Magnificat* (or "The Song of Mary"; Luke 1:46–55). Other traditional but less frequently used canticles are "The Song of Miriam and Moses" (Exod. 15:1–6, 11–13, 17–18), "The First Song of Isaiah" (Isa. 12:2–6), "The Second Song of Isaiah" (Isa. 55:6–11), "A Song to the Lamb" (Rev./Apoc. 4:11; 5:9–10, 13), "The Song of the Redeemed" (Rev./Apoc. 15:3–4), and "The Song of Hannah" (1 Sam. 2:1–10). Two ancient, nonbiblical hymns, the

Gloria in excelsis and *Te Deum laudamus* (*BCP,* pp. 94–96) are also commonly counted as canticles.

Modern liturgical renewal has prompted the publication of collections of canticles, the musical settings of which are within reach of most congregations.[31] Many of these collections contain settings of less traditional canticles. Prompted by literary critical identification of hymns and fragments within the Bible, modern collections of canticles are exploiting a broader range of texts. Long-dormant texts are at last receiving what they so richly deserve—melody. Some examples are: Philippians 2:5–11 (*Worship3,* # 92; Series 3, Evening Prayer, Church of England); Colossians 1:12–20 (*Worship3,* # 93); Jeremiah 31:10–14 (*LBW,* # 14); 1 Peter 2:21–24 (*Worship3,* # 95); and Revelation/Apocalypse 19:1–7 (*Worship3,* # 99; *PGS,* pp. 305–7).

In addition a profusion of canticles, known colloquially as "Scripture Songs," is expanding the repertoire further. Many of these have even ventured into prose passages of Scripture. Without questioning their popularity, which is considerable, or the principle that underlies the form, which is sound, we note that many of these compositions await judgment as to their literary, musical, and liturgical merit.

As a direct proclamation of Scripture, canticles are a rich form of liturgical participation. Their interiorization places God's word within the memory, there to shape the mind. The setting of Scripture to melody enables the soul to magnify the Lord and the spirit to rejoice in God, our Savior.

Liturgical Music

Liturgical music has as its core five hymns of great antiquity and stature. These "ordinary hymns," so-called because they are part of the *ordinaria* or regular parts of the *Ordo Missae,* the Roman Catholic Order of Mass, are *Kyrie eleison* ("Lord, Have Mercy"), *Gloria in excelsis Deo* ("Glory to God in the Highest"), *Credo* ("Creed"), *Sanctus* ("Holy, Holy, Holy Lord"), and *Agnus Dei* ("Lamb of God"). These hymns have often been rendered chorally as musical compositions that bear the name "Mass." From a historical, Western perspective they are normative to the sung liturgy. Obviously, there are many exceptions to the norm: textual variants (e.g., Luther's *Sanctus*); differing orders (e.g., the 1552 *Book of Common Prayer* placement of the *Gloria* at the end of the communion service or the *Credo* at the fraction in the Mozarabic Rite); alternate texts (e.g., the Eastern Orthodox *Trisagion,* "Thrice Holy," instead of the *Gloria*); supplemental compositions (*LBW*'s "Let the Vineyards Be Fruitful, Lord"); and deletions (the *WB* omission of the *Agnus Dei*). Nonetheless, these five hymns form a core of liturgical hymnody that links Christians of many traditions across the ages.

A striking feature of worship in our time is the abundance of congregational settings for these venerable hymns. This profusion is due in part to a recovery of the concept of the congregation as choir. Correlatively, the ensemble of trained voices is increasingly viewed as an auxiliary choir whose primary purpose is to assist the singing of the congregation, which is the main choir. Although modern musical settings of the Mass cannot compare in quality with the classic choral works, they serve an expanded function: they enable the entire congregation to participate actively in the praying of these portions of the liturgy.

Kyrie eleison

The *Kyrie* originates in Eastern liturgies where it remains as an opening litany or *ektene.* A shortened form of this Eastern *Kyrie* litany has recently been revived in the *LBW* services of Holy Communion. The reception of the *LBW Kyrie* settings, especially the natural blend of text and melody in setting 2 (*LBW,* pp. 78–79), has been enthusiastic. In the late fifth century, the *Kyrie* litany was introduced into the Roman Rite. Not long thereafter, it became the practice to omit the petitions, leaving only the invocations, each repeated three times:

> Lord, have mercy.
> Christ, have mercy.
> Lord, have mercy.

The use of the *Kyrie* responses in the Greek preserves a link with early Christian liturgies similar to the link that *Amen, Alleluia,* and *Hosanna* provide with Hebrew worship.

Gloria in excelsis Deo

The *Gloria in excelsis,* based on Luke 2:14, is also Eastern in origin and is used for the Eastern Orthodox Orthros (Morning Prayer-Lauds). It was probably brought to the West by Hilary of Poitiers (d. 367), where in the fifth century it became a part of the Roman Pontifical Mass (mass when a bishop is present). When this restriction to Pontifical usage was removed in the twelfth century, its usage became much more widespread. The *Gloria* traditionally occurs at the beginning of the liturgy, immediately following the *Kyrie.* However, the 1552 *Book of Common Prayer* moved it to the conclusion of the Eucharist where it functions as an expression of praise and thanksgiving. This placement has had widespread influence on many traditions. In its preferred position before the lessons, the *Gloria* resonates with the angels over Bethlehem, who proclaimed good news of a great joy: Christ, the Word of God. Thus heralded, the people listen as the good news is read.

Credo

Creeds are summaries of the faith that is held and proclaimed in common by Christians throughout the ages. In condensed language the entire framework of Christian truth is recapitulated. The Nicene and Apostles' Creeds are the most universally accepted. The Nicene Symbol was introduced into regular use in the fifth century as a Monophysite protest against the Council of Chalcedon. Later the practice spread to the West. The older Apostles' Creed is traditionally a baptismal creed.[32]

Creeds should contribute to that catholic backdrop that expands liturgical participation. For this reason, local or private formulations or variants of the great creeds should not be used. Because creeds affirm the universal faith of the church, those used should have formal ecclesiastical approval. The imposition of unsanctioned creeds upon a congregation dissipates participation in that it presumes a level of comprehension or adherence that may not be actual. However, a credal hymn drawn from Scripture (e.g., Phil. 2:6–11; Col. 1:15–20) may be used in lieu of the classic creeds.

A confession of faith is appropriately sung, for doctrinal confession is above all praise to God, the knowledge of Whom exceeds all human comprehension. While there are lovely musical settings for the creeds, their technical difficulty places them beyond the abilities of most congregations. Hence, unison recitation is a common method in parish celebrations. The regular use of a creed will commit a summary of Christian faith to memory, setting up the possibility of retroactive engagement by the power of the Holy Spirit.

Sanctus

The "Holy, Holy, Holy Lord" acclamation within the Eucharistic Prayer is a hymn of adoration based upon Isaiah 6:3 and Revelation/Apocalypse 4:8. Its origins possibly lie in the *Kedûshāh* of synagogue worship, in which case its introduction into Christian worship would have been quite early. The hymn symbolizes the mystical unity of the Church Militant with the Church Triumphant, a role indicated in words that typically introduce it:

> And therefore we praise you, joining with the heavenly chorus, with prophets, apostles, and martyrs, and with all those in every generation who have looked to you in hope, to proclaim with them your glory, in their unending hymn of praise:
>
> > *Holy, holy, holy Lord, God of power and might,*
> > *heaven and earth are full of your glory.*
> > *Hosanna in the highest.*
> > *Blessed is he who comes in the name of the Lord.*
> > *Hosanna in the highest. (BCP, pp. 370–71)*

The *Sanctus* is the major element of congregational participation in the Eucharistic Prayer, one that clearly identifies the church as a priestly body, offering the sacrifice of praise and thanksgiving to God in unity with the saints in glory.

Agnus Dei

The "Lamb of God" entered the Roman Rite in the seventh century as a hymn to accompany the breaking of bread:

Lamb of God, you take away the sins of the world,
    have mercy on us.
Lamb of God, you take away the sins of the world,
    have mercy on us.
Lamb of God, you take away the sins of the world,
    grant us peace.

A modern translation unfolds the multivalence of the Latin:

Agnus Dei, qui tollis peccata mundi:	Jesus, Lamb of God,
miserere nobis.	have mercy on us.
Agnus Dei, qui tollis peccata mundi:	Jesus, bearer of our sins,
miserere nobis.	have mercy on us.
Agnus Dei, qui tollis peccata mundi:	Jesus, redeemer of the world,
dona nobis pacem.	give us your peace.

(ICET, 1986)

The referent "Lamb of God" in the context of communion reception applies both to the risen Lord and to the real presence of Christ in the sacrament. It does not endorse any particular theory of presence.

In addition to the five ordinary hymns, there are numerous other portions of the liturgy that the congregation may sing. The responses to God's word, the *Sursum corda*, Lord's Prayer, eucharistic acclamations, *Amen, Alleluia,* and *Hosanna* deserve melody and properly belong to the entire congregation. The choir's purpose should be to teach, not monopolize, them.

Of the abundance of settings of the ordinary hymns that are suitable for congregational use, those contained in hymnals usually offer two advantages. (1) Often these have undergone a trial use in an earlier publication and are thereby well-worn and proven successes. (2) Because of the length of some of the hymns, a congregation needs to have printed music in hand if it is to learn the setting. The hymnal setting provides music that is lucid and eliminates concerns over copyright infringements.[33]

The congregation that is shopping for a hymnal should regard the liturgical music section as a necessity and examine it carefully. How many settings a congregation should have in its repertoire is difficult to say, since factors of attendance, musical abilities, and the degree of assistance available from the choir and music ministers vary widely. However, the use of liturgical music should be conservative. The goal is not to expose a congregation to a great deal of liturgical music, but to discover only those few settings that will serve it well. Considerable effort is expended in the teaching of a setting of liturgical music. The same congregation that feels restless with one setting under its belt may feel overwhelmed trying to handle two. This is the tension out of which are born the long-term successes of this type of music.

Liturgical music need not always be conventional in its form. Chorale services in which hymns are substituted for the liturgical hymns and responses have been attempted with some success (see *LBW*, p. 120). The reformed Taizé Community in France has derived an innovative style that straddles the distinction between liturgical music and hymnody. The Taizé responses, litanies, acclamations, and canons grew out of an unusual need: liturgy for very large numbers of Christians making pilgrimages to the community, who do not necessarily share a common language or liturgical tradition. In order to enable diverse congregations to participate actively in a common experience of prayer, Jacques Berthier constructed this music upon the *ostinato,* a short musical unit sung in continuous repetition. (Examples follow.)

Meditative repetition is not unknown in Christian tradition; the Jesus Prayer of the ancient Greek church fathers and the Rosary are earlier examples of the same principle. The advantage of this approach to prayer is that it promotes an inner unity of the person, which allows the spirit "to be more open and more attentive to what is essential." To guard against repetition being overtaken by tedium, the Taizé texts are in Latin. Not only is this a neutral language for a multilingual congregation but also, because it is a dead language, it is less likely to become threadbare. To add variation and depth to the singing, the *ostinatos* are embellished with accompaniments (keyboard, strings, and other instruments), litanies, and chorales sung by cantors. The effect is stunning—a sonority of multiple harmonics that translates into a vivid experience of gathered prayer.[34]

JUBILATE, SERVITE

Rejoice in God all the earth. Serve the Lord with gladness.

Canon (2 voices)

Ju - bi - la - te De - o om - nis ter - ra.

Ser - vi - te Do - mi - no in lae - ti - ti - a.

Al - le - lu - ia, al - le - lu - ia, in lae - ti - ti - a.

Al - le - lu - ia, al - le - lu - ia, in lae - ti - ti - a!

Accompaniments

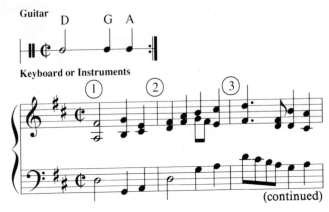

(continued)

(Accompaniment continued)

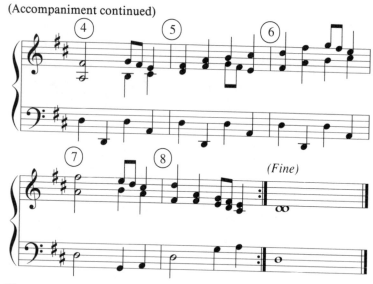

Hymns

As has often been observed, hymns are the most popular form of English poetry. Hymnody is postbiblical psalmody. Hymns, like psalms, display an awesome variety of intentions: praise, historical recapitulation, catechesis, confessions of faith, confessions of sin, thanksgiving, exhortation, evangelical proclamation, and petition. Hymns, like psalms, are the sung prayer of a community of worshipers, which owns them. Hymns, like psalms, are inspired by the Holy Spirit. Unlike psalms, however, hymns do not enjoy canonical status as Scripture. Consequently, the body of hymns in current usage is ever-evolving. Whereas the Psalms are the hallmark of biblical prayer, hymnody is more fluid and more expressive of contemporaneous and local spirituality, as this is discerned by the community under the guidance of the Spirit.

Community discernment is often vested in the hymnal commission whose task is to sift through the hundreds of thousands of hymns to determine which are suitable for inclusion as corporate expressions of prayer.[35] A starting point for this work is often a list of hymns that are found in other major hymnals (e.g., in the U.S. a list of 227 hymns chosen in 1976 by the Consultation on Ecumenical Hymnody). The selection process of a hymnal commission is of utmost importance, for it will profoundly impact upon the spiritual formation of many.

A hymnal should nobly display the note of catholicity by containing a representative historical selection of texts and tunes. A preponderance of hymns from any one period, including the modern, reflects and promotes a parochialism of piety.[36] The well-rounded hymnal will contain hymn texts from all ages: antiquity, plainsong hymn settings from the Middle Ages, hymns and tunes from the sixteenth century to the present. The modern hymnal should also contain representative portions of the different styles and traditions of hymnody. Plainsong, Lutheran chorales, metrical psalms, hymns from the Wesleyan tradition, evangelical, folk, spiritual, non-Western, Protestant, Catholic, Orthodox hymns—they should all be there. Obviously, one would expect denominational hymnals to continue to emphasize the particular traditions they represent. Methodist hymnals will feature Wesleyan hymns, Lutheran hymnals will contain a generous portion of chorales, etc. Such rich traditions deserve to be so emphasized and will thereby replenish hymn collections outside of those traditions. Yet any hymnal ought to contain at least a sampling of the world's hymnody as a celebration of the universal family of God, which is made one in Christ. Hymn singing makes one a co-participant with others across time and space who pray through the same hymn. A catholic hymnal will also be sensitive to inclusivity of language, symbols, and images. Age, race, gender, and physical limitations are factors that impinge upon the inclusion and editing of hymns today.

The most successful hymns owe their stature to many factors, not the least of which is a happy marriage of text and tune. The great hymns of the church also possess theological and artistic integrity. Because hymns are poetry, it is difficult to say precisely why some succeed more than others. For sure, the most popular hymns contain a certain boldness of imagery, which often resonates with biblical overtones, such as these beloved hymns:

"Crown Him with Many Crowns" (Rev./Apoc. 19:12); "Immortal Love, Forever Full" (Mark 5:27); "The Church's One Foundation" (1 Cor. 3:11; Eph. 5:25–27); "Glorious Things of Thee Are Spoken" (Ps. 87[88]:3; 1 Peter 2:9; Rev./Apoc. 1:5); "Guide Me, O Thou Great Jehovah" (Exod. 16:4; 17:6; 40:38); "At the Name of Jesus" (Phil. 2:11–12); and "Swing Low, Sweet Chariot" (2 Kings 2:11–12). In other cases the boldness of imagery arises from poetry that contains genuinely captivating metaphors: "O For a Thousand Tongues to Sing"; "Open Now, the Gates of Beauty"; "Now, On Land and Sea Descending"; "Creator of the Stars of Night"; and "All Creatures of Our God and King." In still other instances poetic language helps to bond one's affections to hymns: "If Thou But Suffer God to Guide Thee"; "There Is a Balm in Gilead"; and "Eternal Ruler of the Ceaseless Round."

The accompaniment of hymns is vital to participation through congregational hymn singing. The organist who assumes that hymns require little or no practice is badly misinformed. Effective hymn playing is neither natural nor easy. It must be cultivated and can only grow out of an acute awareness of the text—its inner meaning and flow, how it breathes, how it articulates, how it prays. The more accomplished musician can introduce hymns using a chorale prelude and accompany them using alternate harmonies, descants, and inter-verse improvisations. An organist can vary the playing of verses through such techniques as solo stops (reeds, etc.), omitting the pedal voice, changes of registration, and the use of other instrumentation, such as trumpets and handbells. Interludes should be the exception, not the norm, and should be a musical statement that is related to the hymn and that adds intensity to the singing of the final verse(s). For extended processions, additional verses can often be found in English and Episcopal hymnals. The degree to which improvisation is possible and appropriate is directly proportional to the familiarity of the hymn to the congregation. The organist should always articulate enough of the melody to carry the congregation's singing. To the extent that such devices inspire hymn singing, they are effective means of hymn accompaniment.[37]

Although musical taste and virtuosity are important, they

must not overshadow the singing itself. Of course, powerful hymn singing, as many Mennonite congregations have long demonstrated, need not be dependent upon musical instrumentation at all. The occasional singing of selected hymn verses a cappella paints a powerful portrait of a church as a living, breathing organism.

The singing of hymns may also be varied through vocal devices, such as the canon. On selected verses, the unison melody line, sung in unison and often unaccompanied, can be echoed, usually at a distance of one measure. The division of voices between male and female gives the canon an interval of an octave. Only certain tunes, because of their harmonic implications, have this potential. In all cases hymns sung in canon must be very familiar to the congregation. The service bulletin can help to avoid problems by clearly indicating what is happening, as the following example shows:

PSALM 23 – HYMN 267 *(RIL)*   "The King of Love
                                                                        My Shepherd Is"
                                                                            St. Columba

1 — All
2 — Adult choir in harmony *(a cappella)*
3 — All in canon; men begin with organ;
        women enter one measure later
4 — Children's choir
5 — All in canon; women begin with organ;
        men enter one measure later
6 — All in unison.

This and similar renditions are aided by a female director bringing in the women and a male director bringing in the men at their respective appointed times.[38]

Welsh hymns may be sung in the style of a Welsh community hymn sing *(Cymanfa Ganu)*. At the discretion of the accompanist or leader, the chorus or final phrase is repeated again and again, with slowing of tempo *(ritardandoes)* and lengthening of notes *(fermatas)* being liberally employed.[39]

Voices may also be woven antiphonally. This is most easily

accomplished through the alternation of verses between choir and congregation, men and women, etc. However, the weaving can be more intricate, as shown by this Paul Manz rendition of "Now the Silence" (*LBW,* # 205):

All:	"Now the Silence . . ."
Men:	"Now the Kneeling . . ."
Choir:	"Now the hearing . . ."
All:	"Now the body . . ."
Choir:	"Now the wedding . . ."
Women:	"Now the Spirit's visitation . . ."
Men:	"Now the Son's Epiphany . . ."
Women:	"Now the Father's blessing . . ."

Such devices should be used regularly, but not to the point of excess (i.e., wherein the experience of prayer through hymn singing succumbs to distraction or triteness). On special occasions, however, fuller demonstrations of creative hymn singing are appropriate. Hymn festivals have recently grown in popularity, due to the creativity of musicians such as Manz. A hymn festival may also be structured as Morning or Evening Prayer.

Attention to hymn singing has as its sole objective the more worthy praise of God. Occasionally this will result in a qualitative breakthrough in which a hymn articulates unrestrained adoration. When the congregation soars together, the singing of a hymn becomes a truly memorable occasion. Without preparation by musicians and worship leaders, this seldom, if ever, happens. With careful preparation, it will occur often enough to make the extra effort well worth it.

The degree of liturgical participation through hymn singing is dependent upon the element of familiarity. This is not an argument for singing only "favorite hymns." It is rather an argument for teaching hymns of quality. People love to sing what is familiar to them. However, what is familiar can be determined to a large extent by what is taught, rehearsed, and sung again and again. Catechesis on hymnody has received short shrift all the way from the curricula of theological seminaries to the local parish. Many clergy would be hard pressed to name a modern hymn writer or do a literary analysis of the hymn of their choosing. The case for hymn catechesis is an obvious one: here is a treasury of spirituality that expresses the heart of the Christian faith and does so in a form that is profoundly formative. Hymns meld the matrix of spirituality. Hymn catechesis should be thoroughly integrated into all areas of the preaching and teaching ministries of a church. Pastors who take seriously their responsibility for the spiritual development of their flock will make the effort to interpret hymns.[40]

Hymnody is illustrative of an important principle of participation in worship: extraliturgical reverberation. Every day hymns are lofted out over communities from church carillons, broadcast over the airwaves, and piped into hospital rooms. They are sung, hummed, whistled, overheard. More than one missionary has recalled with nostalgia the distant sound of native Christians singing hymns to ease the toil of the day. Concertgoers may recognize hymns embedded within symphonic works and silently pray the words they know and love as the orchestra plays. And what would Christmas be without the greetings of carolers or the sounds of Salvation Army brass ensembles? Hymns are one of the more transportable elements of the liturgy. Popular and easily recognized, they are often an extraliturgical link to the worship of the church. When recalled to mind, they prompt an occasion of prayer. In so doing, the place that these hymns hold within the fabric of spirituality is deepened.[41]

The Gates of Prayer

Music is indispensable to participation. It provides more than an ambience. It throws wide the gates of prayer, ushering the worshiper into the presence of the Holy One. Indeed, music is God's second greatest gift to humanity. The church has at its disposal a veritable wealth of sacred music, a repertoire so lavish that it is hard to imagine how this wealth could be further enriched; yet, it continues to grow. Moreover, all across the land, Christians engage in the act of singing together—even those who, from a musical standpoint, have no business singing. In fact, wherever you go, if you find Christians, you will find singing.

This phenomenon tends to be taken for granted. However, in looking about, there is little singing elsewhere. Unquestionably, there is plenty of music around. But there is very little active singing. The behavior of Christians is striking indeed! Moreover, this singing is consistently better and more frequent than anywhere else. Why *do* Christians sing?

1. We sing because it is a way of praying together. It shows forth our unity in Christ. It is a way of praying together as the body of Christ, one in purpose and in spirit. St. Ignatius writes:

> Your accord and harmonious love is a hymn to Jesus Christ. Yes, one and all, you should form yourselves into a choir, so that, in perfect harmony and taking your pitch from God, you may sing in unison and with one voice to the Father through Jesus Christ. Thus he will heed you, and by your good deeds he will recognize you are members of his Son.[42]

The positive relationship of music to church unity exposes an incongruity: the opinions voiced by some that would delimit musical expression. To wit:

"Hymns should not be sung in worship for they are of human composure. Only psalms should be sung, for they are God's very word! If hymns are sung, psalmody will be eclipsed."

Or: "Chant has no place among us. We are a hymn-singing tradition. Chant belongs to the lifeless church that we left behind at the Reformation."

Or, conversely: "Hymns actually constitute an alternate liturgy that runs in competition with our rites. They are alien to the ethos of our liturgy, whose only natural idiom is chant."

Or: "Liturgical music does not belong in the free church, where ritual is eschewed. Scripture songs, yes, but no canticles."

Or: "Spirituals are subjective and should not be allowed to contaminate our tradition of purely objective hymnody."

Throughout the church apathy, if not downright hostility, can be found toward major forms of participatory music. A presupposition that often underlies this lack of concern is that liturgy should reflect the purity of a tradition. However, the study of the history of worship quickly dispels this notion as myth. Liturgy is eclectic and proud of it, for this eclecticism is its badge of catholicity. Here we do not intend to endorse clashes in musical styles or bad taste in musical decor. Rather, we recognize the simple fact that worship can be enriched from the larger Christian family, if the temptation to delimit musical options is resisted. Liturgy offers a place for each form of music in worship, a proper balance of psalms, canticles, liturgical music, and hymns. The balance dissolves perceived competition or incompatibility among them and instead establishes a relationship of cooperation and complementarity.[43]

Christians sing together as one choir because they are one body and drink of one Spirit. They sing to demonstrate their unity.

2. Christians sing because they are God's new creation. Song is necessary to expressing faith more fully. In the Bible the verb *to sing* appears over 146 times. Thirty-two of these occurrences are joined with the word *praise*. When you want to praise God, when you stand in awe before the Lord, *words alone simply won't do*. Prose is fine. Poetry is better. But poetry set to music can be sublime. "Those who sing," it has often been said, "pray twice." That is what song does for words. It enriches and expands them, investing in them a whole new depth of meaning.

Christians have an irrepressible urge to sing. This is wonderfully illustrated by the story of Paul and Silas, imprisoned in Philippi, feet in stocks (Acts 16:19–34). What does a person do in that sort of predicament? For these early Christians, the answer was to start singing and praying (16:25)! Everyone in the jail was listening to them, some no doubt wondering about their sanity: "Who can sing in a place like this?" The jailer had surely seen more than his fair share of misfits and ne'er-do-wells and perhaps regarded the apostles as a couple of lunatics. But after the earthquake, which opened all the cells, there the jailer was, standing outside of the cell whence had come the singing, crying out, "What must I do to be saved?" Singing transforms our little prisons into cathedrals! Christians sing to give full expression to their faith and to fill dungeons with the light of Christ.

3. Christians sing because heaven sings. The Bible says that the angels of heaven sing day and night without ceasing: "Holy,

holy, holy, is the Lord God Almighty, who was and is and is to come!" (Rev./Apoc. 4:8). In the Orthodox liturgy, when the gifts of bread and wine are brought to the altar, the choir sings:

> We who mystically represent the cherubim, who sing to the life-giving Trinity the thrice-holy hymn, let us now lay aside all earthly care. . . . That we may welcome the King of all invisibly escorted by angel hosts. Alleluia! Alleluia! Alleluia!

The singing of Christians is a mystical representation of cherubim and seraphim who chant in ceaseless praise. Heaven is filled with song. The saints in glory sing to the Lamb upon the throne. Angel cries out to angel. Archangels and all the heavenly host sing out:

> Holy, holy, holy Lord
> God of power and might,
> heaven and earth are full of your glory.
> Hosanna in the highest.

Heaven is filled with singing. The persons of the trinity sing to each other: the Father sings to the Son; the Son to the Spirit to the Father. The triune God is a perfect harmony of divine love that reverberates throughout heaven and all of creation.

Christians sing. We just can't help it.

Patterns of Interiorized Verbal Participation

The covenant is God's promise to remember His people. The covenant obligates the elect to remember God. In the dialogue between heaven and earth, human memory is the avenue to encounter with God. Memory permits the soul to live. It invokes communion with God.

The heart of the worship experience is the beholding of the Lord, high and lifted up, glorious in majesty, Whose train fills the Temple, Whose glory covers the earth. Before this Holy One, awesome in power and might, the steps of pilgrims become tentative and uncertain. Thankfully, the pilgrims are not alone! A great cloud of witnesses surrounds them with the language and music of prayer, prayer that remembers the covenant before the Lord, prayer that invokes God's saving presence anew.

Participatory prayer is collective prayer: prayer that is offered to God through Christ, the church's High Priest; prayer that is uttered in the Spirit of Jesus; prayer that transcends time and space, mystically uniting the communions of earthly and heavenly saints in a triumphant *Te Deum*. Interiorized Verbal Participation provides God's people with a common expression of prayer, wherein they might enter His gates with thanksgiving and His courts with praise. Not only does the prayer of the church unite saints above with saints below. Indeed, whenever a thousand tongues chant hymns and psalms of praise, there is a counterpoint: the song of all of creation—floods clap their hands and hills sing for joy together.

Participatory prayer is transformative prayer. It is prayer that is beloved and familiar, prayer that resounds within the spirits of those who are living memorials to a gracious God. Interiorized Verbal Participation melds the matrix of the spiritual life. It places God's word near the heart, there to await the ministry of the Holy Spirit. Capitalizing on familiarity through repetition, it is the prayer of those who in deepest mystery are being transformed from one likeness into another. Remembered prayer is used by the Spirit to effect the renewal of minds in order to prove what is good and acceptable and perfect.

Study Guide

1. Before the group meeting have the leader of the study group select twenty familiar hymns, Scripture passages, liturgical responses, spirituals, psalms, etc., AND twenty familiar commercial jingles. Mixing the religious set with the secular set, devise a contest to determine the depth of interiorization. For example, how does the group respond to these oral fill-in-the-blank statements?

Miller Lite has a third less calories, AND it tastes _____.
(sung) A mighty fortress is our God, a bulwark never _____.

Devise a scoring system to compare the strength of religious versus secular responses. What do these results suggest?

2. If your organist refused to play the *Amen* at the end of hymns, would you object?

3. What are some advantages and disadvantages to the use of a prayerbook in worship?

4. Do you pray through the Psalms? Which musical idioms assist your prayer? Which inhibit it?

5. How does repetition help to transform you "by the renewal of your mind"?

6. In what ways might hymn singing become more participatory for you?

For Further Reading

Prayerbooks and Liturgical Texts:

ASB. Cambridge, UK: Cambridge University, 1980.

BCP. New York, NY: Church Hymnal Corporation and Seabury, 1977.

Prayers We Have in Common: Agreed Liturgical Texts Proposed by the International Consultation on English Texts. Philadelphia, PA: Fortress, 1970. A 1988 English Language Liturgical Consultation (ELLC) revision of these texts contains language that is gender-inclusive as well as other slight modifications. The ELLC is located at 1275 K St., N.W., Suite 1202, Washington, DC 20005–4097.

Sac. Collegeville, MN: Liturgical, 1974.

SLR. Philadelphia, PA: Westminster, 1984–.

SWR. 12 Vols. Nashville, TN: Abingdon or United Methodist Publishing, 1972–82.

On the Psalms:

Anderson, Bernhard W. *Understanding the Old Testament*. 4th ed. Englewood Cliffs, NJ: Prentice-Hall, 1986. Pp. 540–67.

Brueggemann, Walter. *The Message of the Psalms*. Minneapolis, MN: Augsburg, 1984.

Gunkel, Hermann. *The Psalms: A Form-Critical Introduction.*

79587

Tr. Thomas Horner. Facet Books, 19. Philadelphia, PA: Fortress, 1967.

Mowinckel, Sigmund. *The Psalms in Israel's Worship.* 3 Vols. Tr. D. R. Ap-Thomas. New York, NY: Abingdon, 1962.

Murphy, Roland E. "Psalms." Pp. 569–602 in *Jerome Biblical Commentary,* ed. Raymond E. Brown et al. Englewood Cliffs, NJ: Prentice-Hall, 1968.

von Rad, Gerhard. *Old Testament Theology.* 2 Vols. New York, NY: Harper and Row, 1962. 1.355–459.

Ringgren, Helmer. *The Faith of the Psalmists.* London, UK: S.C.M., 1963.

Weiser, Artur. *The Psalms.* Old Testament Library. Philadelphia, PA: Westminster, 1962.

Westermann, Claus. *The Praise of God in the Psalms.* 2nd ed. Tr. Keith R. Crim. Richmond, VA: John Knox, 1961.

The Music of Worship:

Anderson, Fred R. *Singing Psalms of Joy and Praise.* Philadelphia, PA: Westminster, 1986.

The Anglican Chant Psalter. Ed. Alec Wyton. New York, NY: Church Hymnal Corporation, 1987.

The ASB Psalter and Canticles. Ed. L. Dakers and C. Taylor. London, UK: Collins, 1976.

Berthier, Jacques. *Music from Taizé.* Vocal ed. (G-2433), instrumental ed. (G-2433-A). Chicago, IL: G.I.A., 1981.

Bishops' Committee on the Liturgy. *Music in Catholic Worship.* Washington, DC: National Conference of Catholic Bishops, 1972.

The Book of Canticles. Church Hymnal Series, 2. New York, NY: Church Hymnal Corporation, 1979.

Congregational Music for Eucharist. Church Hymnal Series, 5. New York, NY: Church Hymnal Corporation, 1980.

Dix, Gregory. *The Shape of the Liturgy.* 2nd ed. London, UK: Dacre, 1945.

LINCOLN CHRISTIAN COLLEGE AND SEMINARY

Diehl, Katharine Smith. *Hymns and Tunes—An Index.* New York, NY: Scarecrow, 1966.

Eskew, Harry and McElrath, Hugh T. *Sing with Understanding.* Nashville, TN: Broadman, 1980.

Five Settings of the Common Texts of the Holy Eucharist. Church Hymnal Series, 1. New York, NY: Church Pension Fund, 1976.

Gelineau, Joseph. *Voices and Instruments in Christian Worship.* Collegeville, MN: Liturgical, 1964.

———. *30 Psalms and 2 Canticles.* Chicago, IL: G.I.A., 1962 (G-1430).

———. *24 Psalms and 3 Canticles.* Chicago, IL: G.I.A., n.d. (G-1424).

Hustad, Don. *Jubilate: Church Music in the Evangelical Tradition.* Carol Stream, IL: Hope Publishing, 1981.

H82. New York, NY: Church Hymnal Corporation, 1982.

LBW. Minneapolis, MN: Augsburg, 1978.

Old, Hughes Oliphant. *Praying with the Bible.* Philadelphia, PA: Geneva, 1980.

PGS. Ed. John Melloh and William G. Storey. Chicago, IL: G.I.A., 1979.

Psalter Hymnal, 1987. Ed. Emily Brink. Grand Rapids, MI: The Board of Publications of the Christian Reformed Church, 1987.

RIL. Grand Rapids, MI: Eerdmans, 1985.

Routley, Erik. *Christian Hymns Observed: When in Our Music God Is Glorified.* Prestige Publications, 1986.

———. *Church Music and the Christian Faith.* Carol Stream, IL: Agape, 1978.

———. *Hymns Today and Tomorrow.* New York, NY: Abingdon, 1964.

———. *The Music of Christian Hymnody: A Study of the Development of the Hymn Tune Since the Reformation, with Special*

Reference to English Protestantism. London, UK: Independent, 1957.

_____. *A Panorama of Christian Hymnody.* Collegeville, MN: Liturgical Press, 1979.

Webber, Christopher. *A New Metrical Psalter.* New York, NY: Church Hymnal Corporation, 1986.

Worship3. Chicago, IL: G.I.A., 1986.

On Creeds:

Farrer, Austin Marsden. *Lord I Believe: Suggestions for Turning the Creed into Prayer.* London, UK: S.P.C.K., 1962.

Gerrish, Brian, ed. *The Faith of Christendom: A Source Book of Creeds and Confessions.* Cleveland, OH: World Publishing, 1963.

Kelly, John Norman. *Early Christian Creeds.* New York, NY: D. McKay, 1972.

Link, Hans-Georg, ed. *Confessing Our Faith Around the World.* 3 Vols. Geneva: World Council of Churches, 1980.

MacGregor, Geddes. *The Nicene Creed, Illumined by Modern Thought.* Grand Rapids, MI: Eerdmans, 1980.

Schaff, Philip. *Bibliotheca symbolica ecclesiae universalis.* New York, NY: Harper and Brothers, 1905.

Traugott, Paul. *An Introduction to the Great Creeds of the Church.* Philadelphia, PA: Westminster, 1960.

6

Fresh from the Word

Prophecy and the Prophetic Voice

And in the last days it shall be, God declares,
that I will pour out my Spirit upon all flesh,
and your sons and daughters shall prophesy,
and your young men shall see visions,
and your old men shall dream dreams;
yea, and on my menservants and my maidservants in those days
I will pour out my Spirit; and they shall prophesy. (Acts 2:17–18; see
Joel 2:28–29)

The resurgence of prophecy is one of the most striking aspects of
the birth of the church. As with the prophets of old, the Spirit
inspires a new expression of the timeless truths of God's covenant. Prophecy is a gift. It is not novelty for novelty's sake. Nor
does it deny that the familiar can also become prophetic, due to
changes in subjective perception. It is the gift of proclaiming
God's unchanging word in an improvisational mode, *so that it
might be recognized anew.*

The prophetic literature of the Bible encompasses a broad
range of genres. Prophecies may contain words of consolation,
ecstasy, knowledge, discernment, edification, exhortation, pre-
diction, encouragement, admonishment, and, at times, judgment. Despite this diversity, what all prophetic utterances have
in common is that they are God's word delivered to the com-

munity of faith (1 Cor. 14:22) through the individual. More-over, the prophetic gift is one addressed to specific and current needs. The community of faith is scarcely passive in this process of communication. It is the responsibility of the community to discern whether or not the prophecy is indeed God's word. This discernment explains in part how some prophecies came to be canonized as Scripture while others were excluded or forgotten.

Prophetic Verbal Participation, the subject of this chapter, occurs interactively with the prophetic voice. In theory, it is possible for the prophetic voice to be heard through any type of participation. However, there are certain contributions to worship the original intent of which is to engender Prophetic Verbal Participation. Preaching is the foremost of these. Worship resources may also be designed to interact with God's word in the prophetic voice.

Prophetic Verbal Participation awards to individual creativity a vital role in shaping the liturgical expression of a community. Worship leaders are given a wide latitude in the selection and composition of liturgical resources. These may either be offered extemporaneously or more deliberately composed, selected, and adapted. The crucial factor is that the sermons, proclamations, prayers, and litanies be shaped for the occasion by the person to whom a community has awarded the exercise of this prophetic ministry.

The call of the community to prophetic ministry through liturgical leadership is a tremendous gift of freedom in the Spirit. It is based in the recognition that God's word is not bound. With this gift of prophetic freedom is incurred an equally tremendous burden of responsibility—to serve the people with energy, imagination, intelligence, and, above all else, love. Prophetic Verbal Participation requires a worship leader who is highly skilled in pastoral sensitivities.

Because prophetic leadership is demanding, it is not surprising that attempts to engender Prophetic Verbal Participation do not always produce the desired effect of interaction with the prophetic voice. For this reason the chapter will discuss considerations that may thwart these efforts. These concerns will focus on three areas: individual creativity, catholicity, and inclusivity. This discussion may appear severe or restrictive to the prophetic voice, which by its very nature is God's word unfettered (2 Tim. 2:9). However, if God's word is to go forth through the prophetic mode, there must be a savvy awareness of the liturgical context within which Prophetic Verbal Participation operates. Hopefully the reader will view the discussion of these concerns as a prophetic word addressed to the prophetic word, arising from the author's concern that the word that goes forth from God's mouth shall not return empty but shall accomplish that which God purposes and prosper in that thing for which it was sent (Isa. 55:11).

The Integrity of Preaching √

Preaching is the primary occasion for interaction with the prophetic voice through Prophetic Verbal Participation. Enhanced liturgical participation necessitates a proclamation that is bold, persuasive, energetic, powerful, animated, insightful, well prepared, faithful, seasoned, proportioned, appropriate to the audience, and, most important of all, biblical. A preacher's task must be taken with the utmost seriousness. Those with the gift to preach must take care to cultivate that gift and to allow for the necessary fermentation, pastoral sensitivity, and preparation that underlie effective preaching. Sermons should be designed and delivered in such a way that listeners will respond—thinking, doing, feeling, deciding for themselves. Preaching that consists of conclusive pronouncements can reduce a congregation into quiet submission and become a form of coercion that hampers participation.[1]

Participatory preaching possesses a transparently human quality. Although addressing a different issue, St. Paul's words are relevant nonetheless:

> When I came to you, brethren, I did not come proclaiming to you the testimony of God in lofty words or wisdom. For I decided to know

nothing among you except Jesus Christ and him crucified. And I was with you in weakness and in much fear and trembling; and my speech and my message were not in plausible words of wisdom, but in demonstration of the Spirit and of power, that your faith might not rest in the wisdom of men but in the power of God. (1 Cor. 2:1–5)

The Apostle's oratorical skills may not have been of the caliber of a Cicero. Nevertheless, St. Paul was an extremely effective preacher. From where does his confession of "much fear and trembling" come? It is more than self-effacement, a virtue in all-too-short supply among some preachers. Paul is referring to the overwhelming task that confronts any preacher, not because that person may be poor at the craft but because the wisdom of God is so vast, so incomprehensible, so indescribable. Preaching is effective not because of human logic but because it bears witness to Logos, the wisdom of God that is apprehended by the power of the Holy Spirit. Any defects in preaching ability, says Paul, highlight the enormous gulf that exists between human wisdom and God's wisdom. The latter cannot be attained through the genius of the former.

There are other "hotter media" that could be substituted for the sermonic efforts of lowly preachers. A high-quality religious movie could be shown. A sermon that a famous preacher has had published could be read. A television monitor could bring the glitter of the Electronic Church into a local parish. Surely such alternative media would be more polished and therefore a more effective means of promoting the gospel through plausible words of wisdom. However, a most crucial dimension of effective preaching would be missing in these alternative media.

Vital preaching comes straight from the heart of the preacher standing there live. The best preaching ministers directly to the hearts of the congregation that a particular preacher is called to know, to love, and to serve. Therefore, it has to be done live. It has to occur in the flesh, for as a "cool medium" it elicits an immediate dialogue of spirits through the Spirit of the incarnate Christ. A preacher must stand up in the pulpit—week in and week out, in fear and trembling, with weaknesses evident to all—for God's word to be credible and to be received in power. Only fully present human beings, in all their frailty and inadequacy, can do this. While the preaching of the Electronic Church serves some limited purposes, it does not deserve to be in competition with the real thing no matter how lacklustre the latter may be. For the proclamation of the gospel, the medium must complement the message. Preaching that is too glitzy is ill-suited to imparting God's wisdom, for the cleverness and polish of the performer and the medium begin to detract from the glory that is due to God alone. Preaching that is overly flamboyant or ostentatious, causing the listener to be more impressed with the preacher than with the Almighty, has defeated itself.

In this sense preaching is sacramental. To be effective it must transport the listener past the preacher and into the presence of God. To accomplish this preachers must keep their egos out of the way. The effectiveness of preaching is measured by the encounter with Christ that occurs only by the grace of God. Evangelist Billy Graham was once introduced with lavish and glowing praise for his pulpit abilities—all very much true. But, to his credit, when he rose to preach, he quickly set the record straight: "Any glory is due to God alone." It is a preacher's responsibility to reveal the secret and hidden wisdom of God and to do it in a fashion that will bring listeners into a saving encounter with Christ.

The Prophetic Voice: Contemporary and Specific

The remainder of this chapter will focus on forms of Prophetic Verbal Participation that are found outside of the sermon. With the availability of inexpensive print media, many of these forms are frequently dependent upon the printed word. In the history of human liberation, the gift of literacy plays a decisive role. Through the printed word the horizons of human expression and experience are greatly expanded. There is no wonder that churches have capitalized on this medium as a means of enhancing liturgical participation.

Prophetic Verbal Participation operates in the prophetic mode. It contrasts vividly with Interiorized Verbal Participation, which is clearly at home in the ritual mode. Whereas Interiorized Verbal Participation is traditional in its outlook, emphasizing the value of repetition, Prophetic Verbal Participation favors a more contemporary idiom. Its forms aspire toward fresh insights and immediate relevance. For this reason, they are often disposable forms of worship, and unapologetically so. Such forms highlight a dimension of God's word that is ever-new, ever-free, ever-fresh, like the breaking dawn.[2] They further demonstrate the obligation of each generation to make its own distinctive contribution to the prayer of the church, for prophecy is the cradle of ritual.

The language of liturgy is the language of poetry. Not every pastor is a poet; in fact, few are. But pastors and worship leaders with literary gifts ought to be provided with free space for their special ministry. Use of these gifts enriches the church in that through them the classical corpus of liturgical resources is replenished. After all, the prayers and materials in prayerbooks were themselves once fresh and new, the creative composition of an individual sometime, somewhere. As rich as is the classical corpus, there is always room for improvement and a need to update. Many attempts at creativity are required to generate those few expressions that will live on. That is how each generation makes its distinctive contribution to the ever-expanding prayer of the church.

The language of Prophetic Verbal Participation needs to be contemporary without being trendy or hackneyed. Note the freshness of expression in this unison Opening Prayer for Christmas Eve in which the Bethlehem personae are creatively woven into an array of petitions:

Lord God of majesty and mangers, send now your angels to lift my burdened heart in joyful song. Send shepherds to show me how to bend my tense and tired knees. Send wise men who can teach my tight shut fists to open and to know the joy of giving. Send gentle Mary who can school my proud rebellious spirit to obedience; quiet Joseph who will show the way to genuine humility; and your Son,

Jesus the babe of Bethlehem, to lighten all my darkness with the warm and steady radiance of your grace. Amen.[3]

The following antiphonal Prayer of Confession for Palm Sunday applies Holy Week themes in trenchant prose, unsoftened by the deliberations of an editorial committee:

Right: On this day of promise and portent we are the crowd—eager to hail a conqueror, and just as eager to curse a loser.

Left: We are the Pharisees—the religious people, resenting this disturbance of our orderly existence, hating this strange, demanding newcomer who overturns our customary ways.

Right: We are the disciples—delirious for a day, dreaming of success and fame and fortune, loyal to a point, but only to a point—and then the cock crows.

Left: We are the fig tree—bearing no fruit, flowering no faith, moving not even our own hearts let alone mountains.

All: FORGIVE US OUR BARRENNESS, LORD, OUR FRUITLESSNESS, OUR BLINDNESS, AND SO WALK WITH US DOWN THE EASTER ROAD THIS WEEK THAT WE MIGHT SHARE BOTH IN THE AGONY OF YOUR CRUCIFIXION, AND IN THE GLORY OF YOUR RESURRECTION. AMEN.[4]

In the life of any congregation there are liturgical moments that call for greater specificity than a classical collection of prayers is able to provide. The following unison Prayer of Confession was composed to complement and support a temporary change in the musical idiom of the worshiping community—in this instance, a jazz pianist who provided the liturgical music. The prayer expresses the ability of the Holy Spirit to minister through sounds that worshipers may be unaccustomed to hearing:

Lord, you are calling us out into new ways, new times. You provoke us with strange rhythms, you challenge us to learn fresh tunes, to sing new songs. Yet we don't want to move. We cling to the old. We love the familiar. We cherish the cozy and comfortable. We know what to expect, and we expect only what we know and it's safer that way. Forgive our caution, Lord, open us now to the surprises that lie hidden within worship. Through Jesus Christ who came, who comes, as your eternal surprise. Amen.[5]

On Christian Unity Sunday the same Presbyterian congregation welcomed a neighboring Roman Catholic monsignor to its pulpit. The unison Prayer of Confession acknowledged the significance of that event:

> You have called us together, Lord, to be your Church. But we have splintered apart, seeking to be our church. You have called us to be your Body, broken in the service of your world. But we have broken your body in our own ways, dividing into rival groups, separated communities each one claiming to be the real body, the true church, the only one in the right. Forgive us, Lord. Break down the walls we have built up to shut each other out. And set us free to love you and to serve your world together. Amen.[6]

Individual Creativity

Because the prophetic voice is heard through the individual's voice, it is necessary to examine the limits of individual creativity, so that attempts to engender Prophetic Verbal Participation do not defeat themselves. The predominant mode in preaching is prophetic. However, the predominant mode in liturgy is ritual. Neither is excluded from the other. The voice of ritual will often be heard in preaching just as the voice of prophecy will often be heard through the liturgy. However, outside of the sermon, the ritual mode normally predominates. This means that the prophetic voice in ritual is properly understood as the leaven in the loaf, not the loaf itself. For the prophetic voice to be effective through the liturgy, the emphasis must be upon quality, not quantity.

The result of overly expansive Prophetic Verbal Participation is excessively verbose liturgy. Contemporary efforts at more participatory worship all too frequently have made disproportionate use of that twentieth-century liturgical anomaly, the mimeograph machine. Access to inexpensive print media has resulted in a proliferation of celebrations that are ever-new, ever-adaptive, and ever-wordier. Forests have fallen as reams upon reams of disposable liturgies have been produced in a compulsive quest for more participation. Worshipers have been handed tomes that in some cases exceed their reading quotas for the week. The verbosity of such worship stifles the religious spirit. Meanwhile,

duplicating and paper companies prosper, the unwitting bene-
ficiaries of "participatory worship."

An overemphasis on this or any type of liturgical participation that is already prominent only produces a greater imbalance.
In promoting participation, more is not necessarily better. One
key is balance, avoiding an exaggerated emphasis. Another key is
complementarity, grasping the fact that the various types of
participation act as checks and balances upon each other—that
each type serves as a corrective, rescuing the others from their
own worst tendencies.

An excess of individual creativity in worship inhibits participation therein. At a large conference, a "liturgy specialist" was
given the responsibility to plan and lead the worship. The substantial liturgy booklet distributed to the conference participants
revealed a curious feature: all of the prayers, litanies, responses,
and even many of the hymns had been composed for that occasion by the worship leader. While this impressed many as a
supererogation of the first order, these liturgies were fundamen-
tally flawed. The prophetic and ritual voices were in utter confusion. The prophetic had far exceeded its proper role and had
inundated the ritual side of the equation. Consequently, as
people celebrated these services, they experienced them as the
liturgist's liturgy rather than as the prayer of the church. It was
impossible to get around the liturgist. Everywhere the congregation turned, there he was. The worship leader had unwittingly
established himself as mediator of the worship. In the name of
participation, he had actually thwarted it.

While that worship leader's example of participatory worship
is an egregious one, there is plenty of "creative worship" around
that displays similar tendencies. Individuals do not write liturgies, at least liturgies that will live to enjoy any larger ownership.[7]
Excessive personal creativity subjects a congregation to the
tyranny of individualism, which is a thinly disguised form of
clerical dominance. Too much individual input into the shape
and content of the liturgy creates an unhealthy dependency upon
a worship leader for the experience of worship itself. Parishioners are thereby put in the awkward position of having to

evaluate their personal feelings about the worship leader in order to worship God. Some mainline churches and the Electronic Church have more in common here than either cares to admit.

Prophetic Verbal Participation will prosper from the healthy recognition that composing worship that has integrity requires special training and gifts. The prophetic voice can succumb to shortcomings of theology, grammar, and syntax. Poor quality materials, especially those turned out in haste, discourage participation through their ineloquence or through their lack of substance, style, imagination, or seasoning. Worshipers also react negatively to prayers that are didactic or manipulative.

Prophetic Verbal Participation may also be defeated by a parochial arrogance that assumes that it can sustain a well-rounded diet of liturgical materials for a congregation. Participation is enhanced when a catholic backdrop is evident, the sense of sharing in an act of prayer with Christians of all times and places. This is an extraordinarily difficult thing for any one individual to generate out of personal creativity. For Prophetic Verbal Participation to prosper it needs to work side by side with the larger tradition of the church, before which the individual's creativity is meager by comparison. The congregation that is fed too exclusively on the creativity of its leader will soon grow restless and dissatisfied with the inevitable malnutrition. Those who are entrusted with the responsibility of planning and leading worship ought to be relieved of the burden of perpetual creativity. There is no need continually to reinvent the wheel. The first gift of liturgical leadership is humility: knowing that one's own creativity pales before that of the larger tradition. The goal is not worship infused with the leader's personality. The goal is worship infused with the prayer of the church, the embraced corporate worship of the church. Here is the secret passageway to participatory worship.

Creativity in worship is wrongly ascribed to the worship planner/leader. That person is not the focus of creativity that enhances participation. Rather, the focus of true creativity is the Holy Spirit, who, as at creation, "broods over the warm earth with, Ah! bright wings" (Hopkins). Creativity in worship is that which is transparent to the creative movement of the Holy Spirit, active throughout all generations, present to all of space and time. It does not lie in the hands of the worship planner or composer, and rightfully so. From the purview of liturgical participation, the Holy Spirit is the provenance of creative worship.

The Context of Catholicity

A celebrant is called to lead the people of God in the church's prayer. A worship leader is ordained as a steward of the mysteries, one who delivers over "that which has been received" (1 Cor. 11:23). A worship leader performs a function for a church, that of leading it in its traditional prayer. Liturgy is not the place for perennial innovation. Participation in worship demands a well-established sense of ministerial propriety. Ministers are called to serve the church by leading the prayer of the church.

In a general sense, the prayer of the church refers to all prayer that is addressed to the Father, in the name of Jesus, through the Spirit. St. Paul notes that it is the Spirit who actually prays through the church:

> We do not know how to pray as we ought, but the Spirit himself intercedes for us with sighs too deep for words. And he who searches the hearts of men knows what is the mind of the Spirit, because the Spirit intercedes for the saints according to the will of God. (Rom. 8:26–27)

The epistle to the Hebrews informs us that the prayer of the church that is offered in the Spirit is united with the prayer of Christ:

> He holds his priesthood permanently, because he continues for ever. Consequently he is able for all time to save those who draw near to God through him, since he always lives to make intercession for them. (Heb. 7:24–25)

The general sense of the prayer of the church is a way of speaking about a larger backdrop to worship. Liturgical participation is enhanced through this sense of solidarity, the knowledge that others in time and space also share in this act of prayer. The prayer of the church projects a universal scope, situating all prayer within the prayer of Christ. Individual creativity must ever be mindful of classical models. Although the prophetic voice is not bound by them, it dare not operate oblivious to them.

The Order of Worship

The experience of participation is enhanced through structures for worship that are transparent to those of the church catholic. Based upon ancient custom, there is today ecumenical consensus on what constitutes the basic structure for Lord's Day worship:[8]

> Reading(s) from Scripture[9]
> Preaching
> Intercessory prayers
> Offertory (the movement of bread and wine to the altar-table)
> Eucharistic Prayer/Great Thanksgiving
> Holy Communion
> Dismissal

Beyond this basic structure, there are other elements, such as the Lord's Prayer, the Nicene or Apostles' Creed, a rite of confession, and the collection of alms, which have traditional locations that should be respected. Still other elements—hymns, anthems, announcements, and the Peace—are less crucial in their placement. Special celebrations like baptism, marriage, ordination, communion, confirmation, and recognitions should normally occur after the sermon and may be related to the elements that follow. For example, when a marriage occurs, the intercessory prayers should focus on the bridal couple and on all marriages and families. The Peace may flow out of the nuptial kiss. The bride and groom may present the gifts of bread and wine at the offertory. The crucial elements for catholic recognition are biblical preaching and Eucharist, about which more will be said in chapter 9.

Calls to Worship

In addition to influencing liturgical structure the concern for catholicity affects the shape of the individual elements of worship. The following Calls to Worship illustrate the importance of an awareness of the larger liturgical context within which the prophetic voice operates:

EXAMPLE A

Leader: Why are we here Lord?
People: *Yes, why are we here?*
Leader: Now is the time to live and say "Alleluia!"
People: *Yes, now is the time to say "Alleluia!"*
Leader: Now is the time to come to the God who creates us;
People: *To sing to the Lord who frees us;*
Leader: And to give ourselves completely to the Spirit who fills us!
People: *Alleluia! Alleluia! Alleluia! AMEN.*

EXAMPLE B

Leader: All the faithful will make their prayers to you in time of trouble;
People: *When the great waters overflow, they shall not reach them.*
Leader: You are my hiding-place;
People: *You preserve me from trouble;*
Leader: Be glad, you righteous, and rejoice in the Lord;
People: *Shout for joy, all who are true of heart.*

Example A is the product of a pastor's individual creativity. Example B is excerpted from the Psalm for the Day (Ps. 31[32]).

Example A is a one-time usage, thereby limiting its impact. Example B builds upon already familiar phrases.

Example A discourages participation through triteness. "Why are we here, Lord?" Goodness, you mean we don't know? Example B encourages participation by capitalizing on the sublime prose of the church's treasurehouse of spirituality, the Psalms.

Example A is manipulative. Who is to say that "now is the time"? Who is assuming that we should feel a certain way? Example B provides a larger backdrop as the curtain rises on the action, drawing the people of God into worship via the prayer of the Spirit as uttered by God's people down through the ages.

Confessions of Sin

The prophetic voice is not confined to contemporaneous expression. Indeed it is possible that interaction with the prophetic voice may be more likely to occur through classical prayers, as this comparison of opening penitential prayers demonstrates:

EXAMPLE C

CONFESSING OUR SIN (*together*)
O God - who cared enough to give us directions; Who cared enough to show us in Jesus Christ what the laws mean; Who cares enough to stand beside us, in the Spirit, to help us with the rules; Who cares enough to keep after us, asking us to be careful. Forgive us all those times and places where we have not been careful enough of your will or of each other. And we have been too careful of ourselves and our resources, withholding what belongs only to you, squandering it on other masters. We pray in the name of our sole Master. AMEN.

EXAMPLE D

Most merciful God, we confess that we have sinned against you in thought, word, and deed, by what we have done, and by what we have left undone. We have not loved you with our whole heart; we have not loved our neighbors as ourselves. We are truly sorry and we humbly repent. For the sake of your Son Jesus Christ, have mercy on us and forgive us; that we may delight in your will and walk in your ways, to the glory of your Name. AMEN.[10]

Example C is the product of the pastor's individual creativity and betrays an individualistic theological perspective. Example D is from a denominational worship resource, which adapted it from the *BCP*.

Example C is a one-time usage, thereby limiting its impact upon participation. Example D enhances participation by building upon familiar lines drawn from biblical phraseology. It reassures the tongue that it has passed this way before and will pass this way again.

Example C is structurally flawed. It places the petition for mercy in the middle of the prayer instead of at the conclusion. It then places a postscript after this petition. The voices of the prayer shift inexplicably. There are distracting errors of grammar. Example D is refined to perfection.

Example C meanders and lacks clarity. Example D is to the point. We have fallen short. We are sorry. We need God's mercy to glorify His name. Its prose is simple, direct, and eloquent.

Example C constricts participation through a coercive and manipulative specificity. Just what is it that I have "squandered on other masters"? Is such a confession authentic? Or, is it "just something to think about"? Example D is a general confession of sin ("what we have done, and what we have left undone"). Its generality creates a free space for the Holy Spirit to prompt an appropriate level of specificity.

Admittedly, these comparisons are oblique. Yet, they highlight the need for the prophetic voice to speak through forms that are biblical, literary, familiar, nonmanipulative, and free from the tyranny of individualism.

Collects

An Opening Collect or Prayer for the Day is properly a presidential prayer, a prayer that is articulated by the one who is presiding. Nonetheless, many congregations use it as a unison prayer. An opening prayer sounds the theme for celebration, often reflecting the gospel lesson for the day. It follows a classic structure:

(a) an address to God the Father;
(b) mention of some divine attribute or act as the basis for the prayer;
(c) characteristic terseness to the prayer proper—short, simple, definite.
(d) a concluding doxology, which indicates that the prayer is offered to the Father, through the Son, and in the Holy Spirit.

This fourfold progression is evident in this Opening Prayer for the Feast of the Transfiguration:

Let us pray:
(Pause for silence)

(a) O God,
(b) who before the passion of your only-begotten Son revealed his glory upon the holy mountain:
   (Pause)
(c) Grant to us that we, beholding by faith the light of his countenance, may be strengthened to bear our cross, and be changed into his likeness from glory to glory;
(d) through Jesus Christ our Lord, who lives and reigns with you and the Holy Spirit, one God, for ever and ever. AMEN.[11]

As previously noted, it is important to pause for the silence of centering after an invitation to pray. The centering prayer is then gathered up or "collected." The collect itself should then be articulated deliberately, unrushed, pausing at the point at which the motive for praise shifts to the petition. Regrettably, such fine points of execution are usually lost when collects are offered as unison prayers. Lastly participation in God's word is reinforced and deepened when the collect or any prayer resonates with images from the lections for the day.

Litanies

More conducive to corporate involvement than collects are litanies, prayers that are punctuated by a fixed, corporate response.[12] If such responses are kept simple and invariable, and if the people are instructed when to respond, litanies need not be printed out in the worship resource, thereby freeing the worshiper from the printed medium. If well composed, litanies can be an effective means of promoting Prophetic Verbal Participation. They are flexible in form and may be tailored to suit any occasion. Typically, they are responsive readings or prayers of praise, thanksgiving, penitence/confession, or intercession. Thematically, they are often precatory, invoking God's aid and comfort for peace, church unity, the nation, or other special concerns. They may be proper to special occasions, such as ordinations, baptisms, the Paschal Vigil, Lent, Rogation Days, or days marking special observances in the life of a congregation. On such occasions they invite creative compositional talents.

Litanies will be most effective when they observe the general guidelines noted for Prophetic Verbal Participation:

—verbal inclusivity
—literary quality
—biblical language and images,
—faithfulness to doctrinal norms
—universal scope, not parochial or individual
—fixed responses
—nonmanipulative generality that allows for the specificity of the ministry of the Holy Spirit.[13]

Verbal Inclusivity

For the prophetic voice to be heard and received as God's word, the verbal language that it employs must be intelligible. This means first of all that it should be in the vernacular.[14] However, because languages are living, evolving systems of communication, the meanings assigned to the vernacular are in constant flux. This fluctuation poses an ongoing dilemma for the language of worship.

The historical tendency in English usage has been for grammatical gender to give way to natural gender. In natural gender males are referred to as "he," females as "she," and all the rest are referred to as "it." The evolution of English contrasts with languages like German and Russian, in which nouns have preserved masculine, feminine, and neuter gender identities and the Romance languages (such as French and Spanish) which have eliminated the neuter.

The preference of English for natural gender has brought some modern expressions of the language to a crossroads with far-reaching implications for participation in worship. Since the late 1960s, some usages of English, primarily American, have evolved in the meanings assigned to certain generic terminology. The effects of this evolution on the language of worship have been considerable. Terms that were previously viewed as inclusive of both male and female genders are now interpreted exclusively by many. For example, the term *man,* which for centuries in English usage could refer to males and females, especially when accompanied by an article as in "man is the Lord of creation," is now increasingly restricted in its meaning to adult males only. Such changes in these expressions of gender specificity have been rapid and probably irreversible, despite the fact that they have not been adopted by all (or even the majority of) English-speaking people.[15]

Language About the People of God

When references are made to the church, they should be made in such a way that all persons will feel addressed, included, and equally valued before God. This immediately excludes the liturgical use of references perceived to be derogatory to race, class, sex, etc. It further requires that traditional generic terms yield to substitute expressions, such as:

Brothers	—sisters and brothers, people, children, friends
Men	—all, they, them, folks, we, us, ones
Fellow man	—humanity, all people
Brotherhood	—communion, community of faith, church, family, God's people
Son(s)	—child, own, children, sons and daughters
Man	—one, all, we
Fathers	—parents, ancestors, mothers and fathers
He	—one, we

The substitution of terms complicates the task of reading Scripture in worship. Traditionally, the office of lector has fulfilled a formal function for the community—that of reading God's word from a version approved for use by the community. Because of the rapid evolution in American English usage, lectors are using authorized versions containing what may now be interpreted as gender-exclusive language. New translations are in preparation, but that process is a slow and necessarily painstaking one.

In the meantime lectors should prepare for their task with great care. Inclusive language may appropriately be substituted where the intention of the original text can be preserved. For example, the Greek word *'adelphoi* in Romans 12:1 may legitimately be translated as "sisters and brothers," which are in some current expressions of English the equivalent of "brethren." It is politic for lectors to seek the permission of and guidelines from the congregation before altering authorized translations.

Some passages (e.g., 1 John 3:4–18) can become so entangled with emendations that they are better left untouched by lectors. They require the deliberations of committees preparing authorized translations. When paraphrases, such as *The Living Bible,* or when unfamiliar translations are used, they should be identified for the congregation. Listeners should not be unduly distracted by unfamiliarity.

Language About God

Liturgical language that refers to God raises more difficult issues. To scrub liturgical language of all gender-specific references is counterproductive, for it narrows the poetic possibilities for liturgical expression. Using a wider range of images is a better approach. Liturgical language about God should be at least as diverse as that of the Bible. The language of much modern worship has tended to favor such terms as Father, King, Master, Creator, Lord, etc. By contrast, the Bible uses an expanded repertoire of similes and metaphors, which, in English, are neuter:

Rock	First and Last	Light
Truth	Helper	Warrior
Refuge	Redeemer	Salvation
Savior	Shepherd	Ruler
Foundation	Creator	Sovereign

The examples provided are neutral in English and themselves demonstrate the painful shortage of feminine biblical imagery for God for the English reader. Nonetheless, utilizing a fuller diversity of biblical images in worship will offset an overuse of masculine images and enrich the perception of God's being.

The liturgical use of *Yahweh* is discouraged out of respect for the time-honored Jewish custom observed by Jesus of silent reverence before the name of God. Traditionally, the name has not been pronounced or even written. At the time of Christ only the high priest of the Temple was allowed to utter the holy tetragrammaton, *YHWH,* and then only once a year. Following the destruction of the Temple, the transmission of the secret pronunciation was broken. It is uncertain how this name for God should sound. The RSV translates *YHWH* with the substitute expression "the LORD." Just as some English terms have *in*creasing gender specificity (e.g., man, brother), *Lord* is a term that has *de*creasing gender specificity in American usage.

The replacement of masculine pronoun references for God is permissible, except where unacceptable levels of repetition and assonance result. The frequent substituting of strong nouns, such as *God,* for pronoun references is also problematical in that meaning is diluted through overuse.

Editing and, in some cases, retranslation of hymn texts are allowable and appropriate. Some regard this change as tampering with the poetry of individuals. However, hymns belong to the church. The precedent for modifying them is as old as the redaction of the hymn in Colossians 1:15–20, which brought it into line with orthodox Christian theology.[16] However, hymn editing is best left to hymnal commissions. The practice of individuals changing the texts of hymns while singing them is distracting and contradictory to the spirit of corporate hymn singing, and it turns a symbol for the church's unity into a symbol of disunity. Quality hymnals are now available whose editors have displayed a commendable level of sensitivity to the need for gender-inclusive language.[17]

The debate over inclusive religious language is most critical where proposed linguistic changes dovetail with theological changes. Some proposed nonsexist references to God imply a reshaping of traditional theology. The doctrines of the trinity, the relationship of Christian faith to nature, and the immediacy of a personal Savior-God are cornerstones of the faith that are being challenged by some in the debate over inclusive language.

The use of *Father* has a special and revered place in Christian worship, it being the distinctive name for God given to the church by Jesus. The richness of this name is enhanced by the fact that *Abba* is an affectionate Aramaic term for *father*. *Father* should continue to be used, and with frequency. Replacing it with a less personal term, such as *Parent,* diminishes the evangelical note of personal immediacy.

Some have suggested the liturgical use of *Mother* as a name for God. While the Bible ascribes "maternal" qualities to God, it does not use this name. Such usage is an example of language that calls attention to itself, which is distracting to participation in worship. Liturgical language should be like a clean window—you look *through* it, not *at* it. Moreover, the use of feminine designations for God for the purpose of balancing masculine imagery poses an additional problem that is frequently overlooked. To assign some qualities to God's "feminine side" and others to God's "masculine side" unwittingly makes human sex-stereotyping even more rigid.

The trinitarian designation (Father, Son, Holy Spirit) is an ancient credal formula and cannot easily be altered without also altering the relational character of trinitarian language. Its significance as an ecumenical unifying point is not to be underestimated. Participation in worship requires a larger backdrop, the sense that the worship is one with that of the church catholic. The custom of replacing the trinitarian names with functions, such as Creator-Redeemer-Sustainer, results in a theological impoverishment. Functional attributes are a diminution of meaning from the names of persons, which alone can embody the mystery behind them. Especially in baptism, which is an introduction of persons at the heart of which is the mutual exchange of names, it is mandatory that the traditional trinitarian formula be used.[18]

The debate over inclusive language is not over, and much work remains to be done on the nature of liturgical language and metaphor. Seeking after verbal inclusivity is a moral imperative, indeed, one that points to the fullness of the kingdom of God and to oneness in Christ (Gal. 3:28). In this pursuit unrealistic expectations of language are not helpful. Given the fact of the evolution of English toward natural gender, it needs to be recognized that the language has a limitation of theological expressiveness. The linguistic shortcomings of English (or, for that matter, any language) ought to serve as reminders of the inadequacy of all theological language. Liturgical language about God stands in the shadow of the final revelation, when it too will be shattered by the reality of the mystery fully revealed. "Now we see through a glass, darkly, but then face to face" (1 Cor. 13:12).[19]

Patterns of Prophetic Verbal Participation

Behold, I am doing a new thing;
> now it springs forth, do you not perceive it? (Isa. 43:19)

Prophetic Verbal Participation, sensitive as it is to the contemporaneous and personalized movement of the Holy Spirit, images the freedom of God. It models for the faithful the steadfast love of the Lord that never ceases, whose mercies are new every morning (Lam. 3:22–23). It expresses the identity of the church as a prophetic community, filled with new wine, whose members are called to claim and proclaim the gospel in a personal way (Acts 2:13–18).

The liturgical materials for Prophetic Verbal Participation may be either appropriated from the classical treasury or freely composed by pastors and worship leaders. Some traditions furnish a plethora of resources and options, with varying expectations about their usage. Others rely more upon the creativity of the local pastor. In either case, the worship leader's attentiveness to the leading of the Holy Spirit will insure a sensitivity to the considerations of individual creativity, catholicity, and inclusivity.

Prophetic Verbal Participation, although it operates within the prophetic mode, cannot exist apart from the ritual mode. It requires a context of structure and familiarity, in competition with which it is all too often held to be. Effective Prophetic Verbal Participation respects the distinction between these complementary voices. The ritual voice is the predominant one in the liturgy. However, in the proclamation of God's word, the prophetic voice takes precedence. Preaching may on occasion find the ritual voice to be an effective medium, just as the liturgy needs on occasion to shift into the prophetic voice, so that what is overly familiar does not become lifeless. But such exceptions in no way alter the primary character that is proper to each.

The basic diet of liturgical materials should for the most part be drawn from the grand old prayers of the church, so that Christians may pray with the saints of all ages. This preference respects the nature of worship as primarily an expression of God's word in the ritual mode. When the basic fare is classical, the stage is then set for improvisation, for the congregation to be "led in prayer with words from its own pastor, who knows and loves that flock, and who, at times, can speak to it and for it more effectively than all the gifted poets, theologians, and liturgical scholars in the Church."[20] Such personalized contributions are similar to a musical cadenza in which a soloist gives free embellishment to the themes of a concerto, while the orchestra remains poised in anticipation of its next entrance.

Study Guide

1. Is linguistic inclusivity a problem in your congregation's worship? What are some problems encountered in the quest for verbal inclusivity? Do you agree with the author that there are limitations to language that may make final solutions impossible? Do you agree that something is lost by not referring to God as Father?

2. Discuss the pros and cons of a worship leader's use of prayer texts versus offering prayer extemporaneously.

3. What is "creative worship"? What are its advantages and disadvantages?

4. Are you able to worship regardless of who is leading the worship? Why, or why not? Who bears responsibility here, the worship leader or you? At what point does the celebrant's individual creativity begin to encroach upon God's creativity?

5. Do you agree with the author's concern for structures of catholicity? How does a sense of solidarity with other Christians affect participation? To what extent is this solidarity dependent upon similarity of liturgical forms?

7

A Priestly Community

Come to him, to that living stone, rejected by men but in God's sight chosen and precious; and like living stones be yourselves built into a spiritual house, to be a holy priesthood, to offer spiritual sacrifices acceptable to God through Jesus Christ.

You are a chosen race, a royal priesthood, a holy nation, God's own people, that you may declare the wonderful deeds of him who called you out of darkness into his marvelous light. Once you were no people but now you are God's people; once you had not received mercy but now you have received mercy. (1 Peter 2:4–5, 9–10)

This passage, the classic proof-text for the doctrine of the universal priesthood of the church, raises difficult questions. Does it imply that all Christians may preach? Who should celebrate the sacraments? Is ordained ministry a holdover from "an earlier period of overly hierarchical church structures"?

Actually, the passage does not address itself directly to such questions. Rather, the main focus of this much-debated text has to do with election and holiness. Its emphasis falls upon the character of the whole church of God, not upon the individual rights and privileges of Christians. It says nothing about who may or who may not exercise priestly rights and functions within the church. In fact, the whole thrust of the passage directs the church as a corporate entity outward into the world to witness to the gospel. It is silent about inner-church matters of office and ordination, stating nothing for or against them. It does not say that individual Christians are called to be priests. Rather, it says that the church is called to be a universal priest*hood*. The emphasis is a collective one, not an individual one.[1]

The Calling of the Whole People of God

On the basis of 1 Peter 2:40–10, it is problematical to state that every Christian is a priest, because the primary emphasis of priesthood is corporate and mission oriented. Nonetheless, we may still ask: to what extent, by virtue of the corporate priesthood of the church, are individual Christians priestly?

1. The priesthood of all believers means that all Christians have direct access to God. They stand in the holy temple of God as priests, consecrated by the Spirit at baptism. They enjoy a direct relationship with God which no human being, institution, or authority can disrupt.

2. All Christians are to offer spiritual sacrifices to God (Rom. 12:1), which include prayer, praise, thanksgiving, penitence, justice, kindness, love, the knowledge of God—indeed, their whole being. These sacrifices are to be offered both within a formal liturgical context and in the liturgy of one's life in the world.

3. The church is priestly in that all Christians are ordained to proclaim the word of God. Christians are to "declare the wonderful deeds of him who called [them] out of darkness into his marvelous light" (1 Peter 2:9). At baptism each Christian becomes an evangelist, one who will give testimony to the faith according to one's gifts.

4. The entire church is given the power to baptize. While for reasons of church order this is customarily administered by an ordained person in behalf of the church catholic, the command to baptize is coupled with the command to evangelize and is given to the whole church (Matt. 28:18–20).

5. All Christians are empowered to forgive sins (Matt. 18:18).

6. The whole church as a priestly community is empowered to partake of the Lord's Supper (Luke 22:19).

7. The royal priesthood serves as a mediator for the world. Each Christian represents God to the world, thereby becoming

the means by which the world might be reconciled unto God. The church is a priesthood, functioning in the world's behalf, offering intercessions for its redemption (1 Tim. 2:1–4). Particularly in the Eucharist, the church exercises its priestly calling by offering in behalf of all of God's creation the praise and thanksgiving that the whole creation longs to give and is properly owed to the Creator (Rom. 8:18–25).[2]

A Variety of Charisms

The corporate and missionary emphasis on priesthood is an extension of Paul's teachings about gifts in the church. According to St. Paul, there are different gifts, but one Spirit. It is the Spirit who distributes and employs these gifts. The community must discern and respect them. The foot cannot say to the eye, "I have no need of you"; nor is everyone an ear. Each needs all the others, and all function harmoniously together because various gifts of the church are orchestrated by the Spirit to the greater glory of God.[3]

In the liturgical gathering of the priesthood of the church, roles are apportioned according to gifts.[4] The leadership of lay-persons in worship is an expression of the community's priest-hood. Leadership is a representative act in behalf of the universal priesthood of the church, one that reminds the church of what it is: a royal priesthood. Such acts are not performed autono-mously, but through the discernment by the church of the gifts of the Spirit. The church acknowledges the diversity of these gifts by the setting aside of individuals for special aspects of liturgical leadership.

Crucifers

The leading of liturgical processions by a cross is a custom dating from at least the fifth century. The gift of the crucifer is to display before a church the symbol that is central to its identity. Leading the procession, the cross declares who the church is as it gathers in God's presence: a community "bought with a price" (1 Cor. 6:20), a people at peace with God by the blood of the cross of

Christ (Col. 1:20). In the exit procession another theme is high-lighted. Here the cross becomes a summary of the church's missionary identity before the world. It challenges the faithful to go out into the world to preach Christ crucified, a stumbling block to the Jews and folly to the Greeks (1 Cor. 1:23).

Thurifers

A thurible, a vessel used for burning incense, is carried by a designated person who is called a thurifer. During the second and third centuries, incense was not used in Christian worship due to its negative associations with the cult of the emperors. In fact, some Christians who apostatized during persecution were contemptuously labeled "incense burners" by those who remained faithful.

The Bible is less hostile to the liturgical use of incense. The Old Testament mentions it frequently (Exod. 30:1–8, 34–38; 1 Chron. 9:29; Ezek. 8:11; Jer. 41:5; cf. Amos 5:22; Hos. 6:6). In the New Testament its use in the heavenly liturgy is assumed by St. John, which likely reflects early Christian liturgical practice as well (Rev./Apoc. 5:8; 8:3–4). The New Testament also alludes to the possible use of incense in liturgy in first-century eucharistic practice (Eph. 5:2; Phil. 4:18), which, were its use actual, would reflect widespread Jewish and Mediterranean table customs.[5]

The liturgical use of incense is honorific and ambient. It honors the presence of the Lord in His temple, the body of Christ. It symbolizes the sacrifice of prayer, as defined by the psalmist:

> Let my prayer be counted as incense before thee,
>   and the lifting up of my hands as an evening sacrifice!
>   (Ps. 140[141]:2)

The thurifer's gift to the congregation is to help create an ambience or atmosphere for prayer, to engage the senses with the mystery of worship.

Servers

The ministry of servers is one of assistance to the celebrant who should be relieved of certain logistical and mechanical concerns. Young people are often used in this ministry, a factor in influencing some of them toward religious vocations.[6]

Deacons

The foundation of all ministry is *diakonia,* service exemplified by that of Jesus, who came not to be served but to serve (Mark 10:45), and exemplified in many churches by a diaconate of persons set apart to minister to the needs of the poor, the sick, and the oppressed. The churches differ in their understandings of the diaconate's relationship to ordained ministry and the liturgy. There is ancient precedent for the use of deacons as lectors, preachers, and leaders of prayer and as presiders in noneucharistic worship when an ordained minister or priest is not present. Within certain traditions, deacons may also have sacramental roles. They may administer baptism. They may assist at the Eucharist and later bring it to the sick and shut-in. Their active role in worship leadership also highlights the interdependence of worship and service in the church's life and mission.[7]

Acolytes

In the Roman Catholic tradition acolytes hold a special relationship to ordained ministry, an association that is very ancient, although the ministry is now open to laypersons as well. In other traditions acolytes are simply torchbearers who carry candles in liturgical processions. Although modern lighting has reduced their practical function, their gift is a symbolic one: to herald "Jesus Christ, the light of the world, the light no darkness has overcome."[8] They may also assist in other duties as defined by local custom and need.[9]

Communion Assistants

The distribution of communion is accomplished through communion or eucharistic assistants. Their gift is a vital one. Through their demeanor, voice, and warmth, they convey the presence of the risen Lord by the power of the Holy Spirit. Communion assistants are, like the women at the first Easter, heralds of the resurrection who exclaim with Mary, "I have seen the Lord" (John 20:18).[10]

Elected Parish Representatives

Members of parish councils, sessions, and the like are often called to perform liturgical duties by virtue of their office. Their gift is a representative one: to show forth the consent of the congregation at an important moment in its life.

Traditions vary widely. Within Calvinist churches elders participate in the examination and presentation of candidates for ordination and also in the laying on of hands, acts that emphasize that ordained ministry arises from the church and has no existence apart from it. In baptism an elder presents the candidate, thereby expressing the consent of the church that this person should be baptized. Similarly, other traditions define roles for parish representatives according to theology and custom.

Sponsors

Life's moments of passage call forth the gift of discernment and support from other Christians. A baptismal sponsor is appropriately one who has served as a spiritual guide or overseer, whose presence at the baptism of an adult is supportive to the candidate. When infants are baptized, the sponsor or godparent assumes a special obligation in behalf of the church, promising to look after the spiritual upbringing of the child. In the rite of marriage the sponsors (best man and maid of honor) indicate by their presence that they assume a special role in behalf of the congregation, pledging to nurture this union so that it may show forth Christ's love for his bride, the church.

Choristers

The gift of musical leadership is vital to worship. The choir is less a performance group than an active leader of the worship of the people. It not only provides special musical selections but also leads in responses (*Amens,* etc.) and the singing of congregational hymns. It also furnishes cues to the congregation through such gestures as standing, sitting, moving to receive communion, etc. Especially when visible to the congregation, the choir through its demeanor communicates a proper spirit for worship.

Cantor

The ancient Jewish role of cantor is being revived in modern Christian worship. This person's gift is a musical and pedagogical one. The cantor introduces new music to the congregation and may serve as its song leader. The modern resurgence of responsorial psalmody has given the cantor new possibilities for the intonation of sacred texts.[11]

Coordinator

In large-scale worship, especially that of festival occasions, it is helpful to designate a person to coordinate the efforts of the various liturgical leaders. This job description is an open-ended one. Much like a stage manager, this person may adjust lighting at one moment and time an entrance at the next. The coordinator should be vigilant to needs as they arise and in meeting them be as inconspicuous as possible.

Discursus on Ordained Ministries

The lay-leadership roles of preacher and presider in sacramental celebrations are gifts that, by long tradition in the church, have been given formal recognition through the rite of ordination. Ordained ministers and priests manifest the charism of special custody for God's word. It is their special responsibility to proclaim the faith of the church catholic and thereby render Christ present.

The one with the gift to preach, a gift bestowed by the Spirit as discerned through the community, thereby becomes a special symbol for God's word. A similar gift is given in connection with the presidential role in sacramental celebration:

> It is especially in the eucharistic celebration that the ordained ministry is the visible focus of the deep and all-embracing communion between Christ and the members of his body. In the celebration of the eucharist, Christ gathers, teaches and nourishes the Church. It is Christ who invites to the meal and who presides at it. In most churches this presidency is signified and represented by an ordained minister.[12]

Lay Readers

Background

The use of lay readers is a venerable tradition, one of many Jewish contributions to Christian worship. According to the Mishnah, when ten or more are present in the synagogue, the Torah may be read by any adult male. This tradition is reflected in Luke 4:16–17. Other sources set a quorum of seven. While women and minors could be counted in the quorum, they could not read out of respect for the congregation, a fact that sheds light on St. Paul's prohibition in 1 Corinthians 14:34–35. In synagogues where Hebrew was not understood, a translator would stand next to the reader. A tenth-century source indicates the presence of a third individual who helps and corrects either the reader or the translator.[13]

In the early Christian church the use of lay readers was continued. St. Paul remarks that individuals should come to worship with a lesson (the Greek word in 1 Cor. 14:26 is *didachē,* meaning a teaching of Jesus or of the Apostles; cf. 1 Tim. 4:13; Col. 4:16). Justin Martyr (c. 155) describes how the "memoirs of the apostles or the writings of the prophets are read as long as time permits." When the reader has finished, the president (presumably another individual) begins the bidding prayers before the Eucharist.[14]

By the third century, readers had become a minor order. They were appointed by the bishop, who gave the reader the book for safekeeping. Since not all in the early church could read, let alone read with public clarity and ease, the position was surely one of some stature.[15] However, the historical tendency has been for members of the clergy to assume the duties of lector. Factors of illiteracy often necessitated this development.

The modern use of lay lectors highlights the fact that the Scripture belongs to all baptized Christians. The practice gives laypersons a sense of ownership over that which is central to the life and witness of the church: God's word. In the priestly community that word is "near you, on your lips and in your heart" (Rom. 10:8). Where women are not ordained or are underrepresented, the use of female readers provides a much-needed although still imperfect balance in liturgical leadership. Participatory worship entails representative leadership, about which more will be said at this chapter's conclusion.

Customs differ with regard to lay readers. Some churches use them for the first and second readings only, the gospel then being read by an ordained person, who is usually the preacher. Others make no such distinction. In many traditions the people stand for the reading of the gospel. If it is read from the midst of the congregation, it becomes a visible sign of Immanuel, God with us. The procession of the gospel book and reader into the congregation may be preceded with torches and accompanied with *Alleluias,* symbolizing the incarnation of God.

In Eastern Rite churches, the gospel reading is a richly participatory event, accompanied by elaborate ceremony that has come to be interpreted allegorically. In what is called the Little Entrance, the drama of the incarnation is recapitulated. Heaven comes to earth. God enters the world of humanity. Christ is present where the good news is heralded.

During the *Alleluia,* the deacon censes the altar (symbol for heaven), the sanctuary (symbol for earth), and the priest (symbol for God the Father). Standing before the altar, the priest prays for illumination:

> O Lord and lover of mankind: Make the imperishable light of thy divine knowledge to shine in our hearts; And open the eyes of our understanding that we may apprehend the preaching of the Gospel. Implant in us likewise awe of thy blessed commandments, that trampling under feet all the lusts of the flesh we may pursue a spiritual life, thinking and doing always such things as are pleasing in thy sight; For thou art the enlightening of our souls and bodies, O Christ our God, and unto thee we render glory, together with thine eternal Father and thine all holy, gracious and life-giving Spirit; now, and forever: world without end. Amen.

The deacon (symbol for Christ) asks for the priest's blessing, who makes the sign of the cross upon him and presents him with the Book of the Gospels. Preceded by a tall candle, the deacon steps forth through the Holy Doors, bearing aloft the Gospels.

With great dignity he moves to the tribune (dais). All stand. A dialogue between priest, choir, and deacon surrounds the reading:

Priest:	Wisdom. Stand steadfast.
	Let us hear the Holy Gospel.
	Peace unto all.
Deacon:	The reading is from the Holy Gospel according to _____.
Choir:	Glory be to thee, O Lord, glory be to thee.
Priest:	Let us give heed.
Deacon:	Wisdom. Stand steadfast. Let us give heed.

(The lesson is read)

Priest:	Peace unto thee that dost preach the good tidings.
Choir:	Glory be to thee, O Lord, glory be to thee.

The deacon then returns to the sanctuary. The doors are again closed. The congregation is seated.[16]

The Gift to Read

Public reading of God's word by nonordained persons is an ancient tradition. The use of lay readers indeed enhances liturgical participation. Moreover, the practice deepens the sense of common stewardship for God's word. However, not every Christian has the gift to read.

A seminary student engaged in fieldwork once asked a bright, young engineer to read a lesson to a gathering of Sunday School children. What could be simpler? The man began on a faltering note and went downhill from there. Within seconds he was sweating profusely. Halfway through, he loosened his necktie. Before he could complete the reading, he left the room for some fresh air.

Those who do not have the gift to read cannot be expected to give it. In this day, when the use of lay readers is becoming more widespread, this note of caution is in order. Does God's word come alive through an unnuanced, listless tone in the reader's voice? Is the boldness of biblical prophecy underscored by a reader who does not project well? Obviously not. The gift to read is rare. Very few possess it. While not all pastors or priests necessarily perform more ably than lay readers, normally they are better trained, more comfortable, and more effective in reading God's word, although it is also true that far too many of them neglect the cultivation of this gift.

The role of lay readers should be looked upon as an office, as a calling that requires cultivation of the gift. Instruction, coaching, rehearsals, and preparation are all crucial to lectors' success. Without such a commitment, most will perform poorly or, even worse, read God's word ineffectively. The regular use of lay readers should occur only where the gift to read is evident.[17]

Particular Uses of Lay Readers

Special circumstances sometimes arise in which a one-time use of lay lectors can be highly effective. Pastoral alertness is needed to exploit this potential. In preparing for the liturgy, consideration ought to be given as to which individuals bear a unique relationship to a given lesson, a relationship that might unfold new meaning for the congregation. Some examples follow.

At the Jesuits' Christmas Eve Vigil Mass at St. Paul's on the Columbia University campus in 1974, a mother-to-be in her third trimester steps to the lectern and reads: "Behold, a young woman shall conceive and bear a son, and shall call his name Immanuel" (Isa. 7:14). The visual impact of this lector, who was very great with child, fittingly complemented the reading and the entire celebration. Yes, that's how Mary was! That's what God had to do to become incarnate!

In a small northern Indiana country parish, an articulate eight-year-old boy reads the Old Testament prophecy for Advent 2A, while his family stands at the Advent wreath, lighting the second candle. His cherubic voice on that bright, crisp, winter morning bespeaks a vision beyond his wisdom, of God's promise of a peaceable kingdom, in which:

The wolf shall dwell with the lamb,
    and the leopard shall lie down with the kid,
and the calf and the lion and the fatling together,
    and a little child shall lead them. (Isa. 11:6)

In an inner-city, integrated parish located within a radically segregated metropolis, where racial and social divisions are severely exacerbated, a black woman, outspoken about issues of racial and social justice, reads with deliberateness from St. Paul's letter to the churches of Galatia: "There is neither Jew nor Greek, there is neither slave nor free, there is neither male nor female; for you are all one in Christ Jesus" (Gal. 3:28).

In 1983 the Southern and Northern Presbyterian Churches merged to form a new denomination, ending a division dating back to the War Between the States. At a Presbyterian church in Oregon a special Eucharist celebrates the reunion. A member whose dialect betrays her origins in the Appalachian foothills of North Carolina reads from Luke: "Men will come from east and west, and from north and south, and sit at table in the kingdom of God" (13:29).

An Ivy League student, struggling with issues of faith, is home for spring break. A seed is planted in his inquiring spirit as he reads:

> For the foolishness of God is wiser than men, and the weakness of God is stronger than men. . . . God chose what is foolish in the world to shame the wise, God chose what is weak in the world to shame the strong . . . so that no human being might boast in the presence of God. (1 Cor. 1:25–29)

In New Jersey a parishioner steps to the lectern. He has recently completed chemotherapy treatments for the cancer in his body. His struggle for health is well known throughout the congregation; the sanctuary becomes charged with emotion as he reads from Psalm 29(30):3, 11–12:

> O LORD, thou hast brought up my soul from Sheol,
>   restored me to life from among those gone down to the Pit.
> Thou hast turned for me my mourning into dancing . . .
> that my soul may praise thee and not be silent.

Not all of these individuals were talented lectors. They performed their tasks with the usual stage fright and butterflies. Yet their particular circumstance compensated for any gift they lacked and added a dimension to the reading of God's word that another reader would not have. In addition, through the relation of biblical themes to their pilgrimages, they themselves participated more deeply in God's word. Such situations are present in any parish. The alert pastor will be sensitive to their existence and potential.

Tongues of Fire

Following the Eucharist, the great Orthodox Easter Vigil concludes with a final gospel reading. John 1:1–14 is read first in the languages of the inscription on the cross: Hebrew, Latin, and Greek (see John 19:20). The vernacular follows, then any other tongues spoken in the congregation. This custom has been adapted to great effect by many Western congregations for use at either Easter or Pentecost.

Typically, readers remain scattered throughout the worship space and stand to read. To simulate the "babble" of Pentecost, they overlap each other. For example, the reading begins in Hebrew. After a few verses, the Vulgate enters as the Hebrew subsides. When the Vulgate has predominated for its entry verses, the next language begins, and so on until all are being read simultaneously. The sequence of readings may follow a historical sequence of evangelization (e.g., Irish, German, Swedish, Russian, Mandarin, etc.). The last entry is in the vernacular, so that the final verses are soloed, perhaps by a child, in a modern version like the *Good News Bible*. Executed in this fashion, the reading should take no longer than four–five minutes.

Even smaller congregations often possess a remarkable diversity of tongues. People relish dusting off dormant language skills and preparing in earnest. Invariably, when this is done there are surprises. In my own experience there have emerged: a former Peace Corps worker to India who arduously translated the lesson into Telugu; a woman who produced her great-grandmother's Hungarian Bible and read with tear-filled eyes; a retired English teacher who uncovered a New Testament in the Middle English of the Purvey Revision of the Wycliffe Bible (c. 1388); a homesick Vietnamese refugee who was delighted to share his native tongue; a graphic enactment of the passage in the sign language of the deaf; a Polish translation read on a Pentecost when Poland was under martial law; a World War II veteran and cryptographer who read in Japanese; a black studies professor who belted it out in Swahili; grade-school children taking their first halting steps in Spanish and French; a child of missionaries who read in Korean.

In one church I served, the organist was a student at a nearby college where many international students were enrolled. Without my knowledge he advertised what was going to happen in the reading. To my surprise and delight that Pentecost morning about twelve of them from all over the world showed up, Bibles in hand, to read in their native tongues.

The overall effect of a Pentecost reading is impressive. Participants have testified to new-found images and associations: the babbling of tongues made intelligible by the Holy Spirit; the birthday of the church in the explosion of Pentecost; an endless caravan of saints, martyrs, and missionaries who have spread the gospel into all the world; the universality of the church of Jesus Christ, whose body is truly a global community. Ten sermons could scarcely have made such an impact. Here again one sees the power of one good symbol.

Lessons and Carols

A service in which lay readers play a primary role is the Advent/Christmas Festival of Nine Lessons and Carols. In its modern form it was first performed on Christmas Eve in 1880 at the Cathedral of Truro, England. At that time Archbishop Benson structured the service so that the lessons alternated with Christmas carols. The order of readers progressed through the various minor orders and concluded with the final lesson being read by the Archbishop. In 1918 the service was simplified and modified for use on Christmas Eve in the Chapel of King's College, Cambridge, England, whence the custom has spread to many Western churches. The nine lessons recapitulate holy history from the fall of humanity in the Garden of Eden to the incarnation. They summarize the loving purpose of God in history. The carols help us respond to but do not necessarily interpret each lesson.

The Service of Lessons and Carols may also be celebrated on the First Sunday of Christmas. This scheduling reinforces the Twelve-Days-of-Christmas concept, widely ignored within cultures that depart from the Christmas theme on the twenty-sixth of December. On this Sunday, often low in attendance and spirit, the Service of Lessons and Carols evokes an enthusiastic level of lay participation and leadership. To avoid lapses, lectors should ready themselves at the lectern while the carol is sung prior to their reading.[18]

Lay-led Worship

In the life of the local congregation there are many occasions that call for worship leadership by laity. It is fitting that committee and judicatory meetings, women's and men's groups, choir rehearsals, youth activities, special congregational gatherings, etc., should pause for prayer. The worship that is ideally suited to most such occasions is the Divine Office in its cathedral form of Morning and Evening Prayer.[19]

Daily Prayer in the Early Church

The tradition of Morning and Evening Prayer is an ancient one. The fourth-century church historian Eusebius remarks:

> The very fact that in God's churches throughout the world hymns, praises, and truly divine delights are arranged in his honor at the morning sunrise and in the evening is surely no small sign of God's power. These "delights of God" are the hymns sent up in his church throughout the world both morning and evening.[20]

What were these celebrations like? While no texts from antiquity are extant, it is probable that they bore a resemblance to the Jewish practice of daily prayer, which Jesus would have shared with his disciples. The focus evolved in the context of the early church, such that Morning Prayer became a celebration of Christ's resurrection, and Evening Prayer a celebration of Christ's passion. The structure of these celebrations was simple and invariable. While different hymns, psalms, and lessons were used, the basic order did not vary. The emphasis of these liturgies was prayer and praise. Morning and Evening Prayer embodied worship for its own sake, centered around hymns, psalms, and prayers, including litanies. Instruction and edification were secondary.

Modern Renewal

Although in its complicated history of development other elements came to be added, five basic elements provide a long-standing structure for Morning and Evening Prayer:

> (a) hymn
> (b) psalm(s)
> (c) reading(s)
> (d) canticle(s)
> (e) intercessory prayers[21]

Morning Prayer begins with a hymn that emphasizes morning and the symbolic spirit of morning, examples of which themes are: the God who is light; Christ the sun of justice; the illumination of the darkness of the world through the coming of Christ, the light of the world; the rebirth of the world; creation; and the future aeon, the Eighth Day, when history will be consummated. An oration from the Maronite morning office expresses this eschatological sense: "Make us worthy, O Lord, of the morning which will not pass away, of the light which will not be darkened, and of your kingdom which will have no end."[22]

Following the hymn is the psalm section. Those psalms traditionally associated with Morning Prayer are 50(51); 62(63); 66(67); and 148—150. Through these psalms the congregation offers prayers of confession, adoration, and praise. The so-called Laudate Psalms (148—150) lie at the center of the morning office and give it a primary orientation of praise.

Following the psalms, a lesson may be read. Then a canticle is read, chanted, or sung. The canticle most frequently associated with Morning Prayer is the *Benedictus,* "The Song of Zechariah" (Luke 1:68–79). Intercessory prayer and the Lord's Prayer follow. The service concludes with a blessing.

Evening Prayer uses the same basic format of five invariable elements but is distinguished from Morning Prayer by its thematic associations with the time of the day. It begins with a hymn in which evening themes are emphasized, the most important of which are thanksgiving and confession. Thanksgiving is expressed for the goodness of the day and for the night that gives rest from the labors of the day. Confession and the petition for forgiveness are expressed so that the sun may not set while hearts are impure. The opening hymn is often accompanied by the lighting of lamps.

Psalms follow the evening hymn. The pattern here is frequently six variable psalms chosen from 110—150 each week. A classic evening psalm is 140(141), which is appropriately accompanied by the burning of incense. Following the psalm(s), a lesson is read, usually one not read in the morning service. The congregation then meditates in silence on God's word. A canticle is sung, the *Magnificat* (Luke 1:46–55) often preferred for Evening Prayer. Intercessory prayers and the Lord's Prayer are offered. The service concludes with a blessing and a sign of Peace.

To summarize, Morning Prayer is characterized by themes proper to morning, Evening Prayer by themes proper to evening, and each by the use of certain psalms and canticles. Both Morning and Evening Prayer have a similar structure of five elements: hymn, psalm(s), lesson(s), canticle(s), and intercessory prayers. This simple structure provides an ecumenical pattern of daily prayer for Christians.

Morning and Evening Prayer are forms of worship that invite a considerable level of lay involvement. Laypersons may organize and lead these services. Their style is highly participatory. In Morning and Evening Prayer the people actively pray together.

The Divine Office and Family Worship

It is in the home where Lay Leadership in worship is most needed. A simplified form of Morning and Evening Prayer provides a structure for family devotional activity. There are many advantages to this pattern, not the least of which is the obvious interrelationship of household, subcongregational, and festival celebrations of Morning and Evening Prayer. When household devotions follow the patterns for Morning and Evening Prayer, they manifest their tie to the corporate prayer of the church, much as table graces before meals resonate with the Eucharistic Prayer. This interrelationship can be charted accordingly:[23]

MORNING PRAYER

Household	Congregation	Festival-Congregation
Verses	Verses	Verses
	Invitatory*	Invitatory*
Psalm 94(95)	Psalm 94(95)	Psalm 94(95)
	Psalm	Psalm
		O.T. Canticle
		Psalm
	The Hymn	The Hymn
Reading	Reading	Readings
		Homily/Sermon
Benedictus	Benedictus	Benedictus
Intercessory	Intercessory	Intercessory
Prayers	Prayers	Prayers
Lord's Prayer	Lord's Prayer	Lord's Prayer
		Paschal Blessing
Blessing	Blessing	Blessing/Dismissal

EVENING PRAYER

Household	Congregation	Festival-Congregation
Lucernarium*	Lucernarium*	Lucernarium*
verses	verses	verses
	Phos hilaron**	Phos hilaron
	("Joyous Light of Glory")	
	Thanksgiving for	Thanksgiving for
	Light (brief)	Light (extended)
	Hymn	Hymn
Psalm 140(141)	Psalm 140(141)	Psalm 140(141) (with incense)
	Psalm	Psalms
		N.T. Canticle

Reading	Readings	Readings
		Homily/Sermon
Magnificat	Magnificat	Magnificat
Intercessory	Litany or Inter-	Litany or Inter-
Prayers	cessory Prayers	cessory Prayers
Lord's Prayer	Lord's Prayer	Lord's Prayer
Blessing	Blessing	Blessing

N.B. It is appropriate that in the celebration of Morning and Evening Prayer, a period of silence should follow each reading, psalm, canticle, or brief sermon. *An *invitatory* is a responsive form of invitation, often based on a psalm, which is used in worship to call to prayer or praise. *Lucernarium* means "lamplighting." **Phos hilaron* ("Joyous Light of Glory") is the Greek title to the second- or third-century hymn that is traditionally sung in Eastern churches at Vespers.[24]

Morning and Evening Prayer provide assistance to family-centered piety and devotions, which are the backbone of Christian worship and liturgical participation. They enrich family worship by providing order, biblical content, and integrity. In turn, this enrichment has a positive effect on Lord's Day worship, without which worship Christianity as we know it would be unrecognizable. Future historians may look upon our era as one that produced excellent Lord's Day resources, but for people whose daily prayer life did not support these celebrations. The disintegration of family piety and personal devotions makes its mark wherever Sunday worship comes to be seen as a strange intrusion into an otherwise secular week. Lord's Day worship and daily prayer are complementary forms of worship. The Christian who is faithful in Morning and Evening Prayer during the week perceives nothing incongruous about Lord's Day worship and is thereby able to participate more fully therein.

Patterns of Lay Leadership

All who participate in Christian worship celebrate the liturgy together, but each according to his or her gifts. Lay worship leadership enhances participation in that it is a reminder to the church of its special calling as a royal priesthood. Lay-led worship also arises out of a vital interaction of spiritual gifts, gifts that constitute the life of the church. The same Spirit bestows these gifts and calls them forth. It is one Lord who acts through them, ministering to the church. Lay Leadership is a sign of God's providence—the love of God that continues to feed and nourish those who are of Christ's body. Lay Leadership also models for the church the priestly ministry to which it is called in behalf of the world.

A plenitude of gifts requires the discernment of the church, the testing of gifts to see that they are the true workings of the Spirit. The recognition of charisms is a delicate undertaking and one that may prove challenging to stereotyped notions of liturgical roles. For example, church traditions notwithstanding, there are neither biblical nor adequate theological reasons to exclude anyone from liturgical roles solely on the basis of sex or marital status. Oppressive forms of social discrimination constitute a sinful quenching of the Spirit. If the gifts have been given, it behooves the church to recognize them, thereby confirming the Spirit's ministry through them.

A final benefit of using lay leaders is that it deepens the level of participation for the lay leaders themselves. They become more aware of their liturgical traditions. Their sense of ownership in worship grows. When they are "back in the pew," their level of participation is often deeper than before.

Study Guide

1. To what extent, by virtue of the corporate priesthood of the church, are individual Christians priestly?

2. The author discusses twelve lay-leadership roles. Are there any in your congregation's worship that could be adopted or strengthened?

3. Discuss the relationship of daily prayer to your church's worship life. In what ways can you strengthen your discipline of daily prayer?

4. Discuss places in your congregational life where Morning and Evening Prayer might be appropriately celebrated.

5. The author contends that the gifts of the Holy Spirit are irrespective of gender and therefore that all liturgical roles should be open to both men and women. Do you agree? Why, or why not?

For Further Reading

Daily Prayer Resources:

BCP. New York, NY: Church Hymnal Corporation and Seabury, 1977. Pp. 37–146, 934–1001.

Chrichton, J. D. *Christian Celebration: The Prayer of the Church.* London, UK: G. Chapman, 1976.

Daily Prayer. SLR, 5. Philadelphia, PA: Westminster, 1987.

"The Divine Office." In *The Study of the Liturgy.* Ed. C. Jones, G. Wainwright, and E. Yarnold. New York, NY: Oxford University, 1978.

LBW. Minneapolis, MN: Augsburg, 1978. Pp. 131–92, 215–89.

Martimort, A. G., ed. *The Church at Prayer, IV: The Liturgy and Time.* Collegeville, MN: Liturgical, 1985. Pp. 151–272. Trans. of *L'Eglise en Prière: La Liturgie et le Temps.* Paris, Tournai: Desclée, 1983.

Mateos, Juan. "The Morning and Evening Office." *Worship* 42 (Jan. 1968) 31–47.

———. "The Origins of the Divine Office." *Worship* 41 (Oct. 1967) 477–85.

Old, Hughes Oliphant. "Daily Prayer in the Reformed Church of Strasbourg, 1525–1530." *Worship* 62 (March 1978) 121–38.

Pfatteicher, Philip H. and Messerli, Carlos R., eds. *Manual on the Liturgy. Lutheran Book of Worship.* Minneapolis, MN: Augsburg, 1979. Pp. 262–304.

PGIS. Chicago, IL: G.I.A., 1979.

The Prayer Book Office. Ed. Howard Galley. New York, NY: Seabury, 1980.

Shepherd, Massey, II. "Implications of Liturgical Prayer for Personal Meditation and Contemplation." *Studia Liturgica* 9(1–2):56–71.

Storey, William G. "The Liturgy of the Hours: Principles and Practice." *Worship* 46 (April 1972) 194–203.

_____. "Parish Worship: The Liturgy of the Hours." *Worship* 49 (Jan. 1975) 2–12.

_____. "The Liturgy of the Hours: Cathedral Versus Monastery." *Worship* 50 (Jan. 1976) 50–70.

Taft, Robert. *The Liturgy of the Hours in East and West: The Origins of the Divine Office and Its Meaning for Today.* Collegeville, MN: Liturgical Press, 1985.

The Taizé Office. London, UK: Faith, 1966.

8

With Heart and Hands and Voices

The Incarnation and Christian Worship

The saving movement of God toward human beings reaches its highpoint in the incarnation. In Jesus Christ the fullness of God is joined to the fullness of humanity: a union of two natures in one person (hypostasis), combined in one substance yet without confusion, change, division, or separation.[1] This union, which shows the depth of God's love and concern for humanity, belongs to the absolute mysteries of faith.[2]

The incarnation provides an analogy for participation in worship. In Jesus of Nazareth the divine nature was not self-evident. God in Christ was at once fully revealed yet also hidden. The divine was veiled by the human. Only those upon whom the Holy Spirit bestowed the gift of faith were able to penetrate the veil of Christ's humanity and thereby perceive the divine nature. This realization occurred in full only after the resurrection.

Liturgy operates in an analogous fashion. The God who chose to communicate to human beings through human flesh continues to approach humanity through sensible things. As Leo the Great said in a sermon for Ascension: "What was visible of our Redeemer has now passed over into the sacraments."[3] Those gifted with the eye of faith are able to discern and participate in the incarnate Christ through these instruments of God's grace. In this sense, the law of the incarnation becomes the law of liturgy. Just as God chose the person of Jesus as the one in whom the word was to become flesh, so God has appointed other sensible things, under which forms God's divinity is hidden. In such a way God has attached a word of promise to sacramental things (specifically, bread, wine, water, oil) so that those who receive them in faith by the power of the Holy Spirit participate in the real presence of the incarnate Christ. God has also attached a word of promise to the body of Christ, the royal priesthood, who, as temples of God's Holy Spirit, are sacraments of God's presence. In this way, the incarnation is archetypical of the liturgy of the church. In worship the encounter with God is an encounter through sensible things—symbols, objects, and people. The Holy Spirit lifts the veil from them so that worshipers may participate in the incarnate and glorified Christ through these means of grace.

Without compromising the uniqueness of the appointed instruments of God's grace, it is possible to extend this sacramental principle based upon the incarnation to all of creation. As Gerard Manley Hopkins writes: "The world is charged with the grandeur of God. It will flame out, like shining, from shook foil." These words echo those of the psalmist: "The heavens are telling the glory of God, and the firmament proclaims his handiwork" (Ps. 18[19]:1). Indeed, the whole cosmos has a sacramental quality. It is laden with God's glory, "for everything created by God is good" (1 Tim. 4:4).

Moreover, the incarnation proclaims that all of creation is an object of God's redemptive work through Christ. In Christ "all things were created, in heaven and on earth, visible and invisible, whether thrones or dominions or principalities or authorities— all things were created through him and for him" (Col. 1:16). The scope of God's redemptive plan is truly universal. God desires not only that all should be saved and come to the knowledge of the truth (1 Tim. 2:4) but also that creation itself should be radically transformed. It is for this change that creation is "groaning in travail" (Rom. 8:22), awaiting the subjection of all things unto Christ, who is subjected to the Father, "that God may be everything to every one" (1 Cor. 15:28). The church, as the first fruits of the new creation, offers a glimpse of the new order. The larger tradition of the church has been lavish in its use of material things in part out of the conviction that God does not want to destroy creation but rather to redeem and transform it. This belief underlies the church's traditional use of art and architecture, music, color, light, incense, ashes, decoration, sculpture, images, icons, vestments, and furniture. Placing such things into the service of Christ and the kingdom not only advances the gospel but also foreshadows the future subjugation of all things unto Christ. The creative use of material things in worship anticipates and fulfills the eschatological direction of God's saving movement (1 Cor. 3:22–23).[4]

Because all cultures and peoples are being subjected to Christ, there are few restrictions as to which styles of art or architecture may be put to the Lord's use. The sole criterion for all liturgical art is that it must be transparent to the mystery of God in Christ. It must be accessible to faith either immediately or through an artistic transparency that patiently awaits subjective human encounter. Liturgical art lends itself to the beauty of holiness (Ps. 26[27]:4). In the church, judgments about the artistic quality of given works of art are necessarily wed to considerations of their effectiveness as vehicles of prayer. Artistic expressions ought normally to reflect local cultures.

The same logic that encourages the use of material objects as instruments of the divine encounter applies to the human body in worship. The incarnation declares the inaccuracy of perceptions of a warring dualism between body and soul. It forever dignifies the human body, giving it a place of importance in Christian worship. Early Christians who came to view the body as evil, as a carnal prisonhouse from which the soul needed to escape in order to experience salvation, created serious tensions within catholic faith and practice. The body, as a temple of the Spirit, is a primordial sacrament of Christ's presence. Through gestures and postures, worshipers extol their Creator with their whole being. They approach that perfect uniting of the outer and the inner that awaits us in a new heaven and earth.

The Shadows of Communication

The positive role that theology awards to the human body in Christian worship is confirmed from an anthropological perspective. Human language consists of verbal and nonverbal modes of communication. One mode appeals to hearing, the other to sight, smell, and the tactile senses. Bodily gestures are fundamental to personal communication. They are a principal means by which humans express their highest forms of intellectual, spiritual, and artistic experiences.

Exclusively verbal patterns of communication can have significant limitations, a fact easily demonstrated through a simple exercise. Attempt to describe, without using any form of bodily action whatsoever, these phenomena: a double helix; a feeling of helplessness; the breathing action of a fish; the perfect golf swing; a most joyful moment.[5]

The nonverbal mode is crucial to much human communication. Nonverbal gestures give to words a greater eloquence and intensity than would be the case if communication consisted of words alone. Moreover, such gestures are often a more natural and authentic expression of inward disposition. Consequently, they may empower or overpower the verbal message that is being delivered by either confirming or denying it.

Worship engages the richest strata of the human spirit. It activates one's inmost confession of sin and belief, one's heartfelt praise and thanksgiving to the Creator, one's openness to the Spirit of God, one's plea for divine assistance. Words alone cannot adequately express these deeper yearnings of the heart. Consequently, a deeper level of profundity requires the use of liturgical gestures and signs.

The nonverbal mode of communication does more than enrich human and liturgical expressiveness. It also can engage the inner person in such a way that it intensifies and even provokes an interior disposition. This fact mitigates some concerns for authenticity of motive in acts of corporate worship. Every liturgical action need not be an immediate demonstration of the interior state of the individual. Indeed, a reluctance to affirm the body's role in engaging the soul with God may be rooted in a rationalistic body-soul dualism that is incompatible with the biblical teaching about the incarnation (John 1:1–14). Scripture upholds the substantial unity of the human body and soul. In so doing, it recognizes that external gestures interact with and are capable of awakening and teaching the internal disposition, and vice versa. For example, the liturgical act of kneeling may initially be lacking in a desired level of authenticity. But the body, through the act of kneeling, can help induce a disposition suitable for prayer. Regarding the cooperative relationship of body and soul in liturgical action, Tertullian writes:

> No soul whatever is able to obtain salvation, unless it has believed while it was in the flesh. Indeed, the flesh is the hinge of salvation. In that regard, when the soul is deputed to something by God, it is the flesh which makes it able to carry out the commission which God has given it. The flesh, then, is washed, so that the soul may be made clean. The flesh is anointed, so that the soul may be dedicated to holiness. The flesh is signed, so that the soul too may be fortified. The flesh is shaded by the imposition of hands, so that the soul too may be illuminated by the Spirit. The flesh feeds on the Body and Blood of Christ, so that the soul too may fatten on God. They cannot, then, be separated in their reward, when they are united in their works.[6]

Liturgical gestures and signs are nonverbal communicators that give rich expression to, intensify, and provoke the deepest religious instincts. They give to the liturgy a power to prompt the human spirit to an awareness of the presence of God. Nonverbal gestures and signs are the distinguishing components of Multisensate Participation. Worship that utilizes nonverbal communicators engages the spirit through the senses. It integrates the full range of human faculties—body, mind, senses, imagination, will, emotion, and memory. It is worship "with heart and hands and voices."[7]

Interpreting Gestures and Signs

Liturgical gestures and signs are, like theological language, liable to varying interpretations and differing perceptions. Christians, especially those caught in polemical contexts, may at times confuse the *de*notative level of meaning with the *con*notative level of meaning. The same phenomenon occurs in marriages and other relationships when communication begins to break down. Misunderstanding compounds misunderstanding. Only a breakthrough arrests the cycle. Often this consists of a return to the denotative level ("You misunderstood me. What I *really* meant when I said this was . . . .").

Denotation refers to definitive content. When a term denotes something, it names a definable class of things or ideas. The denotation of a liturgical gesture is its definitive content, its precise definition, the meaning intrinsic to it.

Life is made more complicated and more interesting by the existence of a second level of meaning: the connotative. To connote means literally "to note together with." Connote refers to ideas, overtones, or associations that are added to a term and cling to it. Such associations are often the result of personal experiences. For example, the term *father* denotes one's own immediate biological progenitor. But connotative meanings may differ sharply. *Father* may connote strength, love, and support to one person, and a radically different constellation of meanings, such as authority, distance, and oppressiveness, to another. Connotative meanings keep religious language, symbols, and gestures in a constant state of flux.[8]

Connotative interpretations of liturgical gestures and signs should in all cases be respected. They are properly viewed as inevitable and even desirable, for, as in the human interaction with art, individual perceptions are the hallmark of human creativity. Of course, when connotations are in conflict with God's word or disrupt the peace of the church, they should be challenged and illumined by the light of Christ who is the foundation for denotative meanings. Three norms help to identify the definitive content of liturgical gestures and signs.

(1) Scripture. Many of the traditional signs and gestures that Christians use in worship have scriptural origins. As a primary source of liturgical theology, the Bible provides guidelines for their interpretation. Those used or instituted by Christ hold

unique value. Study is required to determine the intentions of Christ with regard to denotations. Liturgical gestures and signs are, like all things, subject to the gospel and must be informed in a way that is consonant with and supportive of biblical faith.

(2) Tradition. Liturgical signs and gestures are a conservative form of speech. While they may remain the same in outward forms, their meanings may shift and evolve. Over time, distortions of meaning may occur through either diminution or complexity. Historians can often recover the origin and development of gestures and signs and isolate them by burning away later accretions, allegorical interpretations, and polemical associations. Liturgical signs and gestures should correspond to original intent. Utilitarian acts that are perpetuated by symbolic interpretation or allegory long after their utilitarian function has expired may assume a disproportionate and confusing role in the liturgy.[9]

(3) Natural aptitude. As a result of the word of natural revelation etched by God upon the human consciousness, some liturgical signs and gestures readily correspond with religious instincts. Gestures such as kneeling are intuitively known, especially when they are basic and unadorned. Depth psychology, sociology, and religious history testify to their universal denotation.[10]

Liturgical Postures and Gestures

Physical Presence

> I was glad when they said unto me,
>   "Let us go into the house of the LORD!"
> Our feet have been standing
>   within your gates, O Jerusalem!" (Ps. 121[122]:1–2)

The first act of liturgical participation is physical presence amidst the worshiping assembly, wherein the identity of the church is most fully revealed. The bodies of Christians are temples of God's Holy Spirit (1 Cor. 3:16; 6:19–20; 2 Cor. 6:16). In a unique way they are sacraments of Christ's presence. When Christians gather for worship, it is actually the body of Christ that is drawn together (1 Cor. 12). The presence of Christ in worship is actualized by individual Christians being physically present to each other.

Regular worship attendance is an obligation for every baptized Christian, an obligation prompted by more than the individual's personal needs for enrichment. It is first and foremost a responsibility to show forth and build up the body of Christ. Christians who have grown lax in their attendance may justify this by complaining that they are not personally benefiting from the experience. Such an excuse avoids the main question, which is one's duty to build up the body. If indeed it is true that the worship life of a congregation is hurting, as these nonattenders may claim, it is all the more important for them to attend, for their congregation needs their support during a difficult period.[11]

Religious broadcasting (the Electronic Church) cannot substitute for the actual gathering of God's people. While these ministries may be beneficial to those who are physically unable to attend services, media worship is antiparticipatory insofar as it assumes that communion is normally possible without the spatial and personal presence of other Christians, who, as temples of the Holy Spirit, are vehicles of God's grace.

Processions

Within the rites of the church, processions serve a practical function: the movement of people and objects to the site of religious enactment. Those in a typical entrance procession should move with solemn dignity, together "as one body," avoiding gaps and changes in pace. The recession is actually an exit procession, marking the transition from the liturgy of the sanctuary to the liturgy of Christian life and witness in the world. It is appropriate that these processions be led by the Bible, to symbolize the intention of Christians to apply God's word wherever Christ leads.[12]

Other processions function more specifically as acts of penitence, praise, witness, and commitment. In funerals the procession of the casket to the front of the church is both a gesture of reverence for the deceased and a bold statement about the reality of the occasion. It is also a witness to the resurrection, which will somehow involve our bodies. In the consecration of a church a procession from the former place of worship to the new sanctuary is a festive celebration of the God Who tabernacles with us. Objects of worship are appropriately carried on such an occasion. In a wedding the symbolism of the procession is often complex, even arcane. The bridal procession, rooted in the veiling of nuns, images the movement of the church (the bride of Christ) toward the Lord (represented by the bridegroom). Because of the vestigial nature of this symbolism and the tendency of modern weddings to be bride-centered instead of God-centered, a procession of the entire bridal party (bride, bridegroom, their parties and families) and worship leaders is much to be preferred.[13]

On special occasions, usually following the preaching of the word, individuals may be invited to come forward as an act of initial faith commitment or renewal. At such times, which may be crucial to the formation of faith, those wishing to give their lives to Christ should be met by Christians prepared to offer personal prayers for healing, conversion, and sanctification.

The procession to receive communion further engages the body and consequently the spirit in the eucharistic offering. Some interpret this bodily movement as a denial of salvation by grace through faith, in that Holy Communion imparts God's gifts to us and we need do nothing to earn them. Such a connotation ignores the degree to which the Spirit works to present the church in splendor, "holy and without blemish" (Eph. 5:27). The procession to receive communion is denotatively perceived as a response, a sacrifice of praise and thanksgiving that is prompted by the Holy Spirit.

As a liturgical gesture, the procession achieves several highpoints during Holy Week. On Palm or Passion Sunday the sanctuary becomes a symbol for Jerusalem, the Holy City, the city of death and resurrection. The faithful gather before the service at a place apart, where palms are distributed. Their entrance into the sanctuary amid acclamations of "Hosanna" identifies them with the crowds that welcomed Jesus into the city. But the act also challenges participants. Are you willing to drink the cup that I drink? Are you willing to be baptized with the baptism with which I am baptized? On Holy Thursday there is a procession of persons to the front for the washing of feet. As this service concludes, there is a silent exit procession in darkness, a fitting orientation for the next liturgy of Holy Week. On Good Friday the entrance is especially solemn. During the service there may be, as an act of reverence and penitence, a congregational procession to a cross.

At the Easter Vigil, the light of Christ is brought into the church as the ancient *Exultet* ("Rejoice Now, Heavenly Hosts") is intoned; later there is a procession to the baptismal font to bless the water, which may also serve as an act of renewal for all; the newly baptized may move from the baptistery to the altar-table, there to receive their first communion. These processions image the entrance of the faithful into the promised land.[14]

Standing Erect

Standing is a natural human posture for respect and vigilance. When someone enters the room and is introduced to us, we stand in honor of their presence. Soldiers stand at attention when receiving their orders. Servants stand in the presence of their masters. Out of respect for the law and its magistrates, those in the courtroom stand when the judge enters.

In the Old Testament standing is the normative posture for prayer (Exod. 33:8, 10; Ecclus. 50:12–13; 1 Sam. 1:26; Ps. 134 [135]:2; Matt. 6:5; Luke 18:11–13). Jesus, following Jewish custom, stood to pray and assumed that his followers would too (Mark 11:25). The ancient Hebrews stood as they listened to God speak (Exod. 19:17; cf. Neh. 8:5). In the synagogue Jesus stood up to read (Luke 4:16).

In Christian tradition standing also reflects respect and vigilance. Standing for the gospel is traditionally a sign of honor to Christ, an attitude of vigilance before his word. In the early church standing further signified the resurrection, whereas kneeling connoted atonement and penance, and it soon became customary to stand for prayer not only on Sundays but also during Easter. Tertullian encourages kneeling for prayer on days of fasting, for the first prayer at sunrise, and for worship on Saturday. But fasting or kneeling during worship on Sundays he considers to be unlawful and adds, "We enjoy the same privilege from Easter until Pentecost." He says that this custom also holds true for the season of Pentecost, which is marked by the same joyous celebration. The First Council of Nicaea (C.E. 325) made this practice obligatory.[15]

As a posture for prayer, standing signifies the freedom and dignity of the new covenant. Adopted as God's children, Christians may stand before God, confident that they have been redeemed. Moreover, standing expresses the confidence of Christians as they await the final coming of the Lord. As the elect, they will be able to stand when God appears (Mal. 3:2). Enraptured in heaven, they will stand before the Lamb (Rev./Apoc. 7:9; 15:2). St. Basil the Great writes that liturgical standing foreshadows the fullness of the kingdom:

> We stand for prayer on the day of the Resurrection to remind ourselves of the graces we have been given: not only because we have been raised with Christ and are obliged to seek the things that are above, but also because Sunday seems to be an image of the age to come.[16]

Praying with Uplifted Hands *(Orans)*

Although science has altered the modern perceptions of the universe, it is still natural to be drawn upward when approaching God in prayer. Religiously speaking, heaven remains the throne, and earth the footstool, of God (Isa. 66:1). The lifting up of hands, forearms extended and palms opened wide, is a natural gesture for prayer. This orante posture was widely known among ancient peoples, and its use is reflected in bas-reliefs, sculptures, and frescoes.

Among the Jews it was used as a gesture of invocation (Exod. 9:29), a plea for God's help (Pss. 27[28]:2; 87[88]:9; 142[143]:6), a blessing of the Lord's name (Neh. 8:6; Pss. 62[63]:4; 133 [134]:2), and a blessing of others (Luke 24:50). It is used to dedicate things into the Lord's service (1 Kings 8:22) and to indicate the offering of one's own self (Ps. 140[141]:2). The lifting up of hands to heaven is an outward sign of the lifting up of the heart as a plea for God's mercy (Lam. 2:19; 3:41). The psalmist writes, "I stretch out my hands to thee; my soul thirsts for thee like a parched land" (Ps. 142[143]:6).

In keeping with honored Jewish customs, Jesus used the orante posture for prayer. The New Testament alludes to its widespread use among early Christians: "I desire then that in every place the men should pray, lifting holy hands without anger or quarreling" (1 Tim. 2:8).[17] Tertullian notes an additional significance for the posture—the imitation of Christ on the cross: "Not only do we raise them [our hands], we even spread them out, and imitating the Passion of our Lord, we confess Christ as we pray."[18]

The orante posture is a splendidly evocative one. Through the uplifting of hands the body urges the opening of one's spirit to God's blessings. When the palms are directed forward, it expresses and evokes a reverence before the presence of God. With arms lifted high there is a suggestion of surrender, not as that of a vanquished person but of one who freely submits to the kingdom of God. With arms bent and palms facing upward, the orante posture expresses entreaty, as if one wished a long drought to be ended by rain.[19]

Although in the early church the posture was widely used by the faithful, it subsequently fell into disuse. In some traditions it survives in vestigial form as a posture used by clergy, especially during the Eucharistic Prayer. In the modern Pentecostal churches it has been revived for general use. Its popularity among mainline Charismatics is a welcome reclamation of a biblical posture of prayer for all Christians.

Raising of Eyes

The eyes are the most expressive of the body's organs. Indeed, they are windows of the soul (Matt. 6:22). The Bible contains over five hundred references to eyes. They are connected with God's favor (2 Kings 12:2; Isa. 49:5), human religious knowledge (Gen. 3:6), pride and lust (Ps. 17[18]:27; 2 Peter 2:14), the conscious memory of the wondrous, saving acts of God (Exod.

13:9), and spiritual blindness or insight (Isa. 6:9–10; John 12:40; Acts 28:26–27).

The lifting up of eyes is a gesture that naturally accompanies an experience of the transcendent. That is why the Bible mentions it in connection with visions, occasions of profound insight into God's eternal realm (1 Chron. 21:16; Ezek. 8:5; Dan. 10:5; Zech. 1:18; 2:1; 5:1, 9; 6:1). Jesus uses the gesture in this visionary, prophetic sense as he unfolds his beatific teachings concerning the kingdom of God (Luke 6:20).

As a posture for prayer and worship, the lifting up of eyes is a pleading for God's help and mercy:

> To thee I lift up my eyes,
>   O Thou who are enthroned in the heavens!
> Behold, as the eyes of the servants
>   look to the hand of their master . . .
> so our eyes look to the LORD our God,
>   till he have mercy upon us. (Ps. 122[123]:1–2)

The raising of eyes is also a gesture of praise and the blessing of God's name (Dan. 4:34). In this same attitude Jesus "looked up to heaven" and offered a eucharistic prayer over five loaves and two fish (Luke 9:16). His high priestly prayer for the church is given with eyes lifted up (John 17:1), as is his prayer of thanksgiving at the raising of Lazarus (John 11:41). Early Christians imitated their Lord by praying with eyes lifted up, for which posture they were chided by pagans.[20]

The lifting up of eyes is a naturally integrating posture for prayer. As eyes are lifted, one's whole being is turned toward God. The lifting up of eyes becomes the look of a child gazing upward into the face of a parent, fully confident of a loving and supportive relationship.

That this gesture could heighten one's awareness of the Holy was well appreciated by the architects of the great Gothic and Baroque churches. How else can one explain their meticulous attention to artistic detail even upon vaultings soaring twenty and thirty meters overhead? Examples of modern architectural interest in this same concern are the magnificent tapestry behind the main altar at Coventry Cathedral, the shimmering glass sculpture that is suspended from the ceiling of St. Mary's Roman Catholic Cathedral in San Francisco, and the crosses and crucifixes that are the focal point at the front of many churches. Such furnishings encourage and support this biblical posture for prayer. In the worship environment visual stimulation helps to transport the spirit unto heaven, there to gaze solely upon Christ (Matt. 17:8), so that our eyes might ever be toward the Lord (Ps. 24[25]:15).

Kneeling

Kneeling effectively integrates body, mind, and spirit for the activity of worship. It is an instinctive attitude for prayer, as evidenced by its widespread occurrence within many non-Christian religions. Scripture testifies to a wide range of examples: Solomon's prayer of dedication for the Temple (1 Kings 8:54); adoration and praise—"Let us kneel before the LORD, our Maker!" (Ps. 94[95]:6); Christ's lonely and anguish-filled supplication in the Garden of Gethsemane (Luke 22:41); Stephen's earnest intercession for and public witness to his persecutors, Saul among them (Acts 7:60); Peter's supplication for Tabitha (Acts 9:40); prayers of leave-taking and blessing (Acts 20:36; 21:5); and Paul's private discipline of prayer (Eph. 3:14).

Despite the diversity of biblical interpretations, kneeling came to be regarded by the patristic writers as a penitential posture. St. Basil the Great writes, "Every time we bend our knees for prayer and then rise again, we show by this action that through sin we fell down to earth."[21] It was in this restrictive sense of sorrow, humble supplication, and penitence that kneeling was introduced into the liturgy. Consequently, it was encouraged during periods of fasting, principally Lent, but discouraged and eventually forbidden during Eastertide, because a penitential gesture is incongruous with the season celebrating the joy of the resurrection.

Despite such strictures, the use of kneeling increased. In medieval Western practice, it became the primary posture for adoration, such as before the reserved sacrament, during the eucharistic canon, and other acts of consecration (e.g., weddings, ordinations), and for the reception of Holy Communion.[22]

Given the diversity of tradition and usage, when should modern worshipers kneel? Certainly it is appropriate during penitential acts and seasons and for acts of private devotion. But what about kneeling versus standing for the eucharistic canon or the reception of communion? These are not matters of crucial difference *(adiaphora)* and need not harden into lines of distinction between Christians. Although sacramental worship thrives on a certain sameness, some variety of postures for the Eucharistic Prayer and communion reception will enrich the experience of the sacrament.[23]

The relative effectiveness of all prayer postures ought to be evaluated theologically and pastorally. From the perspective of psychological integration, standing with uplifted hands is preferable to merely standing, and kneeling better than sitting. Beyond this general guideline local and individual customs should be respected. Uniformity in such matters is unnecessary. The twentieth-century church is increasingly a pluralistic one, more tolerant not only of differences between communions but also of variations within them.

Kneeling is recommended as a thoroughly biblical posture that belongs in Christian worship. As St. Paul noted, it is a present image of the lordship of Christ and the destiny of the human race: "God has highly exalted him [Christ] and bestowed on him the name which is above every name, that at the name of Jesus every knee should bow, in heaven and on earth and under the earth" (Phil. 2:9–10).[24]

Genuflection

The term *genuflection* is from the Latin *flecto* ("to bend") and *genu* ("the knee"). It refers to the honorific gesture of briefly kneeling on the right knee with the body erect. Genuflection holds the same outward significance of penitence and supplication as does kneeling, but its history gives it a distinctive meaning. Originally, genuflection was a pagan salutation or act of homage made in front of a temple or statue of a god or before deified rulers and their images (note Gen. 41:43). Understandably, early Christians refused to perform such gestures of obeisance. After the accession of Constantine in the fourth century, however, it was appropriated as a Christian gesture of veneration and reverence before sacred objects (e.g., church-houses, altar-tables, relics, images of saints, crucifixes) and prelates.[25]

In reaction to the eucharistic controversies surrounding the eleventh-century theologian Berengar of Tours, genuflection evolved into a gesture of adoration for the sacrament. Only in the sixteenth century was it formally introduced into the Mass. Common among Roman Catholics, genuflection is not used by Eastern Rite Christians or Protestants. It is best understood as a gesture of respect.[26]

Bowing

A more biblical and catholic gesture of adoration is the bow. Performed either as an inclination of the head or as a deep bending forward from the hips, it is a natural expression of honor and reverence.

Scripture assigns numerous significations to bowing. In Temple worship it was a gesture of reverence:

> O come, let us worship and bow down,
>   let us kneel before the Lord, our Maker!
> For he is our God,
>   and we are the people of his pasture,
>   and the sheep of his hand. (Ps. 94[95]:6–7)

Bowing is one of the body's antidotes for pride, a means of humbling one's spirit before God. All the proud of the earth shall bow down before the Lord (Ps. 21[22]:29). Bowing can also be an expression of thankfulness (Ps. 137[138]:2), an acknowledgment of the presence of the Holy (Pss. 21[22]:9; 44[45]:11), an attitude for worship and adoration (Gen. 24:26; Exod. 12:27; 34:8; 1 Chron. 29:20; 2 Chron. 29:29; Neh. 8:6), a posture of lament (Ps. 34[35]:14), a gesture of supplication (Exod. 11:8), or a reverential greeting exchanged between human beings (Gen. 33:3, 7; 43:28).

Bowing can also express subordination. Subjects bow before a monarch (Esther 3:2, 5); God's vanquished enemies will bow down before Israel (Gen. 27:29) and before Yahweh (Ps. 71[72]:9; even their gods will bow before the Lord (Ps. 96[97]:7). All the peoples of the earth, in recognition of the universal lordship of God, will glorify the Lord by bowing (Ps. 85[86]:9). Bowing is also a sign of ultimate allegiance, which is why the Bible expressly forbids bowing before any other deity (Exod. 20:5; 23:24; 1 Kings 19:18; Ps. 80[81]:9; Mic. 5:13; Rom. 11:4). Jesus expresses his acceptance of God's will when, at the moment of his glorification upon the cross, he bows his head (John 19:30).

The bow or inclination has long been a part of Christian worship. In the Eastern tradition it continues as the normal gesture of respect and adoration. In the West it has at many points been replaced by genuflection (a half-bow), perhaps because this gesture was more seemly for priests, who had begun to celebrate the Mass in the eastward position (with their backs to the people). Some traditions have preserved the medieval custom of bowing during the *Gloria Patri,* at the mention of the name of Jesus and the Holy Spirit in the Nicene Creed, and at the *Sanctus* in the Eucharistic Prayer.[27]

The bow is a reverential gesture that acknowledges the presence of God as mediated through objects and people. For centuries Christians have bowed before altar-tables, the cross of Christ, and each other. This tradition reflects an appropriate recognition of the sanctity of individual Christians who are temples of God's Holy Spirit.

Prostration

The Bible makes more references to prostration *(proskynēsis)* than to any other prayer posture. In the Old Testament prostration denotes: abasement, humiliation, utter depravity, conviction, penitence, forsakenness, and desolation (Deut. 9:18; Pss. 37[38]:6; 43[44]:25; Judith 9:1; 10:2); fear and reverence before heavenly intermediaries (Gen. 18:2; 19:1; Judg. 13:20; Dan. 8:17) and before the Lord (Gen. 17:3; Josh. 5:14; Ezek. 1:28; Tobit 12:16); subjugation (Isa. 49:23); worship, awe, and adoration (Ps. 94[95]:6; 2 Chron. 7:3; Num. 22:31; 2 Macc. 10:4);

honor and obeisance (Gen. 23:7; 42:6; 43:26; 1 Sam. 20:41; 24:8).[28]

There are many New Testament references to prostration, even though the RSV frequently translates *proskynēsis* simply as "worship." Prostration is the posture of Jesus' prayer of desolation in the Garden of Gethsemane (Matt. 26:39; Mark 14:35). Following the resurrection, the disciples worship accordingly at Christ's feet (Matt. 28:9, 17; Luke 24:52, variant reading). St. Paul alludes to prostration in early Christian worship (1 Cor. 14:25). In the apocalyptic vision of St. John, the saints in glory throw themselves down before God's throne (Rev./Apoc. 4:10; 5:14; 7:11; 11:16; 19:4).

Liturgical occurrences of prostration are infrequent. In the Roman Rite of ordination, candidates for the priesthood prostrate themselves while the Litany of the Saints is intoned. At the solemn entrance in the Good Friday liturgy, celebrants prostrate themselves with profound effect. The silent gesture confesses the magnitude and gravity of the human dilemma.

Among Eastern Rite Christians prostration is more common than it is in the Roman Rite and is not limited to clergy. It is encouraged in acts of private prayer and devotion. During penitential seasons, especially Lent, it occurs at celebrations of the Divine Office on weekdays. (It is not done on the Lord's Day, the day of resurrection.) Those who are willing and able prostrate themselves with knees tucked to the breast, outstretched palms and foreheads touching the floor. The gesture also occurs in modified form as a *metany* (from the Greek *metanoia*, meaning "a penitential turning around," "having another mind"). In this form one makes a deep bow, with the right hand touching the ground. In either form the gesture is a penitential one.[29]

Sitting

In the early church the bishop preached while seated on his *cathedra*, or throne, as the congregation stood and listened. The modern custom is usually the reverse of this (two exceptions are the Copts and Ethiopians, who continue to lean upon their prayer staffs for the duration of their lengthy liturgies). There are biblical and early church precedents for sitting during readings and instruction.[30] The child Jesus was seated among the teachers in the Temple at Jerusalem (Luke 2:46) and taught while seated in the synagogue at Nazareth (Luke 4:16–20; cf. John 8:2). Mary sat at Jesus' feet while being instructed (Luke 10:39). The apostolic church allowed sitting during prophecies (1 Cor. 14:30).[31]

From a biblical standpoint, sitting is an anomalous prayer posture despite the fact that it is widespread among modern Protestants. In some traditions sitting was not always the custom. For example, only when pastoral prayers grew into mini-sermons of exhausting lengths (longer than twenty minutes) did nineteenth-century American Presbyterian worshipers elect not to stand. (One traditionalist, Samuel Miller, resisted the new trend and continued to stand for prayers despite the fact that everyone around him was sitting.) This innovation in prayer postures drew barbs from Episcopalians who twitted Presbyterians in language adapted from the latter's catechism: "Presbies, Presbies, do not bend, always sitting on man's chief end."[32]

Some congregations perpetuate the Reformation custom of sitting either in pews or at the Lord's Table to receive communion. The practice denotes that the grace appropriate to the sacrament comes as the unmerited gift of God. Care should be taken that this posture does not connote polemical views of justification or priestly orders. The seating of communicants at one or many tables may require extensive preparation time and unduly prolong the liturgy. For example, in some Scottish churches a table is set, complete with tablecloth, across the back of each pew. Such elaborateness unwittingly reinforces an infrequent pattern of eucharistic celebration.[33]

The inability of some elderly persons to stand at length has prompted some pastors to ease social awkwardness by minimizing the time spent standing by all. Unfortunately, this solution deprives the great majority of their right to a prayer posture better suited to the worship of the Lord's Day. It is preferable to give elderly persons the option of not standing whenever they so desire.

Sitting is the desired posture for the footwashing of Maundy

Thursday (John 13:3–14). This richly participatory act has long been solemnly practiced by whole congregations of Mennonites and Dunkards. Within congregations less accustomed to this ritual, it cannot be assumed that all will wish to have their feet washed. It is better to begin with preselected volunteers (twelve is an appropriate and realizable number) and a symbolic rinsing of one foot only. Participants should be informed ahead of time to wear easily removable footwear (sandals or clogs). Feet should be bare—no socks or pantyhose. The celebrant is assisted by at least two deacons. Chairs may be placed around the altar-table, allowing ample space for movement. An empty chair may be offered to any others in the congregation who wish to participate. Those washing feet should rehearse together beforehand, so that time will not be lost and clean towels and water supplied and removed as needed. Uncertainty, confusion, or accidents will heighten any sense of awkwardness already present. The decorum of those washing should be both reverential and yet disarming of social embarrassment. A cappella singing by the congregation will accentuate the stark beauty of the footwashing. Various settings of the hymn *Ubi caritas* ("Where Charity and Love Prevail") have been used to great effect. This humble gesture is also a powerful reminder to clergy of the nature of their calling as servants of the servants of God.[34]

The Striking of the Breast

This gesture, in which the hands are crossed over the chest, was known in Jewish and pagan usage. It is the reaction of the Jews to the crucifixion of Christ (Luke 23:48). St. Augustine testifies to its use in the early liturgy at the *Confiteor,* the opening act of confession of sin.[35] The modern Roman Rite suggests that worshipers strike their breasts in the opening prayer of confession at the words, "I have sinned through my own fault in my thoughts and in my words, in what I have done, and in what I have failed to do." The striking of one's breast accentuates one's awareness of sin. It is a sorrowful and forthright admission of guilt, the breast being struck in symbolic recognition of the heart as the source and seat of sin. It is a gesture of penitence and humility that is naturally expressive of the prayer of the publican: "God, be merciful to me a sinner!" (Luke 18:13).[36]

The Kiss of Peace

Earlier we commented on the Peace (chap. 3), a thoroughly biblical gesture long sanctioned by tradition. From the standpoint of Multisensate Participation, the Peace reverences the indwelling of Christ in the church. It communicates God's affirming love through the warmth of human touch and helps to dissolve divisions and to unite the body of Christ. Communion with Christ is inextricably interwoven with the communion of the body of Christ, the church. The gesture used to exchange the Peace may vary from culture to culture. It is vital that the gesture be sincere, as St. Augustine writes, "When your lips draw near to those of your brother, do not let your heart withdraw from his."[37]

The Reverencing of Sacred Objects

Just as the Kiss of Peace reverences the body of Christ, the church, the kissing of sacred objects reverences Christ who, although corporeally absent, is present through the modes of word and sacrament. The kissing of objects that are intimately associated with these modes of presence (e.g., the Bible, altar-tables, crosses) is an ancient custom often related to the cultures wherein such practices originate. Scriptural justification is lacking for such actions, which may account for the hesitancy of some modern Christians to reverence holy objects. However, the crucial consideration is the *object* of reverence. It is not the Bible as such, but Christ the Word who is being honored when the Bible, which contains God's definitive self-revelation, is kissed or otherwise reverenced. The dynamic is similar to that of the person who, when separated from loved ones, lavishes affection upon a picture of them.

In passing, it may be noted that scriptural justification is also lacking for the kind of hairsplitting and church schism that has resulted from elaborate and precise theories of biblical inspiration. The simple liturgical gesture of kissing the Bible after the reading can reverence God's word far more than such overheated argumentation. Because of the symmetry of word and sacrament (chap. 9), objects related to sacramental practice may similarly be reverenced. Such gestures are moving displays of affection with intentions similar to those of the woman who anointed Jesus' feet (Luke 7:37–47).

The Laying On of Hands

Next to the eyes, the hands are the most expressive vehicle of human emotion. The Bible suggests clapping as an ecstatic outburst of joy in the Lord (Ps. 46[47]:1; cf. Ps. 97[98]:8; Isa. 55:12). To signify the purity of the heart's intentions, hands are ritually washed (Exod. 30:19–21; Ps. 23[24]:4; James 4:8; cf. Matt. 15:2, 20; 27:24; Mark 7:2, 5). Hands are laid upon the sacrificial victim, signifying identification with it and the transference of guilt to it (Exod. 29:10–25). Hands are laid upon others as a means for transmission of power and authority (Deut. 34:9; Acts 6:6; 8:17–19; 19:6; 1 Tim. 4:14; 2 Tim. 1:6). Christ laid hands upon children as a special act of blessing them (Matt. 19:15) and upon many of those that he healed (Mark 6:5; 8:23; 16:18; Luke 4:40). This gesture is also used in apostolic healings (Acts 28:8). The early Christians laid hands upon those who undertook special missions for the church (Acts 13:3).

In modern practice the laying on of hands is used for leave-takings, commissionings, reconciliations, and crisis prayer. The Charismatic Movement has revived this biblical prayer gesture to great effect. In some traditions certain or all laypersons may be invited to share in the laying on of hands at the ordination of elders, deacons, and ministers. This action recognizes that pastoral office is derived from the Holy Spirit through the community of faith.

The Folding of Hands

Despite modern popularity, the joining or folding of hands for prayer is a posture that is unknown in biblical and early Christian traditions. It likely originated from feudal rites in which vassals joined their hands between the hands of their lord. Consequently, folded hands may be understood to express submission to God's will. The pointing of joined hands upward seems to express the raising of the soul to God.[38]

The Mark of God's Name/The Sign of the Cross

The touch of God leaves an indelible imprint upon the human soul. The spiritual marking of the Christian is accomplished by the Holy Spirit. It is natural and befitting that this inward and invisible grace should be expressed through an outward and visible sign.

The sign of the cross (in Latin, *signatio crucis*) is an ancient custom, very probably baptismal and apostolic in origin.[39] Tertullian testifies to its widespread popularity:

> We make the sign of the cross on our foreheads at every turn, at our going in or coming out of the house, while dressing, while putting on our shoes, when we are taking a bath, before and after meals, when we light the lamps, when we go to bed or sit down, and in all the ordinary actions of daily life.[40]

The sign of the cross has a rich and fascinating history. It is a multivalent gesture, bearing multiple denotations that are determined by the liturgical context.

The Mark of God's Ownership

According to the prophet Ezekiel, members of the future Israel will be marked upon their foreheads with a seal in the form of a *Tāw* (9:4–6). As the last letter of the Hebrew alphabet, the *Tāw* signifies God. The most ancient form of this letter is a slanted cross, ×.

Ezekiel's prophecy about the new Israel is woven into the intricate symbolism of Revelation/Apocalypse. According to St. John's vision, the elect, in order to be spared the effects of the tribulation, will be marked on their foreheads with the seal of God (Rev./Apoc. 7:3–8; 9:4–6; 14:1). This seal is a reference to the *Tāw* of Ezekiel.[41]

Considering the liturgical character of the book of Revelation/Apocalypse, it is possible that reference to this *Tāw* seal reflects existing liturgical practices in John's church. If such is the case, the sign of the cross with which these earliest Christians were being marked, was actually a *Tāw,* denoting the name of the God who "owns" all those having this mark. In this early stage of symbol development, the sign of this cross meant being branded with the name of the Lord. Those marked with the *Tāw* are the Lord's elect. They bear the seal *(sphragis)* of God's ownership, a protection for the day of judgment (cf. Eph. 1:13; 4:30). Similarly, the sign of the cross at baptism means that henceforth this person belongs to Christ as a child of the covenant.[42]

As Christianity moved away from its Hebrew and Aramaic origins into a Greek context, a transformation of meaning is likely to have occurred. The Hebrew × came to be identified with the Greek letter *Chi* (X), which also served as a symbol for Christ whose name in Greek (Χρίστος, "Christos") begins with this letter. *Christos* means "anointed one" or "messiah." In the baptisms of the early church, signing and anointing were probably combined into one sealing gesture (cf. Eph. 1:13; 4:30). Consequently, signing with a Greek *Chi* preserved the primitive ownership theme in which a person was signed with a *Tāw,* a symbol for the name of God. An alternative form of the *Tāw,* a +, became associated with the Greek *Tau* (T) and Latin *Tee* (T). Removed from its Hebrew context, this form came to be identified with the gibbet upon which Christ was crucified.[43]

Although vestiges of the earlier denotation of being branded with the name of God remain, the modern interpretation is primarily that of a reference to the instrument of Christ's passion, hence the appellation "The Sign of the Cross." Christians who sign themselves with the cross understand that they are identifying themselves as Christians and are giving an outward demonstration of the mark made upon them by the Holy Spirit. Understood as such, the gesture is a prayer for the renewal of God's claim upon their lives.

The Sign of God's Protection

As God marked Cain so that no one would kill him (Gen. 4:15), so the Holy Spirit brands Christians so that evil will not overcome them. The mark *(sphragis)* seals a promise of God's abiding protection. To signify this spiritual event, early Christians were signed with the cross in the exorcisms before baptism. The Evil One has lost the power to claim any Christian who is thus marked. When tempted, a Christian need only make the sign of the cross in faith to put the demons to flight. Hippolytus regards the sign of the cross as the fulfillment of Passover imagery:

> Imitate him [Christ] always, by signing thy forehead sincerely; for this is the sign of his Passion, manifest and approved against the devil if so thou makest it from faith; not that thou mayest appear to men, but knowingly offering it as a shield. For the adversary, seeing its power coming from the heart, that a man displays the publicly formed image of baptism, is put to flight.[44]

The cross, a symbol for Christ's triumph over the powers and principalities, was a potent weapon in the Christian's spiritual arsenal and has prompted much martial imagery. St. Chrysostom advises making the sign of the cross frequently, so that the devil will not harm those who have taken the seal as Christ's soldiers. He writes:

> Everything is done by the cross. Baptism is given by the cross—we must receive the *sphragis*—the laying on of hands is done by the cross. Wherever we are, travelling or at home, the cross is a great good, a saving protection, an impregnable shield against the devil.[45]

Cyril of Jerusalem urges catechumens to sign the cross openly upon the forehead "so that evil spirits beholding the royal cipher may fly far from you, terrified."[46] This signing, he writes, is a privilege given by our Lord: "After my battle upon the cross, I give to each of my soldiers the right to wear on their foreheads the royal sphragis." Because of such emphases, Christians facing martyrdom fortified themselves with the sign of the cross, as did soldiers preparing for battle.[47]

An Index of Religious Belief

The first Christians made the sign of the cross by tracing it upon the forehead with a finger or the thumb of the right hand. By the end of the fourth century, there is evidence that it was being made upon the breast as well as the forehead. Among early

Christians the act of signing oneself with the cross was understood as a profession of Christian faith. Augustine writes that Christians should make the sign as a bold testimony of faith: "Upon the forehead we bear his sign; and we do not blush because of it, if we also bear it in the heart."[48]

Doctrinal controversies prompted the further evolution of the gesture. Probably at the time of the fourth-century Arian controversy the sign of the cross came into use by the laity within corporate worship. At that time it began to be accompanied by the trinitarian formula: "In the name of the Father, and of the Son, and of the Holy Spirit."[49] In the sixth century, as an act of protest against the Monophysite heresy, Eastern Christians began making the sign of the cross with either two fingers, signifying the two natures of Christ, or three fingers, signifying the trinity. The custom passed over to the Western churches, where the making of the sign of the cross on the forehead with two fingers and a thumb was formalized by a ninth-century synod.

The larger sign of the cross, made by touching the forehead, the breast, and each shoulder, was used in private devotions at least as early as the fifth century.[50] Pope Innocent III (1198–1216) directed that it be made with three fingers from forehead to breast and from right to left shoulder. Later, Western Christians reversed the sequence, touching the left shoulder before the right, and began to use the whole hand with the fingers extended. Eastern Rite Christians continue to use the earlier pattern, touching the right shoulder before the left, extending the middle finger, forefinger, and thumb (signifying the three persons of the trinity) and closing the ring and little fingers to the palm of the hand (signifying the hypostatic union). This precise configuration of fingers actually became a contributing factor to a nineteenth-century schism among the Russian Orthodox.

The sign of the cross has long been an index of religious belief. In the earliest period it denoted a profession of Christian faith that distinguished one from Jews and pagans. After Constantine, the sign of the cross indicated one's acceptance of an orthodox Christology. In the second millennium it came to identify distinctions between communions, Eastern versus Western, Protestant versus Catholic.

A Dedicatory Act or Blessing

When made as an act of consecration, the sign of the cross denotes the setting apart "from all common uses to (a) holy use and mystery."[51] This usage is an ancient one, rooted in a theology of the incarnation and derived from the baptismal consecration of persons. Augustine insists that the sign is essential to sacramental rites:

> What else is the sign of Christ but the cross of Christ? For unless that sign be applied, whether it be to the foreheads of believers, or to the very water out of which they are regenerated, or to the oil with which they receive the anointing chrism, or to the sacrifice that nourishes them, none of them is properly perfected *(nihil eorum rite perficitur)*.[52]

Against Augustine, it is preferable to describe the gesture as a *dramatic* necessity. Care must also be taken that the sign of the cross as an act of blessing does not contradict biblical teachings regarding spirit and matter.

A Gospel Proclamation

The cross is a symbol for the atonement (Col. 1:20). Christians are called to deny themselves and to follow Christ by carrying a cross (Matt. 10:38; 16:24; cf. Gal. 2:19). The sign of the cross is a nonverbal reminder of the source of grace and the radical cost of discipleship. As G. W. H. Lampe states, it reassures the believer of being

> sealed for a day of redemption, branded as one of Christ's flock, marked with a sign of his membership of God's people, assured of a talisman against the powers of darkness, and given a password, as it were, which would ensure his reception by the angels into the gates of Paradise and his acceptance among the "sheep" at the right hand of the heavenly Judge.[53]

The sign of the cross is a rich form of liturgical participation. Whether as a mark of God's ownership, a sign of God's protection, an index of religious belief, a dedicatory act or blessing, or a gospel proclamation, it is a bold statement about the nature of God's holiness, which issued forth in the incarnation of Christ and which defines creation and the human body as objects of

God's redemptive love. The Christian faith cries out to be so shaped![54]

Patterns of Multisensate Participation

Multisensate worship images God's holiness, which permeates all of creation. Although fallen, the goodness of the created order is nonetheless affirmed by Scripture and sealed by the fact of the incarnation. The glorification of God through the environment of worship exclaims with the psalmist that the earth cries out with the goodness of God. All of creation is the object of God's redeeming love. The liturgical dedication of sensible things to the cause of Christ and his kingdom foreshadows the subjection of all things to Christ, who is himself subjected to God the Father.

For this reason Christian faith is able to affirm the goodness of the human body. In worship, the body may appropriately be used to give expression to, intensify, and provoke the experience of openness to the presence of God. The denotation of gestures and postures is given by Scripture, tradition, and natural aptitude.

The liturgical encounter with God is not a direct one. An effective environment, like nature, facilitates the encounter with God by providing, out of deference to God's holiness, an artistic veil. Those with the Spirit's gift of faith are able to discern the transcendent within the mundane.

Worship that integrates body, mind, and spirit arises out of and participates in God's holiness. From the world's perspective, it is a scandalous declaration that the holy has to do with the things of this order: life, matter, suffering. All are objects of God's redemptive grace. Worship "with heart and hands and voices" images a church that by God's grace is a new creation, exulting in the fullness of the Creator who continues to look upon His handiwork and say, "That's good!"

Study Guide

1. What is the impact of the incarnation upon Christian worship?

2. Pick a liturgical gesture or symbol that you have difficulty accepting or appreciating (e.g., the sign of the cross, the altar-call, the lifting up of hands). Discuss the basis of your negative feelings. Are they based upon denotations (intrinsic meanings) or connotations (associated meanings)?

3. How does your body help to engage your soul in worship? Create a quasi-liturgical environment within which to experiment with unfamiliar gestures and postures. Is it possible that their meanings might deepen through repetition?

4. The sixteenth-century Protestant reformers set out to recover biblical worship. Yet the typical prayer postures for many Protestants today (i.e., sitting, hands folded, eyes closed, heads bowed) are nonbiblical. What, if anything, should be done about this?

5. What steps may be taken to help insure that gestures do not degenerate into mere formalities?

For Further Reading

Bäuml, Betty J. and Franz H. *A Dictionary of Gestures.* Metuchen, NJ: Scarecrow, 1975.

Bishops' Committee on the Liturgy. *Environment and Art in Catholic Worship.* Washington, DC: National Conference of Catholic Bishops, 1978.

Cabrol, Fernand. *Liturgical Prayer—Its History and Spirit.* Westminster, MD: Newman, 1950. Chap. 8: "Attitudes during Prayer and Liturgical Gestures," pp. 80–87.

Casel, Odo. *The Mystery of Christian Worship.* Westminster, MD: Newman, 1962. Pp. 9–48.

Dalmais, I. H. *Introduction to the Liturgy.* Tr. Roger Capel. Baltimore, MD: Helicon, 1961. Pp. 114–24: "The Liturgy and Things."

Daniélou, Jean. *The Bible and the Liturgy.* Liturgical Studies, 3. Notre Dame, IN: University of Notre Dame, 1956. Chap. 3: "The Sphragis," pp. 54–69.

––––––. *Primitive Christian Symbols.* Baltimore, MD: Helicon, 1964. Chap. 9: "The *Taw* Sign," pp. 136–45.

Daniels, Harold. "The Sign of the Cross." *Reformed Liturgy and Music* 21 (Winter 1987) 39–44.

Eisenhofer, Ludwig and Lechner, Joseph. *The Liturgy of the Roman Rite.* Tr. A. J. and E. F. Peeler. New York, NY: Herder and Herder, 1961. Chap. 3: "The Actions of the Liturgy," pp. 85–96.

Gy, Pierre-Marie. "La fonction des laics dans la liturgie." *La Documentation Catholique* 82 (3 March 1985) 24–97.

Howard, Thomas. *Evangelical Is Not Enough.* Nashville, TN: Nelson, 1984.

Kavanagh, Aidan. "A Rite of Passage." *Liturgy 70* 8,8 (1977) (published at 155 E. Superior St., Chicago, IL 60611). The article is from a lecture delivered at Holy Cross Abbey, Box 351, Canon City, CO 81212.

Lampe, G. W. H. *The Seal of the Spirit.* London, UK: S.P.C.K., 1967. Chap. 13: "The Seal of the Cross," pp. 261–84.

Lubienska de Lenval, Hélène. *The Whole Man at Worship: The Actions of Man before God.* New York, NY: Desclée, 1961.

Martimort, A. G., ed. *The Church at Prayer, I: Introduction to the Liturgy.* New York, NY: Desclée, 1968. Chap. 7: "Sacred Signs," pp. 146–79. Trans. of "Les Signes." Pp. 150–83 in *L'Eglise en Prière.* Paris: Desclée, 1961.

Micks, Marianne H. *The Future Present.* New York, NY: Seabury, 1970.

Mitchell, Leonel. *Baptismal Anointing.* Notre Dame, IN: University of Notre Dame, 1978.

Rahner, Hugo. "Das mystische Tau." *Zeitschrift für katholische Theologie* 75 (1953) 386–410.

Troeger, Thomas H. "Theological Considerations for Poetic Texts Used by the Assembly." *Worship* 59 (Sept. 1985) 404–13.

Vagaggini, Cyprian. *Theological Dimensions of the Liturgy: A General Treatise on the Theology of the Liturgy.* Tr. Leonard J. Doyle and William A. Jurgens. Collegeville, MN: Liturgical, 1959. Pp. 49–50, 300–334.

White, James F. *The Cambridge Movement.* Cambridge, UK: Cambridge University, 1962 and 1979.

———. *Protestant Worship and Church Architecture: Theological and Historical Considerations.* New York, NY: Oxford University, 1964.

9

Participation in the Mystery of Christ

The Pursuit of Symmetry

In the years following Albert Einstein's famous discovery of the relationship between energy and matter, numerous physicists and mathematicians have renewed the search for a unified field theory. Such a theory would explain the essential unity of the fundamental forces of nature, i.e., gravity, electro-magnetism, and the nuclear forces of strong and weak (as well as any others not yet discovered). Their quest arises out of the belief that "the universe runs according to a single, simple, breathtakingly elegant mathematical principle." Inspired by the symmetry that is abundant in the natural world, these scientists are motivated by a vision of supersymmetry. They seek a single equation that would contain all of nature's secrets, a master formula for the universe.[1]

The research for this venture is highly speculative, producing theories for which no known methods of verification exist. Consequently, physicists have been forced to depart from scientific procedures. To assume the veracity of their research, they must rely upon a principle of metaphysics, well summarized in Keats' dictum: truth equals beauty, beauty equals truth. As one scientist has stated, the challenge to twentieth-century physicists is to open the door that will "expose the glittering central mechanism of the world in [all] its beauty and simplicity."[2]

Such a "regime of simplicity" would be akin to that which

existed naturally in the first split second after the big bang, the primordial state of ultra-simplicity from which God fashioned all of space, time, and matter. According to this perspective, the apparent complexities of the physical world are the result of the universe "cooling out," following the first moments of creation. The universe as we know it is a "complexity frozen out of simplicity," analogous to the way in which the glassy simplicity of the ocean waters freezes into a tangled ice flow. The diversity that we see in the physical world is only superficial, "purely the result of our sampling physical systems at relatively low energy." The prevailing belief among scientists engaged in the search for a unified field theory is that by raising the level of energy in the processes under study, the unity and simplicity will become more and more apparent.[3]

Liturgical Symmetry

Our study of liturgical participation follows an analogous path. It has isolated six fundamental types of liturgical participation, examining each in detail. Although this approach has been fruitful, a danger is inherent in the method. Whenever a study focuses intently upon the trees, it can easily lose sight of the forest. Hence, to avoid being left with "a complexity frozen out of simplicity" it will be necessary to refocus, to shift from a latitudinal to a longitudinal cross section.

Although there are distinct modes of liturgical participation, they are neither mutually exclusive nor even in conflict. In fact, the relationships between the various types of participation are complementary. Each holds a venerable place in the history of worship. Moreover, each type is essential to a balanced liturgical life, for each lifts up an image of the nature of God, the Christian faith, and the church.

1. Spontaneous Involvement arises out of God's immanence. The new life in Christ is one of personal immediacy by the indwelling power of the Holy Spirit. It is the Spirit who bestows gifts upon the church and orchestrates them to the edification of the body, which is the communion of the Holy Spirit.

2. Silent Engagement ponders God's transcendence. The ways of this majestic and wholly other God are not our ways. God's wisdom is not our wisdom. Through its silent contemplation of the Ground of our Being, the One in whom we live and move and have our being, the church images itself as an obedient flock, patiently attentive to the Holy Spirit. Its prayer becomes one with that of Mary: "Behold, I am the handmaid of the Lord; let it be to me according to your word."

3. Interiorized Verbal Participation memorializes God's graciousness. Slow to anger and abounding in steadfast love, God receives the church's intercessions offered through Christ its high priest. The church is the elect, God's chosen ones, and its memory of God's wondrous saving works prompts anew the saving presence of the Lord.

4. Prophetic Verbal Participation witnesses to God's freedom. His mercies are new every morning. By grace, the church lives in the freedom of God's word. By the Spirit, it is empowered to proclaim to all the world the "new thing" that God has done in Christ.

5. Lay Leadership models God's providence. Each Christian is a recipient of gifts of the Spirit. These are called forth by the Spirit to the edification of the church, that the body of Christ may function as a royal priesthood for the sake of the world.

6. Multisensate Participation resonates with God's holiness, which permeates all of creation. The scandal of the Christian faith is that the divine became incarnate in a human being, dwelling fully in the material world. The church that worships in body, mind, and spirit touches this holiness, exulting in God's goodness, being at one with God's redemptive purposes toward a fallen but redeemable order.

Multiple combinations of these modes of participation have allowed the Christian family to develop a diversity of worship styles. The weaves are rich and varied and should remain so. However, worship at a higher level of energy requires a symmetry of participatory patterns. Regardless of the tradition or worship style, each and every type should be present in abundance. This symmetry is a necessary demonstration of the breadth of God, the catholicity of the church, and the fullness of the gospel. Pursuit of this symmetrical ideal may indeed challenge cherished styles and churchly identities. It may require new ways of thinking in order to rise above the false polarities of the past. But faithfulness to the gospel includes a welcoming of Christ's healing presence into the midst of these painful divisions within the church.

The art of participatory worship is born out of a legitimate spiritual goal: an ardent love for the whole body of Christ, the church catholic. The breadth of vision required for ecumenical or catholic leadership in the church is a lonely and difficult calling. The church's dividedness and parochialism are powerful indications of the lingering hold that sin yet has upon us as we await the redemption of our bodies. But the God who decisively conquered evil in the resurrection of Christ empowers us to be peacemakers and reconcilers. For the sake of the oneness of the church, we are free to risk passing over into other Christian traditions. The healing of the fractured body of Christ, so much a scandal to our common witness, will be slow and difficult. Yet the mandate from our Lord for this is clear (John 17).

To strive for liturgical symmetry is to strive for spiritual wholeness as a way of embracing the catholicity of the body of Christ. The presupposition here is that all churches are called to be catholic churches: i.e., to be inclusive, to preach the gospel unto all the world (Matt. 28:19); to exult in the rich diversity of the human family that is to be reconciled to God; to intercede for all creation. Liturgical symmetry is a way of embracing the unity of God's nature, for all Christians are called to comprehend the breadth and length and height and depth of God and so be filled with the fullness of God (Eph. 3:18–19).

Liturgical symmetry enhances participation by strengthening those types that are neglected or underdeveloped, in contrast to giving an even greater emphasis to those types that are already dominant. An imbalance of types contributes to a theological distortion in the life of the community as it is grounded in Christ. Conversely, a balance of types conveys the fullness of the gospel and the Spirit's ministry in the church.

The complementarity of participatory types provides every motivation to search for a supersymmetry that will dissolve the apparent distinctions at "a higher energy level." To conclude this study, we must seek out the "master formula of persuasive elegance" that will both encompass and unveil the underlying significance of all forms of liturgical participation. The key to this formula lies in a New Testament word: *koinōnia.*

Participation and Koinōnia

Three New Testament words that derive from the Greek root word *koinos,* which means "common," are of particular concern for this study. The verb form *koinōneō* means "to participate in," "to have a share in something with someone," or "to give a share in something to someone" (Rom. 12:13; Gal. 6:6; 1 Peter 4:13). It is used to describe the incarnation as a divine partaking of human nature, as Christ's sharing in the flesh and blood of human beings (Heb. 2:14).[4]

The noun *koinōnos* means "partaker," "one who takes part in something with someone as a partner or companion." In describing redemption as a liberation from the corruption that is in the world, 2 Peter 1:4 refers to Christians as partakers *(koinōnoi)* of the divine nature. St. Paul writes that the church, having been grafted onto the olive tree, which is Israel, is now a joint partner *(synkoinōnos)* in the covenant and its blessings (Rom. 11:17).

The noun *koinōnia* means "participation" in the sense of an intimate association, fellowship, or communion (2 Cor. 13:14).[5] The Apostle Paul uses this form when he describes the relationship of the Christian to Christ and to the church in the Eucharist:

> The cup of blessing which we bless, is it not a participation *[koinōnia]* in the blood of Christ? The bread which we break, is it not a participation *[koinōnia]* in the body of Christ? Because there is one bread, we who are many are one body, for we all partake *[metechomen]* of the one bread. (1 Cor. 10:16–17)[6]

The Christian life is a personal *koinōnia* or participation in Christ. This relationship becomes the occasion for participation in the body of Christ, the *koinōnia* of fellow believers. The church is not a voluntary association of similarly minded religious individuals. The communion of saints is created only through the divine initiative of *koinōnia* in Christ (2 Cor. 1:7; Phil. 3:10; 1 John 1:3, 6–7). Personal participation in Christ enables one to share in Christ and his blessings (1 Cor. 9:23; 1 Peter 1:4) as a partner in faith (Phil. 1:5). The vertical dimension of participation in Christ creates the horizontal *koinōnia* that unites Christians (1 Cor. 1:9).[7]

The life of the Christian is one of participation in Christ by the power of the Holy Spirit. Participation in worship is a manifestation of this life in the Spirit. For this reason liturgical participation is not simply participation in the liturgy. It is participation *in the saving mystery of Christ through the liturgy,* which is merely a vehicle. Moreover, participation in Christ makes one a participant in the body of Christ, the church. Consequently, Christian worship is normatively a shared experience with other Christians. Participation in the corporate worship of the church is the visible manifestation of the participation that Christians enjoy in Christ and the church. Indeed, it is constitutive of the church.

The mystical basis of liturgical participation is most vividly displayed in the Eucharist. According to St. Paul, the experience of participation in Christ is actualized in the Lord's Supper. Although participation in Christ is known perfectly and basically in faith, the sacrament is a means of grace through which this participation is given. Paul is insistent that participation in the sacrament creates *koinōnia.* By implication, this is the basis for his adamant opposition to Christians partaking of Jewish or pagan sacrificial rituals. Do not be partners *(koinōnous)* with demons, he writes (1 Cor. 10:20). You cannot partake of both the table of the Lord and the table of the demons (1 Cor. 10:21). To share in a religious meal makes you a companion of the deity in whose name the celebration is offered. The same is true, he believes, of the Lord's Supper. Those who share in it without "discerning the body" of the Lord risk their very lives and health (1 Cor. 11:30).[8]

Paul's eucharistic theology is hardly a bare memorialism. For the Apostle, the Lord's Supper involves much more than mere mental recollection or a psychological sense of presence.[9] Although the Eucharist is not a guarantee of entrance into the promised land (1 Cor. 10:1–13), through participation in it one actually becomes, by grace through faith, a participant in Christ and a companion of the God who is revealed in Christ. The elements of bread and wine are vehicles of Christ's real presence. The sacrament is a true participation in the body and blood of Christ (1 Cor. 10:16–18), a sharing in the fullness of the mystery of Christ (Col. 1:24; Phil. 3:10; 1 Peter 4:13; 5:1; 2 Cor. 1:5, 7). Those who partake in faith drink of one Holy Spirit (1 Cor. 12:13; 2 Cor. 13:14; Phil. 2:1; Heb. 6:4).[10]

The Symmetry of the Lord's Day

The centerpiece of liturgical participation is the Eucharist. In participatory worship, it is the altar-table of the Lord that is frontal. The Lord's Supper is the "glittering central mechanism" of Christian worship and participation therein.

Those who share in the Lord's Supper participate in the totality of Christ. The Eucharist is a constellation of Christian truths. Whenever the Lord's Supper is celebrated, particular aspects of its meaning are brought into focus through the occasion, the season, the hymns, the lessons, and the sermon for the day. An expansive eucharistic theology challenges the practice of the preacher who selects special "communion texts" for use on "Communion Sundays." Every Lord's Day is appropriately a Communion Sunday. Every lection holds the potential of illuminating the Eucharist, for the sacrament is a grand recapitulation of God's redemptive activity. Within the context of a well-developed Christian Year, the Lord's Supper unfolds layer upon layer of the Christ mystery. Each major theme of Christology is in turn accentuated, through variations in the texts of lections and prayers, the music, colors, and appointments.

Those who partake of the Holy Communion share in the totality of the church. By the power of the Holy Spirit, communicants are mystically joined to all of God's people, throughout time and space. The Eucharist is a foretaste of the world that is to come. It is the messianic banquet, the eschatological feast. Participation in the communion of saints means that God's people of the past, present, and future become one in the Spirit. Together with angels and archangels, prophets, martyrs, apostles, and saints, they worship the one whose glory above the heavens is chanted:

> Holy, holy, holy Lord, God of power and might,
> Heaven and earth are full of your glory.
>> Hosanna in the highest.
> Blessed is he who comes in the name of the Lord.
>> Hosanna in the highest.

As we have often noted, liturgical participation requires this sense of true catholicity. The ambience of Christian worship must be transparent to the unity in Christ that transcends even barriers within the church. It must create a sense of universal solidarity that will open the gates of the New Jerusalem.

Those who together celebrate the Eucharist intercede as a royal priesthood for the whole world. The offering of the church is "in the name of every creature under heaven."[11] The Christian faith boldly proclaims Christ as the master formula for the universe. He is the "mystery hidden for ages and generations but now made manifest to his saints" (Col. 1:26). The church makes known this manifold wisdom of God "to the principalities and powers in the heavenly places" (Eph. 3:10–19). In the Eucharist the priesthood of the church, in behalf of creation, worships the majesty of the Creator.

The Eucharist is the glittering central mechanism of Christian worship and participation therein, a stature owed to Christ's paschal mystery. It is the resurrection of Christ that confirms his lordship over all. Death is not the final word. The gates of hell shall not prevail against it. Justice shall be vindicated. The Lamb, seated upon the throne, is the Alpha and the Omega, the origin and destiny of all creation (Rev./Apoc. 22:13). Indeed, the resurrection is the reason why Christians worship on Sunday, the

Lord's Day, the First Day, the Eighth Day. On this day Christians are bidden to dine with the risen Lord. For this reason every Sunday is a little Easter (making Easter the Great Sunday). The Lord's Day is glorified as Christians gather around the Lord's Table.

The object of all liturgical participation is communion with God in Christ by the power of the Holy Spirit. The biblical witness is clear: in the Lord's Supper, one becomes a participant in Christ and thereby shares in the fullness of God. Does this biblically rooted assertion slight the word? Not at all. On the contrary, it elevates the word to new esteem. Any question of which is stronger or superior, word or sacrament, introduces a tension that is inappropriate. The two are not antithetical, for the word has a sacramental dimension and the sacrament a word dimension. Far from being in competition with each other, they are but two sides of the same coin: the proclamation of the One Word who is Jesus Christ.

The Eucharist, as the glittering central mechanism of Christian worship and participation therein, is joined to the word, read and proclaimed. Indeed, the Eucharist is incomplete without the word and is strengthened by it. If the Lord's Supper is the centerpiece of liturgical participation, then preaching is the light that illumines it and without which the sacrament languishes in darkness. The symmetry of the Lord's Day is lost wherever preaching must stand alone, wherever the sacrament is celebrated merely as an obligation, wherever only a few of the faithful present commune, indeed, wherever preaching and sacrament are not held in equally high regard. The symmetry of the Lord's Day emerges when the word of God is purely preached and heard and when the sacrament is rightly administered and received.[12] This complementary structure for Lord's Day worship, in all its beauty and simplicity, both constitutes in a distinctive way the church of Jesus Christ and raises the energy level of liturgical participation.

Many arguments may be made in support of a word-sacrament symmetry for the worship of the Lord's Day. Historically, such was clearly the practice of the early church. Sixteenth-century Protestant reformers, notably Calvin, insisted that preaching and Lord's Supper should be normative for each Lord's Day.[13] From a theological perspective, the symmetry is even more compelling. Preaching helps to unfold the great mystery of the Eucharist and helps to keep the celebration thereof within the limits of Christian faith. For its part, the sacrament is properly viewed as a fitting complement to preaching. It is a more graphic and vivid representation of the word. It closes the communication gap created by the inadequacy of the verbal medium to express the inexpressible mystery. It seals the preached word by the power of the Holy Spirit. It provides an occasion for an immediate response of faith. In contrast to preaching, which is a general word inasmuch as it may or may not be specifically applicable to the person, the sacrament is a specific word in that it personally addresses God's word to each communicant.[14]

The relationship of word and sacrament is not unlike that of two people in a marriage. While each partner has a distinct personality and is uniquely individual, each is also a complement to the other; each has covenanted to serve the other, to sacrifice for the other, to compensate for the other, to love and to cherish "for better for worse, for richer for poorer, in sickness and in health." Competition simply doesn't belong within the marriage of word and sacrament. In the lovingly deferential language that is unique to marriage, word and sacrament may each claim the other as its better half. Together they share a mysterious unity of purpose: they joyously celebrate the One Word who is Jesus Christ, the Logos of God. The Lord's Day marriage of preaching and the Lord's Supper is one in which each is fulfilled in the other. That which God has joined together let no one put asunder!

The late twentieth-century movement of churches toward a balance of word and sacrament is a hopeful sign of church unification and liturgical renewal. The ministry of the Holy Spirit is evident as sectarian identities, which for too long have polarized the church, are being set aside. The movement toward the symmetry of the Lord's Day may be observed from two directions.

The Second Vatican Council has given considerable impetus to biblical renewal among Roman Catholics. Stated the Council, the Bible teaches "firmly, faithfully, and without error that truth which God wanted put into the sacred writings for the sake of our salvation."[15] "The Church has always venerated the divine Scriptures." They are the "supreme rule of faith." They impart the word of God and

> make the voice of the Holy Spirit resound in the words of the prophets and apostles. . . . The force and power in the Word of God is so great that it remains the support and energy of the Church, the strength of faith for her sons, the food of the soul, the pure and perennial source of spiritual life.[16]

This lofty view of Scripture led the Council to call for certain reforms: a devotional life for all Christians centered in the Bible;[17] the diligent study of Scripture by the clergy;[18] the continuation of efforts of biblical scholars;[19] renewed preaching, the main content of which is to be drawn from the Bible;[20] preaching as a regular feature of Lord's Day and festival worship;[21] a more lavish use of Scripture in the liturgy itself.[22]

Having envisioned these reforms, the bishops expressed a fervent hope:

> Through the reading and study of the sacred books, let "the word of the Lord run and be glorified" (2 Th. 3:1) and let the treasure of revelation entrusted to the Church increasingly fill the hearts of men. Just as the life of the Church grows through persistent participation in the Eucharistic mystery, so we may hope for a new surge of spiritual vitality from intensified veneration for God's word, which "lasts forever" (Is. 40:8; cf. 1 Pet. 1:23–25).[23]

This optimism has not been unfounded. The post-Vatican II Roman Catholic emphasis on the ministry of the word has prompted a powerful tide of renewal within that great tradition. For Catholics throughout the world, these reforms have augmented the level of participation in worship and will continue to bear rich fruit in the years to come as the emphasis on the word continues to grow.

By contrast, for many Protestant churches the symmetry of the Lord's Day is emerging from a slightly different direction.

For historical reasons, many of these churches have de-emphasized sacramental worship. It is now clear that, for those congregations that do not yet celebrate the Eucharist each Lord's Day, a weekly sacrament would do more than any other reform to raise the energy level of participation. This suggestion is more than an abstract appeal to history and theology. The experiences of congregations that have recently moved to weekly communion are surely no less persuasively elegant.

One such congregation, a member church of a Protestant denomination in which monthly communion is the norm, arrived at a weekly Eucharist but not as the result of abstract considerations. Rather, the decisive factors were experiential. The congregation had entered upon difficult days. Tensions among members were high. Hopes for the direction and future of the church were painfully divided. Criticisms were being aired about the leadership of the congregation. Long, anguished meetings of the church council were ending in frustration. The pastor recommended a respite in the form of a communion season, consecutive Sundays upon which the Lord's Supper would be celebrated as the climax of worship. During this season, all would refrain from criticism and rancor, so as to allow the period to be a time of healing. Although skeptical, the congregation agreed to the experiment.

When it was over, to the astonishment of many, the communion season had proven indeed to be a time of healing and spiritual discernment. The tone of congregational life had been noticeably transformed. The church now found itself ready to make important decisions. The result was not only harmony in the fellowship but also an appreciable increase in the stature of the Eucharist within the life of the congregation.

Other factors were also influential in this experiment. Some of the members were former Roman Catholics and Episcopalians, who had been attracted to the congregation because of its vitality and hospitality. In the new climate of openness and sensitivity, they felt free to express their liturgical-spiritual needs, rooted in the richness of ancient traditions. The congregation responded and, in so doing, identified these needs as their own. They came to see that more traditional structures of worship could also breathe the warmth of Christ's risen presence. In addition, as an outreach ministry, the congregation helped to establish across the street a halfway house for the mentally ill. Before long, some of the residents there began attending services. In ministering to them, many of the members observed that the Eucharist provided a greater opportunity for the residents' participation in worship than did the more verbally dominated parts of the liturgy. The combination of these factors encouraged this congregation to make a shift to a weekly Eucharist. Various needs had led the congregation to do this. The change was not imposed but freely embraced, the key to genuine and permanent liturgical reform.

While the events and needs within this congregation are not untypical, its response is highly significant. Christ's little flocks are not without their difficulties. The struggle to be faithful launches them upon paths that demand growth. The good news is that the pilgrimage of any congregation is an open invitation to partake of the real presence of the risen Lord by the power of the Holy Spirit. The path to participatory worship lies in the discovery and rediscovery of the Eucharist, illumined by God's word, as the glittering central mechanism of the life and mission of the church. Through the Eucharist the church participates in the mystery that is central to its existence and ongoing renewal: the death and resurrection of Jesus Christ its Lord. Here indeed is the master formula that will unlock the secrets of the universe.

> For this reason I bow my knees before the Father, from whom every family in heaven and on earth is named, that according to the riches of his glory he may grant you to be strengthened with might through his Spirit in the inner man, and that Christ may dwell in your hearts through faith; that you, being rooted and grounded in love, may have power to comprehend with all the saints what is the breadth and length and height and depth, and to know the love of Christ which surpasses knowledge, that you may be filled with all the fulness of God.

> Now to him who by the power at work within us is able to do far more abundantly than all that we ask or think, to him be glory in the church and in Christ Jesus to all generations, for ever and ever. Amen. (Eph. 3:14–21)

Study Guide

1. Using the chart on the following page, rate your congregation's worship according to the author's six types of participation from 1 (minimum) to 10 (maximum). Do you agree with the author's contention that liturgical participation is enhanced through a balance of types?

2. The author contends that the Eucharist/Lord's Supper is the centerpiece of liturgical participation. Do you agree? Why, or why not?

3. All marriages need work. In your parish, is the marriage of word and sacrament one in which each partner is coequal? Or, is it a lopsided pairing?

4. How can your congregation enrich its celebration of preaching? Discuss this from the standpoint of both the preacher and the listener.

5. How can your congregation enrich its celebration of the Eucharist/Lord's Supper? Discuss this from the standpoint of both the celebrant and the communicants.

For Further Reading

von Allmen, J.-J. "The Time of the Cult." Pp. 213–239 in *Worship: Its Theology and Practice*. New York, NY: Oxford University, 1965.

Bacchiocchi, Samuele. *From Sabbath to Sunday: A Historical Investigation of the Rise of Sunday Observance in Early Christianity*. Rome: Pontifical Gregorian University, 1977.

Botte, Bernard. "Les dénominations du dimanche dans la tradition chrétienne." In *Lex Orandi*. Paris: Editions du Cerf, 1944. 1.127–49.

Daniélou, Jean. *The Bible and the Liturgy*. Notre Dame, IN: University of Notre Dame, 1956. Pp. 222–24, 242–86.

_____. "Le dimanche comme huitième jour." In *Lex Orandi*. Paris: Editions du Cerf, 1965. 39.61–89.

Heschel, Abraham Joshua. *The Sabbath: Its Meaning for Modern Man*. New York, NY: Farrar, Straus, and Giroux, 1951.

Spontaneous Involvement is prompted by the Holy Spirit directly from the heart for the edification of the church. It includes spontaneous singing, prayer, greetings, overt responsiveness to preaching, and charismatic prophecies and glossolalia.

1   2   3   4   5   6   7   8   9   10

Silent Engagement. The Holy Spirit ministers through the silence of preparation, centering, confession, listening, adoration, and communion.

1   2   3   4   5   6   7   8   9   10

Interiorized Verbal Participation operates in the ritual mode, stressing the value of repetition. It employs prayers, responses, and music that is familiar, classical, and oftentimes memorized.

1   2   3   4   5   6   7   8   9   10

Prophetic Verbal Participation emphasizes contemporaneous and individually creative expression, employing unison and responsive prayers, litanies, and readings that are composed, selected, or adapted for the occasion.

1   2   3   4   5   6   7   8   9   10

Lay Leadership is an expression of the priesthood of the church. The community, under the direction of the Spirit, acknowledges the diversity of gifts that the Spirit has bestowed by the calling forth of individuals for special aspects of liturgical leadership.

1   2   3   4   5   6   7   8   9   10

Multisensate Participation engages and integrates the full range of human faculties—body, mind, senses, imagination, will, emotion, and memory, together. It employs a variety of bodily gestures, movement, colors, symbols, art, and environmental stimuli.

1   2   3   4   5   6   7   8   9   10

Porter, Boone H. *The Day of Light: The Biblical and Liturgical Meaning of Sunday.* Greenwich, CT: Seabury, 1960.

Rordorf, Willy. *Sunday: The History of the Day of Rest and Worship in the Earliest Centuries of the Christian Church.* Philadelphia, PA: Westminster, 1968.

Verheul, Ambroise. "Du sabbat au Jour du Seigneur." *Questions Liturgiques* 51 (1970) 3–27.

Notes

PREFACE

1. The book is based upon "Liturgical Participation and the Renewal of the Church," *Worship* 59 (May 1985) 231–43. Material in chap. 4 appeared as "The Still, Small Voice of Calm," *Reformed Liturgy and Music* 21 (Winter 1987) pp. 34–38.

CHAPTER 1

1. The roles of clergy and laity in worship and the problematical association of 1 Peter 2:1–10 with the doctrine of the priesthood of all believers will be discussed in chap. 7.
2. Robert J. Daly, *The Origins of the Christian Doctrine of Sacrifice* (Philadelphia, PA: Fortress, 1978), pp. 1–10.
3. *"Ideo sacris pastoribus advigilandum est ut in actione liturgica non solum observentur leges ad validam et licitam celebrationem, sed ut fideles scienter, actuose et fructuose eandem participent,"* from par. 12 of "Constitutio de sacra liturgia," *Acta Apostolicae Sedis* 56 (Rome, 1964) 102–3; for Eng. trans. see "Constitution on the Sacred Liturgy," 11, in *The Documents of Vatican II,* ed. Walter M. Abbott (New York, NY: Guild, 1966), p. 143.
4. See Jean Daniélou, *The Bible and the Liturgy* (Liturgical Studies, 3; Notre Dame, IN: University of Notre Dame, 1956).
5. *Purity of Heart Is to Will One Thing* (New York, NY: Harper and Row, 1956), pp. 180–81.
6. Josef A. Jungmann, *The Early Liturgy* (Liturgical Studies, 6: Notre Dame: University of Notre Dame, 1959), p. 13; and Gregory Dix, *The Shape of the Liturgy* (2nd ed.; London, UK: Dacre, 1945), pp. 141–55.

CHAPTER 2

1. Gerard J. Mangone, "Cultural Empathy," in *Assignment Overseas,* ed. Stanley J. Rowland, Jr. (New York, NY: Crowell, 1966), p. 80.
2. Julius Melton, *Presbyterian Worship in America: Changing Patterns Since 1787* (Richmond, VA: John Knox, 1967), pp. 79–83.
3. J. G. Davies, "Ritual," *The New Westminster Dictionary of Liturgy and Worship* (Philadelphia, PA: Westminster, 1986), p. 469.
4. The image of God is most profoundly evident when the will is directed to love. The work is entitled *Clothespin,* by Claes Oldenburg, from the school of "sculpture made with found objects." A forty-foot version stands across from City Hall in Philadelphia. Oldenburg compared his *Clothespin* to Brancusi's *The Kiss,* because "both contained two structures pressing close together and held in an embrace." "I have created," he said, "a symbol of things coming together and rising into a higher plane, rising and curving out into the heavens—into the higher realm." Cited from *Oldenburg: Six Themes* (Minneapolis, MN: Walker Art Center, 1975), pp. 59–68.
5. *Letters to Malcolm: Chiefly on Prayer* (London, UK: Harcourt, Brace, Jovanovich, 1964), p. 4.

CHAPTER 3

1. See the author's Ph.D. diss. *Sacramental Theology among American Presbyterians: 1945–79* (Notre Dame, IN: University of Notre Dame, 1982), pp. 30–36.
2. A simple *berākôth* is a short blessing, e.g., upon dressing: "Blessed are you YHWH, our God, King of the Universe, who clothes the naked." Such formulae were frequently used by pious Jews of Jesus' time. See Louis Bouyer, *Eucharist: Theology and Spirituality of the Eucharistic Prayer,* tr. Charles Underhill Quinn (Notre Dame, IN: University of Notre Dame, 1968), chap. 4.
3. *Songs of Zion* (SWR, 12; Nashville, TN: Abingdon, 1981), # 167; for an ethnographic description of this type of singing and prayer see Shirley Brice Heath, *Ways with Words: Language, Life, and Work in Communities and Classrooms* (Cambridge, UK: Cambridge University, 1983), pp. 201–10.
4. For a summary of this debate see Horton Davies, "Congregationalist Worship," *The New Westminster Dictionary of Liturgy and Worship,* pp. 191–92.
5. Dix, *The Shape of the Liturgy,* pp. 42–47.
6. See also "The First Apology of Justin, the Martyr," 65, 67, in *Early Christian Fathers,* ed. Cyril C. Richardson (New York, NY: Macmillan, 1970), pp. 285–88.

7. Some have referred to the Pastoral Prayer as "a sermon with your eyes closed."

8. For a collection of intercessory prayers that complement the lectionary readings see Richard Mazziotta, *We Pray to the Lord* (Notre Dame, IN: Ave Maria, 1984).

9. The so-called *a, per, in, ad* formula: *A Patre, per Filium eius, Iesum Christum, in Spiritu Sancto, ad Patrem.* See Cyprian Vagaggini, *Theological Dimensions of the Liturgy: A General Treatise on the Theology of the Liturgy,* tr. Leonard J. Doyle and William A. Jurgens (Collegeville, MN: Liturgical, 1976), pp. 191–246.

10. Dix, *The Shape of the Liturgy,* pp. 105–10. See also Robert Taft, *The Great Entrance* (Orientalia Christiana Analecta, 200; Rome: Pontificium Institutum Studiorum Orientalium, 1975), pp. 374–78.

11. Dix, *The Shape of the Liturgy,* p. 105.

12. Cited from *Early Christian Fathers,* p. 178.

13. On the varieties of the world's customs for greeting see Betty J. and Franz H. Bäuml, *A Dictionary of Gestures* (Metuchen, NJ: Scarecrow, 1975).

14. Hans Küng, *The Church* (New York, NY: Sheed and Ward, 1967), p. 188.

15. The ecumenical implications of the modern charismatic renewal should not be underestimated. Many of the Christians involved display a commendable level of openness to other liturgical traditions, a result of their fruitful participation therein. Numerous statements by Roman Catholic bishops and Pope Paul VI have maintained a tone of cautious encouragement about charismatic renewal. The hospitality of the Roman communion toward charismatic renewal is exemplary. See E. D. O'Connor, "Charismatic Renewal, Catholic," *NCE,* 17.104–6.

16. W. R. Davies, "Glossolalia," *The Westminster Dictionary of Christian Spirituality,* ed. Gordon S. Wakefield (Philadelphia, PA: Westminster, 1983), pp. 176–77.

17. See Küng's description of a church without vocal prophets, *The Church,* p. 433.

18. *Baptism, Eucharist, Ministry* (Faith and Order Paper, 111; Geneva: World Council of Churches, 1982), p. 20, par. 5.

CHAPTER 4

1. John Greenleaf Whittier's phrase, based on the Elijah story of 1 Kings 19:11–12. See *WB,* # 350, "Dear Lord and Father of Mankind."

2. "To the Romans," 4:1—5:1; see *Early Christian Fathers,* p. 104.

3. "To the Ephesians," 15:1–2; see *Early Christian Fathers,* p. 92; on

the idea of silence in Ignatius' letters see William R. Schoedel, *Ignatius of Antioch: A Commentary on the Letters of Ignatius of Antioch* (Hermeneia; Philadelphia, PA: Fortress, 1985), pp. 56–57, 77, 91, 120–22, 170–71.

4. Presbyterian Church (U.S.A.), "Directory for the Service of God" (New York, NY: Office of the General Assembly, 1985), p. 164, S-2.0300; see also 1 Cor. 10:24—11:1.

5. See Robert F. Morneau's *Mantras for the Morning: An Introduction to Holistic Prayer* (Collegeville, MN: Liturgical Press, 1981); *Mantras for the Evening: The Experience of Holistic Prayer* (Collegeville, MN: Liturgical Press, 1982); and *Mantras for the Midnight: Reflections for the Night Country* (Collegeville, MN: Liturgical Press, 1985).

6. Opening prayer for the Third Sunday of Easter, *Sac*, p. 278.

7. Emily Dickinson, "There's a Certain Slant of Light."

8. *LBW*, "Prayer of Confession," p. 56.

9. Fred B. Craddock, *Preaching* (Nashville, TN: Abingdon, 1985), pp. 25–26.

10. Gerard Manley Hopkins, "God's Grandeur."

11. John Calvin, *Institutes of the Christian Religion*, tr. Ford Lewis Battles (LCC, 20–21; Philadelphia, PA: Westminster, 1960), IV.17.7.

12. *Seasons of Celebration* (New York, NY: Farrar, Straus, and Giroux, 1965), p. 210.

CHAPTER 5

1. *Man Is Not Alone* (New York, NY: Farrar, Straus, and Giroux, 1951), p. 162.

2. *A Passover Haggadah: The New Union Haggadah* (New York, NY: Central Conference of American Rabbis, 1974), p. 34.

3. Nils A. Dahl, *Jesus in the Memory of the Early Church: Essays by Nils Alstrup Dahl* (Minneapolis, MN: Augsburg, 1976), pp. 15–17.

4. Odo Casel, *The Mystery of Christian Worship* (Westminster, MD: Newman, 1962); see also J.-J. von Allmen, *Worship: Its Theology and Practice* (New York, NY: Oxford University, 1965), pp. 21–41; Peter Brunner, *Worship in the Name of Jesus*, tr. M. H. Bertram (St. Louis, MO: Concordia, 1968), pp. 143–50, 160–81, 283–84; B. Faivre, "Eucharistie et mémoire," *Nouvelle revue Théologique* 90 (1968) 278–90.

5. Wolfhart Pannenberg, "Redemptive Event and History," in *Basic Questions in Theology: Collected Essays,* tr. George H. Kehm (2 vols.; Philadelphia, PA: Fortress, 1970), 1.15–80; Dietrich Ritschl, *Memory and Hope: An Inquiry Concerning the Presence of Christ* (New York, NY: Macmillan, 1967).

6. Exod. 13:8, emphasis mine; see *A Passover Haggadah*, p. 32.
7. Brevard S. Childs, *Memory and Tradition in Israel* (Studies in Biblical Theology, 37; London, UK: S.C.M., 1962); Nils A. Dahl, "Anamnesis: Mémoire et Commémoration dans le christianisme primitif," *Studia Theologica* 1 (1948) 69–95; M.-J. Dubois, "Mémoire et présence dans la prière," *La vie spirituelle* 126 (July/Aug. 1972) 544–55; J. M. R. Tillard, "Le mémorial dans la vie de l'église," *La Maison-Dieu* 106 (2nd Trimestre 1971) 24–45.
8. This theological principle is embraced by the adage: *lex orandi est lex credendi* ("the rule of prayer is the rule of belief"). The formula is first attributed to St. Prosper of Aquitaine in C.E. 435–42. Its first recorded application was to a particular case, not as a general principle. Through the centuries various forms of the adage have been used: the subjunctive, *legem credendi lex statuat supplicandi* ("let the rule of prayer determine the rule of belief"); the declarative, *legem credendi lex statuit supplicandi* ("the rule of prayer determines the rule of belief"); *lex credendi legem statuat supplicandi* ("let the rule of belief determine the rule of prayer"); *lex orandi lex credendi* ("the rule of prayer is the rule for belief"); *lex precendi lex credendi est* ("the rule for prayer is the rule for belief"). See Herman Schmidt, "lex orandi lex credendi in recentioribus documentis pontificis," *Periodica* 40 (1950) 5–28.
9. Melton, *Presbyterian Worship in America,* pp. 81–92, 110–11; Stephen Augustus Hurlbut (ed.), *The Liturgy of the Church of Scotland Since the Reformation* (Washington, DC: St. Alban's, 1947); Charles Woodruff Shields, *The Book of Common Prayer and Administration of the Sacraments . . . As Amended by the Westminster Divines in the Royal Commission of 1661, and in Agreement with the Directory for the Public Worship of the Presbyterian Church in the United States of America* (New York, NY: Asson D. F. Randolph, 1864); David Rodney Bluhm, *Trends of Worship Reflected in Three Editions of the "Book of Common Worship" of the Presbyterian Church in the United States of America* (Ph.D. diss., University of Pittsburgh; Ann Arbor, MI: University Microfilms International, 1956), p. 198.
10. *BCP,* "Morning Prayer," I, "General Thanksgiving," p. 58; "Post Communion Prayer," p. 365; "Prayer over the Newly Baptized," p. 308; Ps. 118(119):174, p. 778; "Eucharistic Prayer B," p. 368.
11. "The First Apology of Justin, the Martyr," 65, in *Early Christian Fathers,* p. 286.
12. *PL,* 46:836; 38:1247.
13. *PL,* 26:355.
14. Erik Routley, *Church Music and the Christian Faith* (Carol Stream, IL: Agape, 1978), pp. 96–99.

15. A better translation of the Latin *et cum spiritu tuo* is "and with your spirit."

16. Thomas Howard, *Evangelical Is Not Enough* (Nashville, TN: Nelson, 1984), p. 46.

17. *RS, LBW, BCP,* SLR, SWR, *ASB.*

18. ICET. The text solves the trespasses/debts impasse and gives a better translation of "lead us not into temptation."

19. *The Book of Occasional Services* (New York, NY: Church Hymnal Corporation, 1979), p. 25. See also *RS.*

20. Bernhard W. Anderson, *Understanding the Old Testament* (4th ed.; Englewood Cliffs, NJ: Prentice-Hall, 1986), pp. 540–67; Gerhard von Rad, *Old Testament Theology* (2 vols.; New York, NY: Harper and Row, 1962–1965), 2.355–459; Roland E. Murphy, "Psalms," in *Jerome Biblical Commentary,* ed. Raymond E. Brown et al. (Englewood Cliffs, NJ: Prentice-Hall, 1968), pp. 569–602.

21. Anderson, *Understanding the Old Testament,* p. 542.

22. Fred R. Anderson, *Singing Psalms of Joy and Praise* (Philadelphia, PA: Westminster, 1986), p. 72. Anderson's texts are gender-inclusive and each is followed by a psalm prayer, making them easily usable for celebrations of Morning and Evening Prayer.

23. For other collections of metrical psalms see Christopher L. Webber, *A New Metrical Psalter* (New York, NY: Church Hymnal Corporation, 1986); *A Psalm Sampler* (Philadelphia, PA: Westminster, 1986); and *Psalter Hymnal 1987* (Grand Rapids, MI: Christian Reformed Church, 1987). Also, numerous hymnals contain metrical psalms and psalm renditions, which may be located by using the index of scriptural allusions.

24. *The ASB Psalter and Canticles,* ed. L. Dakers and C. Taylor (London, UK: Collins, 1976), p. 58. See also *The Anglican Chant Psalter,* ed. Alec Wyton (New York, NY: Church Hymnal Corporation, 1987).

25. *LBW,* pp. 263, 290–91.

26. The major U.S. publisher of responsorial psalmody is G.I.A., Inc. (Chicago, IL) which, because of its ecumenical marketing, lists its psalms according to both Latin (Roman Catholic) and Hebraic (Protestant) numberings.

27. *PGIS* (organ edition), p. 6.

28. *Psalm 32* (Minneapolis, MN: Augsburg, 1979), # 11–0682.

29. Introductory note to *30 Psalms and Two Canticles* (Chicago, IL: G.I.A., 1962).

30. See bibliography at end of chap. 5. Well worth the investment for would-be performers is the LP album, "The Gelineau Psalms," as sung by the Choir of the Cathedral Church of St. Mary, Edinburgh

(Chicago, IL: G.I.A., M/S-122). G.I.A. also markets cantor training tapes.

31. See *The Book of Canticles* (Church Hymnal Series, 5; New York, NY: Church Hymnal Corporation, 1980); *PGS* (see list there on p. 327); *Worship3,* ## 82–89; *H82,* S 177–S 288); *LBW* (see list there on p. 960); Christopher L. Webber, *A New Metrical Psalter,* pp. 1–39 (metrical settings); *The ASB Psalter and Canticles* (see index there on p. 5); SLR, 5, pp. 255–78.

32. Previously, the Nicene Creed had only been used on Good Friday. Robert Taft, *The Great Entrance,* p. 398.

33. For hymnal sources of liturgical music, see *LBW,* pp. 57–119; *H82,* S 76–S 176 and S 272–S 281; *WB,* pp. 211–71; *Worship3,* pp. 259–354.

34. Jacques Berthier, *Music from Taizé,* Vocal ed. (G-2433), Instrumental ed. (G-2433-A) (Chicago, IL: G.I.A., 1981), p. x.

35. Commissions are by no means immune to political pressures. In 1987 the United Methodist hymnal commission announced that "Onward Christian Soldiers" would not be in its new hymnal, due to its excessive martial imagery. A storm of protest and some quick research into biblical imagery succeeded in reversing the decision.

36. For example, over fifty-five percent of the tunes and texts in the 1955 *Hymnbook,* still in use in many U.S. Presbyterian churches, are from the nineteenth century, an imbalance especially glaring on this the eve of the twenty-first century.

37. Preludes on hymn tunes and free organ accompaniments (alternate harmonies) are abundant. Worth examination are the works of Paul Manz, John Ferguson, John Walker, D. DeWitt Wasson, David Johnson, Fred Swann, and Gerre Hancock. For descants, in addition to the numerous hymnals that contain them, see the work of Hal Hopson, Lois Fyfe, Richard Proulx, Michael Young, and Robert Powell.

38. For a list of hymns that may be sung in canon, see *Worship3,* # 1208.

39. Four Welsh tunes commonly found in hymnals are: *Ar hyd y nos, Hyfrydol, Cwm Rhondda,* and *Bryn Calfaria.*

40. Some hymnals have companion volumes that give the history of hymns and their composers. Hymnal commissions can budget for these volumes, which are indispensable to hymn catechesis. See *The Hymnal 1940 Companion* (New York, NY: Church Hymnal Corporation, 1940) and Albert C. Ronander and Ethel K. Porter, *Guide to the Pilgrim Hymnal* (Boston, MA: United Church, 1966). Some parishes follow a "Hymn-of-the-Month" emphasis, which is especially helpful when a new hymnal is being introduced.

41. Two hymns, "Amazing Grace" and "Morning Has Broken," were on

their way out of modern hymnbooks when suddenly their renditions by popular recording artists gave them a meteoric revival.

42. "To the Ephesians," 4:1–2, in *Early Christian Fathers,* p. 89.
43. See Horace T. Allen, Jr., "Songs for Word and Sacrament," *Liturgy* 6 (Winter 1987): 21–25.

CHAPTER 6

1. Fred B. Craddock, *Preaching* (Nashville, TN: Abingdon, 1985), pp. 25–26.
2. The title of this chapter is taken from the first stanza of Eleanor Farjeon's hymn, "Morning Has Broken," *Worship3,* # 674.
3. J. Barrie Shepherd, 12/24/85 service bulletin for the Swarthmore Presbyterian Church (U.S.A.) in Swarthmore, PA.
4. *Idem, 3/31/85* service bulletin.
5. *Idem, 9/29/85* service bulletin.
6. *Idem, 2/20/85* service bulletin.
7. This includes the historical liturgies that bear the names of individuals (e.g., St. Chrysostom or St. Basil), but which were actually shaped by many hands over hundreds of years.
8. See "The First Apology of Justin, the Martyr," 65, in *Early Christian Fathers,* pp. 285–86.
9. The use of an ecumenical lectionary is most helpful in building a sense of a catholic backdrop to participation.
10. Source of the prayer printed in the worship bulletin, *BCP,* p. 79.
11. *BCP,* p. 217. Catholic models of the collect may also be found in *Sac* and *LBW.*
12. The origin of litanies in Christian worship dates from the fourth century or earlier.
13. Examples of litanies may be found in two collections: *Be Our Freedom Lord: Responsive Prayers and Readings for Contemporary Worship,* ed. Terry C. Falla (Grand Rapids, MI: Eerdmans, 1985); and Jeffrey W. Rowthorn, *The Wideness of God's Mercies: Litanies to Enlarge Our Prayer* (2 vols.; Minneapolis, MN: Seabury, 1985). The Falla collection displays a didactic proclivity.
14. Examples of when the vernacular may appropriately yield: carols in other languages on Christmas Eve, as a symbol for the unity of Christians; Scripture read in different languages on Pentecost; bilingual or multilingual assemblies; choral settings in which the original language is musically superior, provided translations are available.
15. See the statement on inclusive language adopted by the Presbyterian Church (U.S.A.) 197th General Assembly (1985), reprinted in *Reformed Liturgy and Music* 19 (Fall 1985) 240–42.

16. Fred B. Craddock, "'All Things in Him': A Critical Note on Col. I:15–20," *New Testament Studies* 12 (Oct. 1965) 78–80; Elisabeth Schüssler Fiorenza, "Wisdom Mythology and the Christological Hymns of the New Testament," in *Aspects of Wisdom in Judaism and Early Christianity,* ed. Robert L. Wilken (Notre Dame, IN: University of Notre Dame, 1975), pp. 17–41; Ernst Käsemann, "A Primitive Christian Baptismal Liturgy," in *Essays on New Testament Themes* (Studies in Biblical Theology, 41; Naperville, IL: Alec R. Allenson, 1964), pp. 149–68; Jack T. Sanders, *The New Testament Christological Hymns: Their Historical Religious Background* (Cambridge, UK: Cambridge University, 1971), pp. 75–87; David M. Stanley, "Carmenque Christo quasi Deo dicere . . ." *Catholic Biblical Quarterly* 20 (April 1958) 173–91; and Bruce Vawter, "The Colossians Hymn and the Principle of Redaction," *Catholic Biblical Quarterly* 33 (Jan. 1971) 62–81.
17. The most noteworthy of the new generation of hymnals are *LBW;* the Reformed Church in America's *RIL;* the American Episcopal *H82;* and the Roman Catholic *Worship3.* On the importance of singing with a unified voice see Ignatius' "To the Ephesians," 4:2, in *Early Christian Fathers,* p. 89.
18. See the author's "The Strong Name of the Trinity," *Reformed Liturgy and Music* 19 (Fall 1985) 205–10.
19. See Wolfhart Pannenberg, "Redemptive Event and History"; and Donald G. Bloesch, *The Battle for the Trinity* (Ann Arbor, MI: Servant Publications, 1985).
20. J. Barrie Shepherd, private correspondence.

CHAPTER 7

1. John H. Elliott, *The Elect and the Holy. An Exegetical Examination of 1 Peter 1:4–10 and the Phrase "basileion hierateuma."* (Leiden: Brill, 1966); *idem,* "Death of a Slogan: From Royal Priests to Celebrating Community," *Una Sancta* 25 (Fall 1968) 18–31; Elisabeth Schüssler Fiorenza, "Cultic Language in Qumran and in the NT," *Catholic Biblical Quarterly* 38 (1976) 159–77; *BEM,* "Ministry," par. 17; J. M. R. Tillard, *What Priesthood Has the Ministry?* (Grove Booklet on Ministry and Worship, 13; Bramcote, UK: Grove Books, 1973).
2. Hans Küng, *The Church,* pp. 373–81.
3. Ibid., pp. 401–2.
4. The assigning of liturgical roles and duties is an ancient tradition. Clement ("First Letter," 41:1), c. A.D. 96, says each must serve in his or her own rank. "We must not transgress the rules laid down for our ministry, but must perform it reverently" (cited from *Early Chris-*

tian Fathers, p. 62). This, he says, is according to Christ's supreme will (40:3).

5. Dix, *The Shape of the Liturgy,* pp. 425–30; Taft, *The Great Entrance,* pp. 149–62.

6. Michael Kwatera, *The Ministry of Servers* (Collegeville, MN: Liturgical Press, 1982).

7. James M. Barnett, *The Diaconate: A Full and Equal Order* (New York, NY: Seabury, 1979); Karl Rahner, "The Theology of the Restoration of the Diaconate," *Theological Investigations,* tr. Karl H. Kruger (vol. 5; Baltimore, MD: Helicon, 1966), pp. 268–314; Robert W. Hovda, *Strong, Loving and Wise: Presiding in Liturgy* (Collegeville, MN: Liturgical, 1980); Aidan Kavanagh, *Elements of Rite: A Handbook of Liturgical Style* (New York, NY: Pueblo Publishing, 1982); *BEM,* p. 27, par. 31; *motu proprio* of Pope Paul VI *Sacrum Diaconatus Ordinem* (June 1967).

8. Based on John 1:5. From *LBW,* "Evening Prayer," p. 142.

9. *Motu proprio* of Pope Paul VI *Sacrum Diaconatus Ordinem* (June 1967).

10. Michael Kwatera, *The Ministry of Communion* (Collegeville, MN: Liturgical, 1983).

11. James Hansen, *The Ministry of the Cantor* (Collegeville, MN: Liturgical, 1982).

12. *BEM,* p. 22, par. 14.

13. S. Safrai and M. Stern (eds.), *The Jewish People in the First Century* (Philadelphia, PA: Fortress, 1976), 2.918–20; Eric Werner, *The Sacred Bridge* (New York, NY: Schocken Books, 1970), pp. 53–54; Abraham Millgram, *Jewish Worship* (Philadelphia, PA: Jewish Publication Society of America, 1971), p. 113.

14. "The First Apology of Justin, the Martyr," 67, in *Early Christian Fathers,* p. 287.

15. *ApTrad:* ed. Bernard Botte, p. 66; ed. Burton Scott Easton, p. 40, par. 12. The Eastern Orthodox and, until 1972, the Roman Catholic communions retained the tradition of lectors as the second of the traditional minor orders after the acolyte. Subsequent reform in the Roman Church has rightly opened this ministry up to laypersons. See Pope Paul VI's apostolic letter *Ministeria quaedam* (15 August 1972).

16. *The Orthodox Liturgy* (Oxford, UK: Oxford University, 1982), pp. 47–50.

17. For lay readers' training manuals see James A. Wallace, *The Ministry of Lectors* (Collegeville, MN: Liturgical, 1981); Paul Harms, *Presenting the Lessons: A Guide for Lectors* (Minneapolis, MN: Augsburg, 1980); and Robert W. Smith, *The Is the Word of the Lord* (Los Angeles, CA: Franciscan Communications, 1985).

18. See *Carols for Choirs* series, vols. 1–4 (London, UK: Oxford University, 1961–80); and *The Book of Occasional Services* (BCP), pp. 29–32, 36–39.
19. The Cathedral Office, the regular, corporate prayer for all Christians, is distinguished from the Monastic Office, derived for use in religious communities (matins, lauds, none, etc.). See Juan Mateos, "The Morning and Evening Office," *Worship* 42 (Jan. 1968) 31–47; *idem*, "The Origins of the Divine Office," *Worship* 41 (Oct. 1967) 477–85; and William G. Storey, "The Liturgy of the Hours: Cathedral Versus Monastery," *Worship* 50 (Jan. 1976) 50–70.
20. Commentary on Psalm 63(64):10.
21. The characterizations are those of William G. Storey, "The Liturgy of the Hours: Cathedral Versus Monastery," *Worship* 50 (Jan. 1976) 55–57.
22. Cited in Juan Mateos, "The Morning and Evening Office," *Worship* 42 (Jan. 1968) 38.
23. See *Manual on the Liturgy: Lutheran Book of Worship,* ed. Philip H. Pfatteicher and Carlos R. Messerli (Minneapolis, MN: Augsburg, 1979), pp. 270–77.
24. It frequently appears in hymnbooks as "O Gladsome Light" (*LBW,* # 279; *RIL,* # 623; *Worship3,* # 12, 679). Other settings of the hymn may be found in *PGIS.*

CHAPTER 8

1. The Chalcedonian formula.
2. Cyprian Vagaggini, *Theological Dimensions of the Liturgy,* pp. 49–50, 300–334; Jaroslav Pelikan, *The Emergence of the Catholic Tradition (100–600)* (The Christian Tradition, 1; Chicago, IL: University of Chicago, 1971), pp. 243–77.
3. Sermon LXXIV, 140, *SC.*
4. Much of the contemporary debate over inclusive language in worship is one-sided. The usual focus of this concern is on *verbal* language. However, inclusivity of *non*verbal language is surely as important if not more so. It is possible to have worship in which the verbal language is thoroughly scrubbed to the most current standards of inclusivity, but which has an exclusive nonverbal language, i.e., a dearth of symbols, sacraments, and gestures. Such exclusivity belies suspicions about the human body, doubts about the goodness of creation, a limited appreciation for the historical ministry of the Spirit in the church, and confusion over the significance of the incarnation. The concern for inclusive language must focus on both verbal and nonverbal forms.
5. Dominic A. LaRusso, *The Shadows of Communication* (Dubuque, IA: Kendall/Hunt, 1977), p. 226.

6. "The Resurrection of the Dead," 8:2–3 (c. C.E. 208–12), in *The Faith of the Early Fathers,* ed. William A. Jurgens (Collegeville, MN: Liturgical Press, 1970), p. 149, # 362.

7. Martin Rinkart, "Nun danket," *LBW,* # 533.

8. The classical distinction between denotation and connotation is not an unchallenged one. Many semiologists, philosophers, linguists, communication theorists, rhetoricians, and even some theologians would argue that such a distinction is artificial and invalid. This perspective would deny the possibility of a formal, objective basis for knowledge and truth and hence for the communication of meaning. As interesting as it may be, that discussion lies beyond the scope of this book. The denotation-connotation distinction is offered merely as a means of specifying the meanings of terms, gestures, symbols, etc., which will avoid misunderstanding and open the door to learning. See David K. Berlo, *The Process of Communication: An Introduction to Theory and Practice* (New York, NY: Holt, Rinehart, and Winston, 1960), pp. 190–216.

9. A classic example is the presentation of the priestly implements (chalice, paten, vial, etc.), the so-called *traditio instrumentorum* ("Tradition of the Instruments") of the late medieval rite of ordination in the West, which presentation had become so elaborate that it obscured what was the central gesture of the rite—the laying on of hands.

10. A. G. Martimort (ed.), *The Church at Prayer, I: Introduction to the Liturgy* (New York, NY: Desclée, 1968), pp. 146–48; Bäuml, *A Dictionary of Gestures.*

11. Hélène Lubienska de Lenval, *The Whole Man at Worship: The Actions of Man before God* (New York, NY: Desclée, 1961), p. 85.

12. *Manual on the Liturgy: Lutheran Book of Worship,* p. 207.

13. "Rite of Marriage" (Washington, DC: United States Catholic Conference, 1969), p. 1.

14. *BCP,* pp. 270–95; *RS,* pp. 207–59.

15. Tertullian, *De oratione,* 23 (*PL,* 1:1191; *FC,* 40:182) and *De corona militis,* 3 (*PL,* 2:99; *FC,* 40:182); First Council of Nicaea, canon 20; Charles Joseph Hefele, *A History of the Christian Councils* (Edinburgh, UK: T. & T. Clark, 1872), pp. 434–35; *NPNF,* 14:42; see also "The First Apology of Justin, the Martyr," 67, in *Early Christian Fathers,* p. 287; St. Cyprian, *De Dominica oratione,* 31 (*FC,* 36:153); Martimort (ed.), *The Church at Prayer,* I: 151; B. I. Mullahy, "Liturgical Gestures," *NCE,* 8.894–97.

16. St. Basil the Great, *De Spiritu Sancto,* 27:66 (*SC,* 17:236–37); Eng. trans., *On the Holy Spirit,* 27:66 (Crestwood, NY: St. Vladimir's Seminary, 1980), p. 100.

17. See also Tertullian, *Liber apologeticus,* 30 (*PL,* 1:422); Clement of Rome, *Epist. 1 ad Cor.,* 29 (*PG,* 1:270; *LCC,* 1:57).

18. *De Dominica oratione,* 14:1 (*PL,* 1:1169–70; *FC,* 40:170); *Liber Apologeticum,* 30:4 (*PL,* 1:422; *FC,* 10:87).
19. Lubienska de Lenval, *The Whole Man at Worship,* pp. 44–54.
20. Tertullian, *Apologeticum,* 24:5; 30:4 (*FC,* 10:76, 86); Lubienska de Lenval, *The Whole Man at Worship,* pp. 19–20; Martimort (ed.), *The Church at Prayer,* I: 155; cf. St. Cyprian, *De Dominica oratione,* 6 (*FC,* 36:131).
21. St. Basil the Great, *De Spiritu Sancto,* 27:66 (*SC,* 17:238); Eng. trans., *On the Holy Spirit,* 27:66, p. 101.
22. See Gilbert Cope, "Posture," *The New Westminster Dictionary of Liturgy and Worship,* pp. 437–40; Mullahy, "Liturgical Gestures."
23. Dix, *The Shape of the Liturgy,* p. 13.
24. See also Isa. 45:23; Eph. 3:14; Rom. 14:11.
25. Theodor Klauser, *A Short History of the Western Liturgy: An Account and Some Reflections,* tr. John Halliburton (London, UK: Oxford University, 1969), pp. 113–16.
26. Mullahy, "Liturgical Gestures"; Ludwig Eisenhofer and Joseph Lechner, *The Liturgy of the Roman Rite,* tr. A. J. and E. F. Peeler (New York, NY: Herder and Herder, 1961), p. 85.
27. Mullahy, "Liturgical Gestures"; Lubienska de Lenval, *The Whole Man at Worship,* pp. 58–61; Martimort (ed.), *The Church at Prayer,* I: 153; Eisenhofer and Lechner, *The Liturgy of the Roman Rite,* pp. 85–87.
28. Peter Brunner, *Worship in the Name of Jesus,* pp. 211–12; Lubienska de Lenval, *The Whole Man at Worship,* pp. 18–19, 43; Eisenhofer and Lechner, *The Liturgy of the Roman Rite,* p. 87; Martimort (ed.), *The Church at Prayer,* I: 153.
29. Lubienska de Lenval, *The Whole Man at Worship,* pp. 43–45, 57–61.
30. "The First Apology of Justin, the Martyr," 67, in *Early Christian Fathers,* p. 287; Johannes Quasten, *Monumenta eucharistica et liturgica vetustissima, pars 1,* "Constitutiones Apostolorum," 8.6.2, p. 199.
31. Fernand Cabrol, *Liturgical Prayer—Its History and Spirit* (Westminster, MD: Newman, 1950), pp. 183–84; Eisenhofer and Lechner, *The Liturgy of the Roman Rite,* pp. 87–88; Martimort (ed.), *The Church at Prayer,* I: 152.
32. A parody of the Westminster Shorter Catechism, Article 1, which reads: "Q. What is the chief end of man? A. The chief end of man is to glorify God and to enjoy him forever." Not to be outdone, some Presbyterians retorted: "Piskies, Piskies, say it again. Stand up, sit down, all over again." See Melton, *Presbyterian Worship in America,* p. 38.
33. David A. Ramsey and R. Craig Koedel, "The Communion

Season—An 18th Century Model," *Journal of Presbyterian History* 54 (Summer 1976) 203–16.

34. Any dilution of this symbol (e.g., shoe-shining or handwashing) is minimalistic and even inappropriate. The latter gesture is unfortunate as it mixes metaphors with Pilate's gesture of self-absolution. See *From Ashes to Fire* (SWR, 8; Nashville, TN: Abingdon, 1979), pp. 120–22.

35. Sermon 67:1 (*PL*, 38:433).

36. For a description of this gesture in Jewish and Islamic use see Kenneth E. Bailey, *Poet and Peasant Through Peasant Eyes* (Grand Rapids, MI: Eerdmans, 1976), p. 153; see also "The Order of Mass with a Congregation" (New York, NY: Catholic Book Publishing, 1970), p. 4; Nah. 2:7; Isa. 32:12; Eisenhofer and Lechner, *The Liturgy of the Roman Rite*, p. 94; Lubienska de Lenval, *The Whole Man at Worship*, p. 20; Martimort (ed.), *The Church at Prayer*, I: 155; Cabrol, *Liturgical Prayer*, p. 84.

37. Augustine, Sermon 227 (*PL*, 38:1101A; *FC*, 38:197–98); for various modes of passing the Peace see Daniélou, *The Bible and the Liturgy*, pp. 133–34; Cope, "Gestures"; Lubienska de Lenval, *The Whole Man at Worship*, p. 60; also see various cultural patterns for greeting in Bäuml, *A Dictionary of Gestures*.

38. Eisenhofer and Lechner, *The Liturgy of the Roman Rite*, pp. 92–93; Lubienska de Lenval speculates that its occurrence in Christian practice may reflect the influence of an Indian sphere, where it is a reverential gesture of greeting (*The Whole Man at Worship*, pp. 54–57); see I. H. Dalmais, *Introduction to the Liturgy*, tr. Roger Capel (Baltimore, MD: Helicon, 1961), p. 116.

39. St. Basil the Great, *De Spiritu Sancto*, 27 (*SC*, 17:233).

40. C.E. 211, *De corona militis*, 3:4 (*FC*, 40:237).

41. Tertullian, *Adversus Marcion*, 3:22,5 (*CC*, 1:539); see G. W. H. Lampe, *The Seal of the Spirit* (London, UK: S.P.C.K., 1967), p. 265.

42. Daniélou, *The Bible and the Liturgy*, pp. 54–56.

43. Tertullian, *Adversus Marcion*, 3:22,6 (*CC*, 1:539); see also Jean Daniélou, *Primitive Christian Symbols*, tr. Donald Attwater (Baltimore, MD: Helicon, 1964), pp. 140–41; Leonel Mitchell, *Baptismal Anointing* (Notre Dame, IN: University of Notre Dame, 1978), p. 24.

44. *ApTrad* (ed. Botte, 42:135–37; ed. Easton, 37:56–57).

45. *Hom.Phil.*, 13 (*PG*, 62:277; *NPNF*, 13:242); Daniélou, *Primitive Christian Symbols*, p. 137; Lampe, *The Seal of the Spirit*, p. 263.

46. *Catechetical Lectures*, 4:14 (*PG*, 33:471; LCC, 4:106).

47. *Catechetical Lectures*, 12:8 (*PG*, 33:736A; *NPNF*, 7:74).

48. *On the Gospel of St. John*, Tractatus 3:2 (*CC*, 36:20; *NPNF*, 7:19);

also *Ennar. in Ps.,* 141:9, 35ss, (*CC,* 40:2052; *NPNF,* 8:649–50, Tractate 142:4).

49. Cabrol, *Liturgical Prayer,* p. 86; Eisenhofer and Lechner, *The Liturgy of the Roman Rite,* p. 95; C. Meinberg, "Cross," *NCE,* 4.473–79.
50. For a third-century usage see *ApTrad,* 36:11.
51. *Book of Common Worship* (Philadelphia, PA: Presbyterian Board of Publication [PCUSA], 1946), p. 161.
52. Tractate in Ioh., 118:27–29 (*CC,* 36).
53. *The Seal of the Spirit,* p. 261.
54. Howard, *Evangelical Is Not Enough,* p. 104.

CHAPTER 9

1. Paul Davies, *God and the New Physics* (New York, NY: Simon and Schuster, 1983), pp. 144–63.
2. John Wheeler, as cited in Davies, *God and the New Physics,* p. 158.
3. Davies, *God and the New Physics,* p. 160.
4. Heb. 2:14 also establishes *metechō* as a synonym for *koinōneō.*
5. In secular literature this noun form is often used to describe marriage, the most intimate of human relationships. Additional uses in the New Testament include: a spirit of generosity, comradeship, and altruism (2 Cor. 9:13); a sign of fellowship and a proof of fraternal unity, such as a gift (Rom. 15:26), both of which are extensions of communion in the Spirit. Derivations from the root *koinos* may also describe intimate associations with evil. Christians are warned of the fatal spiritual consequences of sharing the sins and immorality of others (1 Tim. 5:22; Prov. 28:24; Isa. 1:23) and false teaching (2 John 11). Such companionship entangles one in a web of guilt and judgment (Matt. 23:30). Christians must separate themselves from evil and avoid partaking of it (2 Cor. 6:14; Rev./Apoc. 18:4). The children of light cannot fellowship with darkness (Eph. 5:11).
6. The RSV translates *koinōnia* as "participation" in three instances: Phil. 2:1 and twice in 1 Cor. 10:16. This translation is not without precedent. The Clementine Vulgate translates *koinōnia* in 1 Cor. 10:16 as *communicatio* at its first occurrence and as *participatio* at its second. See the *NeoVulgate,* a recently commissioned revision of the Vulgate, which uses *communicatio* at both occurrences. See *Novum Testamentum Graece et Latine,* p. 895.
7. For this reason the modern custom of referring to the parish social room as a "fellowship hall" is, by biblical standards, a misnomer. Fellowship in the church is not centered around the coffee table. Rather, it is established and grounded in the fellowship of the Lord's

Table. See Werner Elert, *Eucharist and Church Fellowship in the First Four Centuries* (St. Louis, MO: Concordia, 1966).

8. St. Ignatius criticizes those who "hold aloof from the Eucharist" because they do not admit to the real presence ("To the Smyrnaeans," 7:1, in *Early Christian Fathers,* p. 114).

9. See Calvin, *Institutes of the Christian Religion,* IV.17.10–11; cf. Ulrich Zwingli, "On the Lord's Supper," in *Zwingli and Bullinger* (LCC; Philadelphia, PA: Westminster, 1953), pp. 185–238.

10. Gerhard Delling, "Das Abendmahlsgeschehen nach Paulus," *Kerygma und Dogma* 10:2 (1964) 61–77; Friedrich Hauck, "koinos," in *Theological Dictionary of the New Testament,* ed. Gerhard Kittel (Grand Rapids, MI: Eerdmans, 1965), 3.804–9; also see G. W. H. Lampe, *A Patristic Greek Lexicon* (Oxford, UK: Clarendon, 1961), pp. 763–64.

11. *Sac,* Eucharistic Prayer IV; see *BEM,* pp. 11–12, par. 8.

12. Calvin, *Institutes of the Christian Religion,* IV.1.9.

13. Ibid., IV.17.43.

14. For a summary of arguments see the author's *Sacramental Theology among American Presbyterians: 1945–79,* pp. 275–322.

15. "Dogmatic Constitution on Divine Revelation," 11, in *The Documents of Vatican II,* p. 119.

16. Ibid., 21, p. 125.

17. Ibid., 25, pp. 127–28.

18. Ibid., 23, p. 126.

19. Ibid.

20. "General Principles for the Restoration and Promotion of the Sacred Liturgy," 35:2, in *The Documents of Vatican II,* pp. 149–50.

21. Ibid., 53, pp. 155–56.

22. This has led to the lectionary that influenced many Western churches; see "General Principles for the Restoration and Promotion of the Sacred Liturgy," 35:1; 51; 92, pp. 149, 155, 165.

23. "Dogmatic Constitution on Divine Revelation," 26, p. 128.

Index of Scripture

Index of Names and Subjects

LINCOLN CHRISTIAN COLLEGE AND SEMINARY

264
ER68

94587